Hostess to the World!
The Life of Irene E. Staples

First Official Hostess of

THE CHURCH OF
JESUS CHRIST
OF LATTER-DAY SAINTS

(The Mormons)

Hostess to the World!

The Life of Irene E. Staples

First Official Hostess of

THE CHURCH OF
JESUS CHRIST
OF LATTER-DAY SAINTS

Kevan Kingsley Clawson
Grandson of Irene Staples

Walking the Line Publications

Other books by Kevan Clawson
Psalms to the Lord
The Atonement of Jesus Christ
The Second Coming of Jesus Christ
A Life of Miracles
Becoming a Great Missionary
Raising a Worthy Missionary
The Enhanced Old Testament

Books by Kevan & Terri Clawson
Obtaining Your Calling and Election

Other books from Walking the Line Publications
Mongolia: The Circle in the Clouds, by John and Nancy Hopkins

Cover Design: Jaime Clawson and Elizabeth Clawson
Electronic Page Makeup: Jennifer Asplund
Editing: John Hopkins
Photographs: Elizabeth Clawson
Printer and Binder: Printed in the USA by Morris Publishing, 3212 E. Highway 30,
    Kearney, NE 68847 (800) 650-7888

ISBN 978-0-9714540-9-5

Introduction

In the history of the Mormon Church, there have been few women who have had such a profound effect upon the world around her as did Irene Staples. Yet, few people in the Church today would even know her name. Irene Staples was the *first* Official Hostess for The Church of Jesus Christ of Latter-day Saints. She was placed in this position just as the Church was beginning to expand from a uniquely American church into the well known international church it is today. Through her help and influence, visitors from around the world—people of great influence and prestige—received their first introduction and spiritual witness of the true Church of God within a cordial atmosphere created so that their acceptance of gospel truths was greatly aided.

There have been many great women in the Mormon Church—Emma Smith, Eliza R. Snow, Belle Spafford, Barbara Smith and other influential Relief Society presidents, for example—yet few of these women could be said to have influenced *the world*, as their sphere of influence was generally within the Church itself. Irene, on the other hand, was placed in a position to influence people both inside and outside the Church. As Official Church Hostess, Irene's testimony was heard by thousands of people from countries around the world. And although she may not be well known by members of the Church today, the effect for good she had upon the Church, and upon the people with whom she came into contact, literally changed the world in which she lived.

As a missionary and teacher of the gospel of Jesus Christ she was without equal, not because she had great doctrinal insights, or because she had personally received great visions or spiritual experiences to inspire and motivate, but because she had a natural ability to touch people's hearts. Upon first meeting someone from any walk of life, from the highest and most proud king or political leader to the humble farmer or blue-collar worker, Irene could *sense* how to make them feel comfortable. She knew just what to say and do to help them feel at home, and then, when they felt most at ease, she would share her testimony of the Gospel, intimately, as though they had been friends all of their lives. Even the most hard-hearted man of the world could be touched by her simple but sincere testimony. And even though not all who came under Irene's positive influence came away converted to the truth, they all came away *changed* by the experience.

In this book I give the reader a glimpse into the life of this remarkable woman. I provide an outline of Irene's famous "Tour of Temple Square," and give you a glimpse into the events that shaped her life. While reading, you will recognize the names of *many* famous people, both in and out of the Church. Although the list will seem impressive—and it is—it displays only the very tip of the iceberg. The number of people with whom Irene shared the gospel will never be known, but my research suggests it would be in the hundreds of thousands!

Through volumes of journals, notes, correspondence, interviews and all other information I could obtain about Irene, I have tried to glean a factual account of the events and times in which Irene lived, and some of the people she was able to touch with her testimony. Since Irene never took the time to write a history of her own life—she was much more concerned with gathering information about her ancestors, and spending her time serving others—I have been left to gather information from such sources as were available. If there are errors, they are mine.

My sincere hope is that those who take the time to read about Irene will be inspired to follow her motto: *Service above self.* Her life can be, and is, an inspiration to all who wonder whether *one* person can change the world in which they live. Irene proved that *anyone* who has a sincere testimony of the Gospel of Jesus Christ, and is willing to share that testimony with others, can not only move mountains, they can change the world!

I want to express my thanks to those who have worked on this book with me. All who participated directly in the production of this book (as listed in the front cover material), and the many readers and proof-readers that took the time to comment about what was written, have been invaluable. I also want to thank the LDS Church Historical Department for permitting access to information about Irene they have gathered over the years (much of which was given to them by Irene herself).

Special recognition needs to be given to MaryAnn Clements (Irene's youngest daughter) and Stephanie Clements (one of Irene's granddaughters) for their help and inspiration. MaryAnn motivated me to write this book, and permitted access to Irene's personal journals and letters. Both MaryAnn and Stephanie spent many hours reviewing the manuscript and cover art, giving suggestions and eliminating errors.

I often felt as though Irene stood over my shoulder as I wrote about her life. My prayer is that this book conveys in some small way the enormous impact Irene had on both the Church and the many thousands of people who had the privilege of hearing her testimony of the gospel.

Although a large portion of this book talks about events associated with The Church of Jesus Christ of Latter-day Saints, and many of the General Authorities of the Church are referred to as a part of this book, it is important to understand that this book reflects my own thoughts and opinions, and does not necessarily reflect the views or position of The Church of Jesus Christ of Latter-day Saints.

Irene Edwards Staples

A Tour of Temple Square

Irene's grandmother, Gwennie Davis, who met with Charles Dickens on the ship Amazon.

The official picture of the Golden Spike ceremony held at the completion of the transcontinental railroad. Irene's grandfather, John Edwards, can be seen on the far right with his hands on the lapels of his jacket.

Irene's father, David Edwards

Irene's mother, Florence Fern Edwards

Irene as a teenager. Irene made the dress she is wearing.

Harold Staples, Irene's future husband, as a teenager.

Harold and Irene prior to Harold's death in 1959.

Harold, Irene, and their children (clockwise): Shirley, John, Richard, MaryAnn.

Irene dressed in a costume she made for the Welsh festival called Gymanfa Ganu.

The pioneer cabin Irene decorated for the first Christmas lights on Temple Square.

Irene sitting in front
of the reflecting
pool of the
Mormon Pavilion
in 1965.

Irene meeting with the Consul General of Israel,
Moshe Yeagar, in 1969.

Irene's "Woman of the Year" picture as seen on the 1973
Mother's Day issue of the Utah Woman's Review.

The sacred oak tree on the hill above Lehi's Cave.

The entrance to Lehi's Cave

The inside of Lehi's Cave

Irene attending the announcement of the Orson Hyde Memorial Gardens at the new church office building, October 26, 1977. On the far left is the Apostle Howard W. Hunter, and second from right is the Apostle LeGrand Richards. To the far right is the Apostle Wendell Ashton.

Irene receiving the Utah National Guard Minuteman Award in 1978. To Irene's left is Governor Scott Matheson.

Irene's History

Hostess to the World!
The Life of Irene E. Staples

First Official Hostess of

THE CHURCH OF
JESUS CHRIST
OF LATTER-DAY SAINTS

Irene's Tour of Temple Square

> This is a poem I wrote many years ago which is sort of my creed:
>
> If any little thought of mine,
> Can make the world seem brighter,
> If any little act of mine,
> Can make a burden lighter,
> God help me do that very deed,
> That in my heart is ringing,
> To make life happier for all,
> That each may go their way singing.
>
> Irene

Irene Staples was the first official hostess for The Church of Jesus Christ of Latter-day Saints (the Mormons). She was a small woman, with fading red hair, who had a passion for the Gospel of Jesus Christ that drove her to move forward with a pace that would leave behind most sprinters. It was always humorous to watch people try to keep up with her as she was walking...her short legs moved so quickly even the tallest men would have to occasionally break into a lope just to keep up! Her frantic pace was set by her busy schedule—people to meet, stories to tell, testimonies to bear, and, most importantly, souls to reap.

Her main task as the Official Church Hostess was to serve as guide to the many guests and VIPs that came to Salt Lake City. General Authorities of the LDS Church, government officials, local businessmen, and desperate friends and acquaintances would all call Irene to "meet and greet" or "host and toast" the visitors that came from around the country and the world to visit Utah.

After being called as the Official Church Hostess, Irene worked seven days a week, 12 to14 hours a day, and was on call day and night for any emergency or need that was brought to her attention. Irene often entertained visitors in her home, sharing home cooked meals and homespun wisdom. At the end of the evening, no one left empty-handed...*everyone* was given a copy of the "Mormon scriptures," the Book of Mormon.

Irene's personal testimony of the truthfulness of the gospel was heard by literally tens of thousands of people. From the most humble farmer to the exalted king, Irene could and did bear witness to the glory of God and the restoration of the gospel in our day.

The list of famous people who knew her by name is simply astonishing and included royalty, heads of state, government officials from presidents to mayors, ambassadors from around the world, captains of industry, movie stars, sports figures...the list goes on and on. All had one common thread: Irene and her humble testimony of the gospel was a shining light that pierced their eye and touched their souls, never to be forgotten.

Irene's home away from home was Temple Square. It was most often here, in the shadow of the temple spires, with the power of the spirit of God surrounding her, filling her, that she would do her best work. After the common greetings and pleasantries were completed, she would begin at the Seagull Monument, located at the south end of Temple Square. It was here she would meet individuals and groups to begin a tour she had perfected, memorized, and filled with insights and moving stories about the Mormon people.

Temple Square and Assembly Hall

After meeting her guests at the Seagull Monument, Irene would begin her tour of Temple Square by describing Temple Square in general, and the Assembly Hall, situated just to the west.

Temple Square is the most visited site in the State of Utah because this area, located adjacent to the headquarters of the Mormon Church, is the home of the granite temple and the world famous Mormon Tabernacle Choir. This ground was set aside for the building of the Temple by Brigham Young after entering the Salt Lake Valley in 1847. Brigham, with a small group of men, had taken a "walking tour" of the valley shortly after arriving. As Brigham walked across this spot of land, he stopped, pondered for a moment, and then said, "Here we will build a temple to our God." The exact location was marked and, in 1852, the wall surrounding Temple Square was built to provide work for new arrivals of pioneers and those who passed through on their way to the gold fields of California. The main purpose for setting apart this "square" of land was to preserve it for a temple. However, as the temple would take over 40 years to build, over time other buildings were erected on the site to accommodate the Saints and visitors that came to Utah.

The first structures to be built on Temple Square were open boweries used for church meetings. Eventually in 1852, a more permanent building, called the Old Tabernacle, was built to replace the temporary open-air structures. In 1877, this building was torn down and the present Assembly Hall was erected using stone left over from the building of the temple. It has a seating capacity of 2,000 and is often used to house overflow from the tabernacle during conferences and programs.

A Star of David appears above each entrance of the Assembly Hall, symbolizing the Church's ties with Israel. Jacob (or Israel) was an ancient Hebrew who had twelve sons. These sons formed the twelve "tribes" that would one day become the Kingdom of Israel. Modern day Jews are descendants of at least one of those tribes, the tribe of Judah. Eleven other tribes were scattered throughout the world as a result of the Assyrian and Babylonian invasions of Israel in about 600 B.C. Mormons believe they are, for the most part, descendants of Joseph who was sold into Egypt.

The Seagull Monument

After finishing her description of Temple Square and the Assembly Hall, Irene would continue her narrative by telling the moving story of the miracle of the seagulls.

"I believe no story in the history of America is more stirring or filled with greater emotion than that of the small group of Mormons that were saved from certain destruction during the great cricket plague of 1848. Mormons strongly accept this event as a 'Divine answer to prayer.' In a most critical period of survival, the Mormons' crops were saved by, of all things, seagulls in the desert! This 'miracle of the seagulls' kept them from starvation and perhaps complete annihilation as a people.

"The Mormon pioneers, driven from their eastern homes because of great persecution, fled to the west—the great American desert—where they felt they would be left alone to worship their God according to the dictates of their consciences. At that time the Salt Lake valley was just an unclaimed territory, not even a part of the United States.

4

"The Mormons had been driven to a place so foreboding and desolate that America's great statesman, Daniel Webster, while a member of Congress in Washington, when approached about appropriating money for a railroad to the west, said, 'I won't appropriate one dime to bring the west any closer to the east than it is. The west is good for nothing except prairie dogs and rattlesnakes. No one can exist there.'

"However, this is where the Mormons had to come, because it was a place unwanted by anyone else. As the first group of Mormon pioneers were nearing their destination, they met Jim Bridger, the great American explorer, in the wilds of the prairies to the north. When he heard that they were going to settle in the great basin of the Salt Lake he told their leader, Brigham Young, that he was taking them to certain starvation. He said, 'I have been there and I know that country. The soil is hard and, due to the dearth of water and unseasonable frosts, nothing can be raised there.'

"But Brigham Young knew where he was taking this band of God-fearing people. Both he and Joseph Smith had seen it in vision long before arriving in the Salt Lake valley, and had a power of faith and an understanding of the hand of God far beyond normal men. He told this great explorer that regardless of what had been said, this was where he had to take this people — to a place no one else wanted, but where they could live in peace and have religious freedom. Jim Bridger replied, 'I will give you a thousand dollars for the first bushel of corn you can raise in that valley. It can't be done.' Brigham Young, who is likened to a modern Moses leading the Children of Israel to the Promised Land, replied, 'I know the Lord will temper the climate so we will be able to raise those things necessary for our needs and to sustain life.'

"That prophetic statement literally came to pass for today —
in one part or another of the state of Utah — you can raise everything from citrus fruits and cotton, grown only in temperate climates, to grains and vegetables, grown in moderate climates, to
apples and fruit trees grown in colder climates. Every necessary
thing is available for the needs of men.

"The pioneers arrived in the Salt Lake valley the 24th of July,
1847. They had to flood the ground with water from the mountains before a plow would cut through the hard soil. They were
the first Anglo-Saxon people in North America to use irrigation.
They immediately planted what seeds they had, and in the short
season they harvested a small crop. How thrilled they were, for
now they had enough food to last them through the winter. But
Brigham Young said, 'No, we must not touch this crop, for we
must save it for seed next spring. There will be many thousands
of our people coming and we must have food for them.' Through
the winter they lived on a starvation diet, eating anything they
could find such as thistle and roots of the sego lily, a flower
growing on the hillside, which is now the state flower. Some
even boiled the leather from their boots to obtain what nourish-
ment they could from the leather.

"The following spring, we can only wonder how they had the
strength to cultivate 5,000 acres of ground and plant it with the
precious seed they had carefully saved. How grateful they must
have been when they saw their fields becoming lush with wav-
ing green stocks of grain! This meant food, and they realized that
for the first time in many years they would soon have enough to
eat and would be freed from the pangs of hunger. How greatly
blessed they felt!

"Then, suddenly, from the hills to the north, there came great
black clouds of insects, a silent flood flowing down upon their
crops. It was vast hordes and swarms of crickets! This black

plague was as deadly to their crops as the plague of locusts spoken of in the Bible. In their tracks they left behind not a single blade or leaf of precious crops. The ground, covered by these myriads of pests, looked as though it had been scorched by fire. They came in a solid phalanx, darkening the earth in their passage.

"Men, women, and children turned out *en masse* to combat the plague, beating, burning, and driving them into ditches in an attempt to drown them, but all in vain. Day after day they toiled until their strength was exhausted. It seemed they were doomed, just like the children of Israel in Egypt in the last days of bondage. Their condition was tragic, for the food they brought with them was all planted and they were nearly 1,000 miles from any other source of food. With winter coming, it meant nothing but starvation, with all of its terrors.

"Just as all their efforts had failed and everything seemed lost, they fell to their knees in fasting and prayer, pleading with God to send deliverance from this devastating plague of crickets, that their crops might be saved and they would be spared from starvation.

"Hardly had they risen from their knees when, from the west, dark clouds gathered again. Hopelessness fell upon the Mormons as they watched the dark clouds move swiftly towards them. As the 'clouds' grew closer they could see that they were great flocks of birds. Where did they come from? They had never been seen in this part of the country before because they were sea birds that live near the water, not in a hot, barren desert. In fact, there had been few birds of any kind here. What would these birds do? Was this just another scourge? Would these birds finish what crops the crickets might leave?

"In fear and trembling they watched as the seagulls settled upon the fields. To their surprise and great joy, the birds pounced upon the crickets, devouring them as they went. Even after they were filled, they still devoured crickets. Going to the ditch banks for water, they would disgorge then fly back to the fields once more to continue their onslaught on this vast plague of destroying crickets.

"For nearly two weeks the birds flew back and forth, devouring crickets until the fields and crops were entirely free of this plague. On the following Sunday, full of thankfulness, the people gathered in religious services and offered thanks to God for their deliverance—for the miracle of the seagulls. Even today one can understand their astonishment over this miracle, because seagulls are not found in deserts...yet they came, and here they are still! These Mormon pioneers knew that the birds had been sent by Divine Providence. Their hearts were filled with the realization that they were Heavenly Father's children, that He loved them and was watching over them, and that He would never fail to answer their righteous prayers.

"As a remembrance of this great miracle, the Seagull Monument was erected on Temple Square, the only monument in the world erected to a bird: 'In grateful remembrance of the mercy of God to the Mormon Pioneers.'"

After telling the story behind the Seagull Monument, Irene let her guests ponder in silence the significance of this great miracle. Then she led them to the next stop on her tour: the great Salt Lake Temple. The group would gather on the west or south side of the temple (depending on the time of day and other crowds gathered at Temple Square) and she would begin her next story.

The Salt Lake Temple

Soon after the pioneers came to Salt Lake, President Brigham Young and a group of men took a walking tour of the valley. At this place, striking his cane to the earth Brigham Young said, "Here we will build a temple to our God."

Four years after the pioneers arrived, the site was consecrated and ground broken. Poor as they were, they didn't hesitate to give everything they had to help build this temple to their God. The temple is designed after a sketch made by Brigham Young that he gave to the architect in 1853. *Forty years* later, the temple was completed.

In Biblical times, the Lord commanded the ancient Israelites to build a temple. The temple was called the "House of God" because it was a place where God himself would visit his children on earth. In our day, the Lord has again asked for a temple to be built where He could come and dwell.

President Brigham Young called men and women to work on the temple, just as though they had been called to serve a mission. These laborers often received no pay except food from the church storehouse. Their whole aim was to finish the temple, not to gain worldly wealth. As many as 150 men might be working on different aspects of the temple at any given time.

The capstone and a statue of the angel Moroni were placed on the temple in 1892, one year prior to its official dedication. The following year was spent finishing the inside of the temple. The interior design of the temple follows a specific plan: each room is decorated with murals depicting different stages in man's eternal progression and journey back to God's presence. There is the *Creation Room* (depicting the creation of the world), the *Garden Room* (depicting the Garden of Eden), the *World Room* (depicting conditions after the fall of Adam and Eve), the *Terrestrial Room* (depicting life as it will be during the millennial reign

9

of Jesus Christ at His Second Coming), and, finally, the *Celestial Room* (representing man's return to the presence of God). The building also includes a lower baptistery where a baptismal font sits on the backs of 12 oxen, similar to the one that Solomon had built for the ancient temple in Jerusalem.

There are rooms with altars where couples and families can kneel and be sealed to each other for time and eternity. The upper floor is one large assembly hall used for special priesthood meetings.

On April 6, 1893, the temple was completed and dedicated. President Woodruff offered the dedicatory prayer. These services were repeated almost daily for 18 days, giving every faithful Latter-day Saint a chance to hear the service. This amounted to about 75,000 people, including 15,000 Sunday School children.

Many saints received manifestations during these prayer sessions. Some who were sick were instantly healed, and angels were seen by others! The power of the Lord was felt by everyone.

There is a great deal of symbolism displayed on the outside of the temple. The six towers represent the restoration of the two priesthoods: the three higher eastern towers represent the Presidency of the Melchizedek priesthood and the three lower western towers represent the Presidency of the lesser Aaronic priesthood. There are stones depicting the sun, moon, and stars, which represent the three degrees of glory in the afterlife: the celestial, terrestrial, and telestial kingdoms, respectively. In addition there are rays of light penetrating clouds, the "all-seeing eye," clasped hands, Ursa Major and the North Star, and, most prominently the words "The House of the Lord" and "I am Alpha and Omega" above the doors.

It took 40 years to build, and since then, baptism and endowment ordinances have been performed for millions, both living and dead.

A Brief Description of the Temple

The temple walls taper from its base below ground to where it supports the roof: the foundation is 16' thick at the footing, at ground level it is 9' thick, at the second story it is 7' thick, and at the top it is 6' thick.

The length of the temple is 186', the width is 91', and the height to the top of the east tower where the angel Moroni stands is 122'.

The temple itself is made of solid granite quarried from nearby canyons. All the stone was hand cut in the mountains, then dragged to this location by oxen. Each stone was cut and numbered so that when it reached the temple it fit right into its place. Transporting each stone was a massive challenge. Eventually, special wagons were built to carry the stone, and special roads were built for the wagons. For a time canals were built and used to "float" the stones part of the distance. Eventually, a railroad spur was installed to speed up construction. Although the stone quarry was less than twenty miles away, it could take a crew of men up to four days to get each stone and bring it back.

There are two doors on the east and two on the west sides of the temple which are used by the authorities of the Church. They are 4' wide and 12' high. They are made of solid white oak, each weighing 600 lbs.

There are four circular stairways inside the temple, one in each corner. Each stairway has 176 hand cut stone steps, each weighing 1,700 lbs., making each stairway weigh 625 tons. If just one stairway weighs that much, one can hardly imagine how much the entire temple would weigh!

The angel Moroni is 12' high and is made of copper, covered with a gold layer which does not tarnish. It is fastened to a granite ball which weighs 6½ tons.

The inside of the temple is beautifully decorated with carvings and paintings. One of the paintings was once owned by Napoleon Bonaparte. It was brought to America by Napoleon's brother, Joseph, was auctioned and sold several times, and finally came into the hands of Hyrum Clawson, who donated it to the Church. It was valued at $75,000 in 1965.

The temple cost more than $4 million to build, not counting the large amount of labor and material that was donated. We can only imagine what the cost would be if the temple were built today!

It should be the desire of every man, woman, and child to live so they will be worthy to go into this beautiful temple. Worthy members of the Church participate in the ordinances of the temple for themselves, and then return to the temple over and over again to do work for the dead. They become "Saviors in Zion" as they bring the saving ordinances of the gospel to their ancestors—those men, women, and children who never had the opportunity to hear or accept the fullness of the gospel while they were living on the earth.

As Irene finished her discussion of the temple, time would be set aside for some questions. Sometimes this "question and answer" period would last quite a while. The temple and the "secrecy" surrounding what occurred inside was a catalyst for wonderful gospel discussions, expertly responded to and guided by Irene.

The Tabernacle

After everyone's questions were answered, the tour would move inside the tabernacle. At this point one of three things might happen. If it were a Wednesday around noon, they would be able to hear an organ recital played on one of the oldest and largest organs in the United States. If it were Thursday afternoon around five, they would be privileged to hear the Mormon Tabernacle Choir practice for their Sunday program. If they came at a time when the building was not in use, Irene would talk to them about the tabernacle, how it was built, and its international reputation for nearly perfect acoustics.

The tabernacle was built between 1864 and 1867 directly west of the temple. It was completed October 6, 1867 and the first General Conference of the Church was held in the tabernacle that same year. In 1870, the upper gallery was built to accommodate more people. The tabernacle can seat about 8,000 people on the main floor and in the choir seats, with additional seating for 3,000 people in the upper gallery.

Irene would take the group to the back of the tabernacle and up the stairs to the gallery. As they rested comfortably on the benches and looked out over the large open tabernacle with its gently curved ceiling, she would tell them about how the tabernacle was built.

The tabernacle is an engineering marvel. It was built using a revolutionary bridge building technology to obtain its unique dome shape. By using a combination of post and beam construction for the building and lattice-truss type construction for the roof, the roof was able to span 150' across and 250' long without center supports. The construction is especially unique because few nails were used in the building.

There were 44 sandstone buttresses, or pillars, built to support the dome (quarried at Red Butte Canyon, then brought by wagon to Temple Square). The dome was then begun using posts and beams that were pinned together using wooden dowels. The timbers were cut into shape, then dowels, smeared with glue made from cattle hooves, were pounded into holes augured out by hand. As an additional securement, and to strengthen and/or repair cracked beams, wet rawhide was wound around the beams. As the rawhide dried, it shrank and tightened. The rawhide, instead of rotting, has over time become like iron.

The post and beams were woven into a latticework that provided the unique curve of the dome and tied the roof together. The roof structure itself was nine feet thick! The building was then capped using 350,000 wood shingles. Later a copper roof and then an aluminum roof were installed for protection.

The interior of the large curved ceiling was covered by lathe and plaster for a finished look. Lime plaster was mixed with animal hair for strength (approximately 100 hairs per square inch), then installed onto the ceiling. After it dried, it was painted white. The Tabernacle is 80' high and contains floor space of 80,000 square feet. The rows of white pine pews on the floor and upper gallery were hand painted to look like oak, and the pine columns that support the upper gallery were hand painted to look like Tennessee marble.

The original cost of the Tabernacle in 1867 was $300,000. Approximately 200 workers (making $2 to $3 per day) toiled for 3 years and 3 months to complete the work. More than 1.5 million board feet of lumber was used, along with 2,500 panes of glass.

After the building of the Tabernacle was discussed, and if time allowed, a small access door would be opened in the wall so people could look at its construction, and see the rawhide strips, still visible today.

As the group looked across the open expanse to the other end of the Tabernacle, their attention was drawn to the large imposing organ on the west side. The original organ was made by hand and had upwards of 700 pipes. The number of pipes has been increased over the years to more than 11,000. The lumber for the organ was shipped by wagon 300 miles from southern Utah. The original organ was powered by hand-pumped bellows, later by water power, and today is powered by electricity. The Tabernacle organ is considered one of the largest and finest in the world.

Finally, Irene would talk about the amazing acoustics of the building. But a demonstration always worked much more powerfully than words! With a wave of her hand, Irene would signal and a young man would appear out of the shadows, walk up to the podium at the other end of the Tabernacle, and with the nod of her head, he would drop a pin onto the wood stage. This "pindrop" could be clearly heard by everyone in Irene's group, sitting more than 170 feet away! After the oohs and aahs died down, she would ask if there were any questions.

The Visitors Center

Sometimes Irene would take people through the Visitors Center herself. However, most of the time she would let one of the young missionaries take over since the center was made so one could almost tour alone. As the group moved among the paintings and panels that explain what Mormons believe and some Church history, visitors were given a brief foundational understanding of the Church's basic tenets and beliefs. Irene would take this time to check her tour schedule and often begin making "special arrangements" for members of the tour that had made requests.

The Christus

As the group neared the end of their tour of the Visitors Center they would walk up a winding ramp towards a large domed area. On the south side of this domed hall is a glass wall looking out over a grass and tree-lined area to the north of the Tabernacle. At the center of the curved hall stood the Christus, a large statue of Jesus Christ, his hands extending downward in an expression of love. This famous statue of Christ is an eleven foot replica of the original statue by Danish artist and sculptor Bertel Thorvaldsen.

As Irene's visitors pondered the information they had received, and the significance of the teachings of Jesus Christ in the lives of the Mormon people, their eyes would move towards the ceiling of the domed room. There, painted in brilliant colors, was a depiction of the universe. Sometimes Irene would point out the splashes of pink in the clouds and note that she had "suggested" the artist put that color there—pink being Irene's color of choice.

Once the group had gathered in front of the Christus, Irene would pause for silence. Then, with humble sincerity and great emotion, she would bear her personal witness of the truthfulness of the Gospel of Jesus Christ. She *knew* that Joseph Smith was a Prophet of God. She *knew* that The Church of Jesus Christ of Latter-day Saints was God's kingdom on earth today. She *knew* that Jesus Christ was resurrected and lived and guided her church leaders today. She *knew* that God was our Father in Heaven; and because we are all God's children He has provided a way for us to return and live with Him again. Then she would close in the name of Jesus Christ. There were very few who heard her sweet, yet powerful testimony that would ever forget Irene Staples!

Man's Search for Happiness

For those who desired to see it, and had the time, a movie called *Man's Search for Happiness* was then shown in the main theater. This film explained the Plan of Salvation, God's plan for His children on earth. After the film, Irene would again make herself available to answer questions, help to obtain literature, and provide a copy of the Book of Mormon to anyone who desired one.

The film, discussed later in the book, is one of the greatest tools the Church has developed for teaching people the plan of salvation in a way that is easy to understand. It takes the viewer from pre-mortal life, through mortality, and into life after death. It *shows* people, in a very real way, that after death they will be greeted by their loved ones on the other side of the veil. What peace this gave to all who viewed the film! They learned that there was life after death, that they would not be alone…there was no longer any need to fear death, because their loved ones would be waiting for them on the other side!

Often, Irene would slip into the theater at the end of the movie for one more chance to bear her testimony to the group about the truthfulness of what they had just seen and experienced. It was true! It was *all* true! And they could know for themselves it was true—by reading the Book of Mormon and praying about it.

During a normal tour of Temple square, people would hear Irene's fervent testimony five or six times. Is it any wonder why people from all over the world remembered a little red haired grandmother from Salt Lake City named Irene Staples?

The VIP Tour of Salt Lake City

One of the "special arrangements" for which Irene was famous was an extended tour of the greater Salt Lake valley. For
special guests that could stay longer, and for government dignitaries and heads of state, Irene would often expand her normal
tour to include many other areas of Salt Lake. These other sites
included: Hotel Utah, Brigham Young Monument, LDS Women's
Relief Society Building, Daughters of the Utah Pioneers Museum,
Utah State Capitol, Mormon Battalion Monument, Old City Hall,
Memory Grove, City Creek canyon, LDS Primary Children's
Hospital, the residential or avenues district, city cemetery, Shrin-
ers Children's Hospital, Governor's home, a typical LDS Ward
building, the University of Utah campus and Medical School,
Fort Douglas, the Veterans Hospital, This is the Place Monument,
Hogle Zoo, Liberty Park, Masonic Temple, Utah Historical Soci-
ety, the local Presbyterian church and the Catholic Cathedral of
the Madeline, the Eagle Gate, Beehive House and Lion House
(Brigham Young's homes), and Welfare Square, among other
places of interest. Each guest requesting an extended tour would
be taken to places that would be of interest *to them* specifically, as
Irene would continue to read their needs, wants, and desires to
insure they had a wonderful and unique experience in Utah.

The Granite Mountain Record Vaults

For those who still couldn't get enough of Irene and Salt
Lake, and who were interested in genealogy, Irene would further
extend her "extended" tour and drive south along the Wasatch
Mountains to the Mormon Church's granite vault, in which
they keep and preserve genealogy records and other important
documents.

The vault is located at the mouth of Little Cottonwood Canyon, near the site of the original rock quarry used by the Mormons to obtain granite for the building of their temple. It is a massive "tunnel" cut some 600 feet into solid granite rock. Built between 1958 and 1963, it consists of two main areas.

There is an office area, with shipping and receiving docks, that sits below 300 feet of granite. Farther back, sitting under 700 feet of granite, is the larger vault area that consists of six chambers, each 190 feet long, 25 feet wide, and 25 feet high.

Specially constructed doors, weighing 14 tons, secure the main entrance. They are designed to withstand a nuclear blast.

Within the six chambers, nature maintains a constant humidity and temperature that are optimal for microfilm storage. Each chamber contains banks of cabinets for the storage of microfilm. Since 1938 the Church's genealogical society has been collecting historical information on rolls of microfilm. These vaults were created to store and protect this sacred information. There are millions of rolls of microfilm, containing literally billions of names, stored safely inside these vaults. The names stored record the history of mankind going back many centuries.

Irene Staples: Hostess to the World

Irene's Pioneer Heritage

> Many years ago there was a group of pioneers coming across the plains. One family had a little baby boy who became very sick. In fact, he became so ill they could not go any farther with him in the cold wagon.
>
> Just then a group of friendly Indians came. One of the Indian squaws, seeing the sick child, picked him up and said she would take him home and make him well.
>
> The father and mother hated to leave their baby, but they knew that if they took him any farther in the cold wagon he would die. So they gave the child to the Indian.
>
> Many years later, a fine big boy came to the door of their pioneer home and said, "I am your son, George. My Indian mother was very good to me, and I have learned to love her, but it is right that I should live with my own people."
>
> So I am thankful for the Indians, because that baby boy, raised by the Indian squaw, was my own grandfather.
>
> Irene

Irene was a 21st century woman, with a 19th century heart, stuck in the quiet calm of the 20th century.

Irene would have been right at home living in the 21st century. In her mind, she was not only equal to, but better than most men she knew. She was career-oriented and not only enjoyed

21

working in a man's world, she excelled at it. Had she lived in an age and time where women's opportunities were not so limited, there is no telling what she may have become. In fact, with her proven social skills and desire to be involved in politics, she would have been a natural politician—who knows, a congress-woman, a governor, perhaps even more. Unfortunately, she was born at the beginning of the 20th century, decades before the modern women's movement would bring greater emancipation. She was raised and nurtured in a time and place that severely limited what a woman could even *think* of doing or becoming. In addition, the poor circumstances of her family prevented her from going to college. It is a tribute to her stubborn desire to make something of herself that she was able to accomplish so much.

There was another problem—or another asset, depending on how you look at it. In her heart, Irene was a 19th century pioneer, crossing the plains with her forefathers. In many ways the women of the 19th century were more liberated than those of the early 20th century. They were forced by the circumstances of the age to experience obstacles and accomplish feats women can even now only shake their head at in wonder. The true pio-neers—those women who crossed the plains with their families, who watched their husbands and children die in their arms—carried on under threat of certain death due to exposure to the elements or the constant danger lurking around them. These are the women that actually did the work, carried the burdens, and birthed the next generation at the same time they were burying the last generation with their own hands! These courageous pio-neer women did what they had to do, and stood shoulder to shoulder with their husbands as they carved out a life for them-selves in the harshest of wildernesses—the desert of the Great Basin. Irene would have fit in well with these women. She was a woman of substance, someone who *acted*, and shaped the world around her by the force of her will. She revered her pioneer ancestors, and often felt as though she "missed out" on the opportunity to truly prove herself, as her predecessors had.

Irene's favorite stories to her children and grandchildren were not about her own accomplishments, but those of her ancestors. They centered on her pioneer grandparents who traveled from Wales across the plains to Utah. There is no doubt that she admired these pioneers and the sacrifices they made. She could have been one of them! But no, she was not born in their time.

Dan Jones

The story of both of Irene's grandparents begins with the last prophecy of Joseph Smith, given to one of his body guards, Dan Jones, the night before Joseph and Hyrum were killed by a mob in Carthage jail.

Elder Jones, a short, sturdy, fiery Welshman, was a bodyguard of the Prophet Joseph Smith and was with the Prophet in Carthage Jail the night before the martyrdom. He was just one of several who had traveled with Joseph to Carthage, out of fear for Joseph's life. The night before the Prophet's death, after the others had fallen asleep, Joseph asked Elder Jones, "Are you afraid to die?"

Dan Jones responded with courage fueled by his faith, "Has that time come, think you? Engaged in such a cause, I do not think that death would have many terrors."

It was then that the Prophet spoke his last words of prophesy in mortality: "You will yet see Wales and fulfill the mission appointed you before you die."

At the request of the Prophet, Elder Jones left Carthage the next day to deliver a letter from Joseph to Orvil H. Browning, asking Mr. Browning to represent the Prophet and Hyrum in their forthcoming trial. Elder Jones rode off through the mob amid gunshots and threats on his life. He arrived in Quincy, Illinois only to learn of the deaths of Joseph and Hyrum that very afternoon.

He was called several months later to go on a mission to Wales with his wife, Jane. There he both preached and presided over the mission for several years in the 1840s and 1850s. Despite intense persecution, he issued numerous publications and achieved astounding success. This success is understandable if one believes what the Prophet Joseph Smith told Dan Jones about the Welsh — that there was more of the blood of Israel in Wales than in any other country in the world!

From 1845 to 1848, approximately 3,600 people were baptized. Some 2,000 more joined the Church in the 1850s during Elder Jones' second mission. Throughout this period of gathering, most of the converts became pioneers and made the arduous trek to Utah.

Among these thousands of converts were two families of importance to Irene: the Edwards and Davis families. John Edwards, Jr. and Gwennie Davis were Irene's grandparents.

John Edwards

After being converted to the Mormon Church, John Edwards, Sr. came directly to Willard, Utah from Wales in 1855. Even though John's wife never joined the Church, she said she would follow her husband and children wherever they would go. The Edwards' had two children, John and Mary. John Jr. would eventually marry Gwennie Davis.

The decision to immigrate to Utah was easy, however the actual event was quite trying. It became well known in Wales that new Mormon converts usually immigrated to America. Therefore, when you became a Mormon it was almost impossible to sell your home and other belongings because people knew you were likely to leave them behind. With much prayer, the family was able to sell their home for just enough money to immigrate to Utah. But of course no one would buy the furnishings, knowing if they simply waited they would have them for free.

It would be a scene seared into the minds of the family until their deaths…and even then passed down to their children and grandchildren. As the family finished packing the few belongings they were able to take with them, they climbed into the wagon and slowly drove away from their ancestral home. As they came to that final bend of the road, they stopped to have one last look at their ancestral home. To their shock, amazement, and disgust, they saw their friends and neighbors rushing into their home to carry away everything that was left behind…like vultures swooping down upon their prey!

They turned their heads away from the sight with heavy hearts. It was hard to see their precious possessions being carried away by the same "friends and neighbors" who had refused to buy any of these cherished articles from a Mormon. But they had no reservations rushing in to steal them! As the emotions of the event settled over them, it simply steeled their souls with greater resolve to make it to Zion.

Their long voyage over the ocean and even longer trip over the plains was not without trial. The small family buried their mother in an unmarked grave somewhere on the plains of Kansas. Upon reaching Utah, they settled in a small northern town called Willard and began raising cattle. Just a few short months after arriving in Utah, John Edwards' son, John Jr., was called by Brigham Young to go back East to act as a guide for other Mormon families coming to Utah. John Jr. would make two trips back to Winter Quarters[1] to guide wagon trains of pioneers to Zion.

---

[1]Winter Quarters, Iowa was a small settlement created by Brigham Young as a way-station for converts immigrating to Utah from the Eastern States and Europe.

Gwennie Davis

Gwennie Davis was very dear to Irene's heart for several reasons, one of which was that it was from Gwennie she inherited her red hair. Gwennie was only fifteen years old when she became a pioneer and traveled to Utah.

Titus Davis was a shoemaker by trade, but his love and passion was to be a concertmaster who conducted a large choir. Unfortunately, music could not feed his family. But it was through his love of music that he met Mary Gwenllian Bowen, Gwennie's mother. Mary possessed a very beautiful voice and was a member of Titus' choir. With a father who loved music, and a mother who sang like an angel, it was natural for Gwennie to develop singing talents as well. In fact, she exceeded her mother in her talents.

Since Titus and his oldest son, David, had to travel as part of his shoe trade, they had the opportunity to visit larger cities and soon became acquainted with the Mormon religion. Both Titus and David quickly realized they had found the truth and joined the Church. Titus' wife Mary was immediately opposed. She had known many people who had joined the Church and left for America, and had heard horror stories of those who died terrible deaths or suffered untold hardships along the way. She was filled with fear that her husband would not only want to follow the Mormons to America, but take their children with him! In time, her worst fears would be realized.

Since the Baptist church to which they belonged believed in baptism by immersion, Mary felt it was not necessary to leave her church for another that practiced the same principle. Unfortunately, after Titus and David joined the Mormon Church, many arguments ensued within the family. Mary continued to take counsel from her minister and relatives, who said with one voice that it was Mary's duty to stay in England. It seemed clear to her that Mormonism, with its doctrine of polygamy, was a mockery. Mary, convinced by her minister that the Mormons were evil, would stay with her own religion until she died.

Gwennie, like her father and brother, was attracted to this new religion, but had reservations because it seemed to be breaking up the unity of her family. Finally the time came that Titus felt he could wait no longer—he was determined to travel to America to join the Saints and find Zion. As one can imagine, this precipitated a lot of discussion concerning who would go with Titus, and who was going to stay in Wales with Mary. Mary was just as determined to stay as Titus was to leave. It was a situation that could not be resolved without the break-up of the family. In the end, Titus and all but one of his children left for America. One young son, Mary's favorite, would stay with her in Wales, to keep her company and care for her in her old age. Gwennie and six other brothers, including Henry, the youngest son only four years old, went with Titus to Utah.

It is hard to comprehend in this day and age of pampered youth, but there was the cold reality staring her in the face: Gwennie Davis, at fifteen years of age, became responsible for the care of an entire family of six small children and her father, when her mother refused to emigrate with the rest of the family.

In May of 1863, eight years after the Edwards had immigrated to Utah, the Davis family started their journey. The family left from London on an American sailing ship called the Amazon. It was not a happy parting. When Titus and Mary were standing at the dock, he sailing to America and she staying behind in Wales, Titus shook her hand and tersely said, "Well, goodbye, Sister Davis."

Not all who planned to go to America made the trip. To their surprise, David, their oldest son, had been called on a mission to Wales soon after his baptism. He stayed in Wales for another year before coming to Utah.

This parting was especially hard on Gwennie. Though convinced that the gospel was true, the trip to America and then to Utah was simply overwhelming for this teen-aged girl. Strong emotions of fear, regret, and loss constantly assaulted her as she thought about leaving her mother, never to see her again. Further, she would have to care for all the children, including four-year-old Henry, all the way across the continent of America. The thought of the trials that lay ahead often caused her to weep uncontrollably.

When they arrived at the ship, they discovered there would be a delay in leaving. They would have to wait on board for almost a week before sailing. This delay seemed to put even more pressure and fear on young Gwennie, as feelings of homesickness grew each day away from her mother. At one point the sorrow, fear, and pressure simply overcame her. Weeping uncontrollably, she asked her father if she could stay in Wales with her mother. Titus was not willing to force any of his children to go with him, and arranged for her to leave the ship and return home.

The Saints on the ship, including such well known brethren as George Q. Cannon, had quickly become a close-knit group. As the Latter-day Saint women watched Gwennie weep, their compassion led them to come and comfort her. Their loving kindness and quiet testimonies changed her mind again. She would be strong! She had to be! She would somehow find the inner strength to make the journey. To pass the time and to bolster their spirits the Saints began to sing. This was soon going to place a great temptation and another difficult decision squarely upon Gwennie's shoulders.

While waiting to sail, Charles Dickens,[2] the famous journalist, came on board to write an article on the Mormons. At first no

---

[2]Charles Dickens included a description of his visit to the Amazon in *The Uncommercial Traveler.*

one knew who he was. He quietly moved about the ship talking to the Captain and passengers, observing the Mormons, their habits, and living conditions. Toward the end of his visit, the Captain introduced Mr. Dickens to the group. Mr. Dickens, having heard them singing while on board, requested another song. Gwennie, with her father, sang again for him in their native language. He immediately pronounced Gwennie's voice equal to any that he had ever heard! Dickens was so enthralled with her voice that he offered to make her his protégé. He said he could make her even greater than Jenny Lind,[3] the reigning coloratura soprano of the day. Dickens claimed that he would take her back to London, where he would make a "prima donna" of her, rather than wasting her talents in the barren deserts of Utah! At this glorious, tempting offer, Gwennie completely broke down and wept again. Life was asking too much of her. On the one hand she could stay home with her mother, and realize not just a young girl's fantasy, but the dream of every great singer of that era — to become a prima donna and sing in the great opera houses of London! After all, couldn't she live the gospel here just as well as she could in America? Her older brother David was staying…On the other hand, Gwennie strongly felt the responsibility of her family, and especially her younger brother, Henry. She knew her father could not make the trip to Utah without her. Who would cook? Who would care for the children? For the second time in days Gwennie had to reaffirm her life-altering decision. She knew she had to give up her worldly dreams and reach inward for her spiritual ones. She knew she had to be the one to ease the burden her father shouldered…she must go and be the little mother to her brothers and especially to baby Henry. Gwennie declined Mr. Dickens generous offer, and sought solace with the other kind women on the ship. How thankful Irene was for

---

[3]Jenny Lind was the first Swedish mega-star, famous for her exquisitely expressive singing. Often called the "Swedish Nightingale," she was one of the most remarkable singers in the world. She earned a fortune and donated large sums of money to charity. There are still hospitals, schools, orphanages, and scholarships, bearing her name today.

Gwennie's decision to stay with her father, to give up fame and glory, and as a result bring great spiritual strength and blessings to her posterity!

As the ship sailed from port, the brass band from Cardiff played "Hail Columbia," "The Star Spangled Banner," and "Yankee Doodle." Many tears were shed as more than a thousand Saints said goodbye to their homeland.

After they arrived in New York, they traveled to Winter Quarters. Upon reaching this departure point for the wilderness of the west, the Davis family was overjoyed because they not only met several people they knew, they were assigned to the wagon company headed by John Edwards, Jr.! What a lovely coincidence, since these families had actually known each other in Wales.

During the journey, as promised and expected, Gwennie did all the cooking, cleaning, and washing for the family, as well as taking care of the children. The trip went quickly for Gwennie, as she and John had plenty of time to become acquainted.

The wagons numbered about 100. The occupants were immediately placed on half rations, for little food, such as fish from the streams or buffalo, was available along the way. They arrived in the Salt Lake valley in October, 1863, five months after leaving London.

After staying a few days at Emigration Square in Salt Lake, which served much like Ellis Island in New York, they set out for Willard, Utah, where many Welsh people had already settled. About two months later, on the 21st of November, 1863, Gwennie became the bride of John Edwards, Jr., who had brought them across the plains. It must have made the difficult trek much lighter to have a romance along the way! Their first home was a two-room log house. Their son, David T. Edwards, would become Irene's father.

The Edwards family raised cattle and sold them to the railroads. John Edwards, Sr. was also involved with building the transcontinental railroad. The east and west lines of the new railroad met at Promontory, Utah, where the golden spike was driven to commemorate the completion of the railroad. An official picture was taken to commemorate the occasion, and John Edwards can be seen in the picture.

Irene Staples: Hostess to the World

Irene's History

> Then, of course, comes prayer: Have family prayer!
>
> "Let prayer be the key to the day, and the lock at night."
>
> "A family that will pray together will stay together."
>
> I remember, as a child coming from a family of 8 children, we would all gather around the big kitchen table and end the evening by all of us kneeling at our chairs around the table and having family prayer.
>
> We all took turns, although the sweet voices of some of the little ones could hardly be heard...I am sure Heavenly Father looked down and saw those 8 little children with father and mother praying for His guidance, and was moved with compassion and answered their prayer a thousand-fold.
>
> Irene

Growing up in a Righteous Family

Irene was born on September 29, 1906, in Malad, Idaho, the fifth of eight children of David T. and Florence Fern Edwards. David had met Florence, a recent convert, while serving a full-time mission in Pennsylvania. David was a dentist by trade.

Like Nephi, Irene was proud to have been "born of goodly parents." In fact, her father had the privilege of being sealed to eternal life by the Prophet of God. From the beginning, Irene and her siblings had a lot to live up to! Like many families, some followed in their parents' footsteps while others wandered off the path.

The family later moved to Preston, Idaho, where Irene's father continued to practice dentistry. One of Irene's earliest memories, and one of her most cherished, was of the entire family — all eight children and their parents — kneeling at their chairs around the table before supper for their daily family prayers. This faithful ritual set an example of righteousness that lasted a lifetime. Even into her 90s, Irene would reflect with great fondness upon that memory of her family kneeling around the table …how could God, looking down upon this scene of a family humbly kneeling in prayer, *not* grant the wishes and blessings they desired of Him? Simple common sense told her He could not! He would not! Irene would often reflect on her mother saying, "Never do anything but what you can ask the Lord's help in doing, whether it is your work, school, or play."

Another vivid memory Irene had was the sound of singing in her home. The family was always singing while doing the usual household chores. They even sang in parts, from the youngest to the eldest. They all attributed their singing talent to their grandmother, Gwennie Davis.

From an early age Irene had a talent for the arts. Arts and crafts, flower arrangements, sewing, writing, decorating, etc., all seemed to come naturally to her. She especially loved to make hats for her dolls (hats were very popular at that time — a lady would not go out in public without a hat!). Of course, as poor as they were, and as young as Irene was, she was reduced to adorning her hats with chicken feathers. Irene also taught herself to play the piano.

Irene started school in Preston, but when her Grandfather John Edwards grew older, he persuaded her father to move back to Willard to help with the farm, which he did in 1917. This was a difficult transition for the family, because they not only left longtime friends but their father's income went down considerably due to working on the farm rather than in dentistry. However, they eventually adapted with the help of their extended family in Willard.

Irene finished grade school in Willard. She had been such a bright and energetic student that she was permitted to skip two grades. Irene went to Box Elder High School, where she graduated in three years instead of the regular four. She was only 15 years old at the time of her graduation from high school! The principal told Irene she was the youngest student to graduate from Box Elder High School, and she was an honor student to boot!

Since moving back to Willard, Irene's parents could no longer afford to buy books, pay tuition, purchase school clothing, etc., so Irene would pick fruit during the summer to earn money to buy clothes and pay for her schooling. She got ten cents a bushel for peaches and five cents for cherries. She would earn up to two dollars a day! Irene was the only one of the five sisters to graduate from high school. She had a great desire to go to college, but without money it was impossible.

Starting a Career

After high school, Irene's father brought her, her sister, and her cousin to Salt Lake City to get work. The Paris Co., a prominent department store, had advertised for an apprentice in the millinery[1] department, so Irene's father took her there. Seemingly out of nowhere, Madam Smith, a tall dark woman with very black eyes strode forward and peered down at Irene. With

---

[1]Millinery is the profession of designing, making, and/or selling women's hats.

35

the gravest look she stared directly at her and said, "Did you make the hat you are wearing?" Irene, almost dying of fright, meekly answered, "Yes, Ma'am."

"Well" she said, weighing her words, "I will hire you at $5 a week, and *if* you prove satisfactory, in six months, I will raise your wages to $7."[2] Then, not even pausing long enough for Irene to respond, said, "Be here promptly in the morning at 9 a.m.!" Too stunned to say anything, Irene simply nodded, and watched this stern woman turn and walk away. Irene was outside on the street with her father before she understood the impact of what had just happened. She had her first job! Her life was about to change dramatically, almost instantly.

This was a dream come true for Irene—she would be moving from chicken feathers to ostrich plumes, from doll clothes to producing the newest fashions of the time for the city's prominent women. The balcony at the Paris where the women worked went around the whole interior of the store, and they could look down on the shoppers on the main floor.

"I loved to make the beautiful big picture hats with flowing ostrich plumes and handmade roses. In those days, a woman wasn't properly dressed without a hat. The women who ordered hats at the Paris were very fussy, but a delight to work with," Irene would say.

On the way to Salt Lake to find work, Irene had only vaguely considered what would happen if she actually found work...she would be forced to move away from her home and family in Willard and move 50 miles south to Salt Lake City! Irene's sister and cousin could not find work and returned home to Willard, but Irene, at 15 years of age, moved from rural Willard to urban Salt Lake City to live with her aunt. Fortunately, her aunt was very good to her, but soon her aunt's family would move to California and bring Irene the first of many trials.

---

[2]This was a *very* good wage for an unskilled female worker.

For now, Irene was excited and happy. The whole world seemed to be opening up for this young woman. It was during this period of time that Irene tried out for, and was accepted into, the Mormon Tabernacle Choir, becoming the youngest member of the choir at that time. She sang in the choir until moving to Idaho four years later. Singing brought such great joy to Irene that all through her life and in every ward she lived, Irene would participate in the choir. Irene's life seemed like a dream come true!

However, her dream was soon dashed. In an instant everything changed. Irene had not known that her aunt did not own the home where she was living. When the owner of the home moved back to Salt Lake, an uncle Irene had never met, the kind aunt Irene had been staying with moved to California, leaving Irene alone to deal with this strange, temperamental relative. Irene's uncle not only demanded that she leave his home immediately, but insisted she pay room and board for the time she had spent in his home! Irene was young, and, intimidated, felt she had no choice but to pay the man the money he demanded. She gave him $30—all the money she had saved. She had been planning to buy a winter coat, and perhaps another dress, as she had only one dress, and no coat at the time, and winter was coming. In tears, she ran downstairs and into the street. Where would she go? She had no money, only one dress, and no coat.

Irene had already been struggling to get by living with her aunt for free. She had been paying $1 for car fare into the city each week, which left her only $4 a week to live on. Irene's father convinced another aunt, who lived in the avenues and closer to Irene's work, to let her stay with them. As it turned out, this was a better option for Irene. This aunt was good to her, and she could walk to the Paris Co., about 12 blocks away. The only downside was the wear and tear on her old shoes. Irene would put cardboard in her shoes to cover the holes that kept appearing. Just when things began to look up again, this aunt also decided to move to California.

Honesty is the Best Policy

By this time Irene's brother, Fern, had found work in Salt Lake delivering milk, so they decided to live together. They got a two-room apartment in a home in the avenues. This solved one problem, but Irene still had no coat for the winter.

It was just at this time of need that Irene's honesty rewarded her with a large amount of money. One night, while going to a 25 cent movie with her brother, Irene found a purse containing money and a large diamond brooch. The owner was stunned when Irene brought her the purse, with all the money and the broach still inside! Impressed with her honesty, she rewarded Irene by giving her $200! It was the most money she had seen in her life, and she could now buy her winter coat!

The money should have given Irene some security, but Irene's father was suffering financial problems—he was too honest and trusting for his own good. Often he would trust people with money and investments, only to lose everything. As the bank came closer to foreclosing on the family farm, Irene was able to rescue her family by giving them the money she had left from her reward.

Another family tragedy happened at this time. Irene's mother went blind from glaucoma. Irene tried to help as much as she could, but in the end there was not much anyone could do. Irene's mother, to her great credit, adjusted very quickly to this devastating event, even learning Braille, and learning how to type. It was *after* she went blind that her mother won awards for her writing, even winning first place in a Church-wide Relief Society writing contest! Irene's mother often said, "My eyes were closed that I might see!"

Irene Begins to Blossom

Two years after Irene started to work, the Paris Co. was sold and new management brought in. Mrs. Smith, the iron-handed woman who had been head of the millinery department, left to work at a competing department store. The new management of the Paris Co. asked Irene to become head of the millinery work room, a wonderful compliment for a girl only 17 years old! Irene had advanced quickly in her millinery skills and in a little less than three years had become head of the department.

The department made beautiful hats for the many wealthy people in Salt Lake who expected to keep up with the newest fashions. Irene's specific job was to design hats and take special orders. Finally, she was able to put her full artistic talents to work and made a real success of the department. The hats had beautiful feathers, plumes, flowers, and velvet and satin ribbons. Irene's hats were the height of elegance. One hat she designed won an award as the "hat of the year," and was worn by the famous Siamese twins Daisy and Violet Hilton.[3] This was a far cry from the "chicken feather" hats she made as a child! However, most girls of today would probably chuckle at these fancy designs, for they were typical of the flapper days[4] of the roaring twenties.

It was also at this time that Irene began to date and socialize with the young people in the city. She often went out with friends on dates and to dances. Irene *loved* to dance, even winning first prize at a dance contest at Lagoon, the local amusement park.

---

[3] The Siamese twins, Daisy and Violet Hilton, were born in England. Their adopted family put them on exhibition as part of a group called Rose's Royal Midgets, They eventually moved to America and spent most of the 1920s on the vaudeville circuit, playing clarinet and saxophone, and singing and dancing. The sisters became a national sensation, and even appeared in the well known cult-classic movie *Freaks.*

[4] The term *flapper* may have derived from a fashion of wearing galoshes unbuckled so that they flapped as the person walked. During the 1920s flapper was used to describe an impetuous girl who was attractive, reckless, and independent. Flappers wore 'kiss proof' lipstick and a lot of heavy makeup with beaded necklaces and bracelets. They also loved to wear fancy hats. Flappers were a new breed of young women who wore short skirts, bobbed their hair (a *bob* was a short haircut that became very popular in the early 1920s); listened to jazz, and flaunted their disdain for whatever was traditional and decent behavior for that era. Flappers pushed the envelope for the women of that generation, and were often seen as brash for wearing makeup, drinking, and smoking cigarettes.

It was at one of these dances at Lagoon that Irene first met Harold Staples, her future husband. Harold and Irene had mutual friends, so Harold had seen Irene and was attracted to her. One night at Lagoon he asked Irene for a dance. Before the end of their first dance, Harold had asked Irene for a date. From then on they dated often. He was nice looking, clean in his dress, and had highly polished shoes. Irene thought he looked like Harold Lloyd, a popular movie star in that day. Irene thought to herself, *"Anyone that keeps his shoes so highly polished must be clean and well groomed all over!"*

These were times of great contentment and fulfillment for Irene, perhaps the very best times of her life. Here she was, a young woman of 17 or 18, totally independent and on her own. She was well into a career she loved, and was making more money than most adult men of the time. She was young, beautiful, carefree, and it showed as she danced across the floor with young men who clamored for her attention. After all the trials and poverty she had endured, it seemed like nothing could break this wonderful spell. She, like many others, was swept-up in the fashions and frenzy of the roaring twenties. Irene bobbed her hair and wore the newest fashions, danced the newest dances, and pushed the conventional envelope as far as her conscience would let her! Little did Irene know her carefree days would soon be over, as a result of a decision she herself would make.

A Time of Decision

At 19, Irene received a job offer to manage the entire millinery department of a ladies' ready-to-wear store in Idaho Falls. They offered $15 a week, with room and board. Those were *really* good wages in those days, especially with room and board added on top of her salary.[5] Irene felt she could not pass up this great opportunity, and so, perhaps without fully understanding the consequences of such a decision, she accepted the job.

---

[5] Highly skilled men at that time earned $30 a week. Most women earned less than $10 per week.

Irene moved to Idaho Falls right after the 1st of January, 1926. As usual, Irene thoroughly enjoyed the work, but, as is common with high-pressure careers, she was so busy working she did not have the opportunity to meet other young people. It wasn't long before her loneliness turned to depression. Although she was making an enormous amount of money, and had experienced a meteoric rise in her career, she was lonesome. The carefree days of friends, parties, and dancing were suddenly gone. She had always thought she would find complete fulfillment in her work, but was facing the stark reality of the lessons she had been taught over and over as a child: that true joy can only come through God and family!

It was Irene's good fortune that Harold continued to write, pleading with her to move back to Salt Lake. In February, as Irene's depression deepened, Harold decided to drive to Idaho to see Irene in person, to convince her to come back to Salt Lake. As Harold drove through Idaho, on his way to Idaho Falls, he had an accident. He immediately called Irene from Pocatello and ex-plained he was stuck — his car had been towed to a local garage to be fixed and there was no way he was going to make it to Idaho Falls to see her.

Harold convinced her to catch the train to Pocatello, which she did. As the two sat together talking, it became clear that Har-old was as lonesome as Irene. He was afraid he would lose Irene forever if she stayed in Idaho.

Harold could see Irene was depressed. He felt this might be his one and only chance to commit her to marriage. Kneeling at her side, and with great emotion, Harold asked Irene to marry him. To his astonishment, she agreed to his proposal. Even years later, Irene could not say exactly why she agreed. Harold's deci-sion to drive to Idaho had made a great difference. It had proven how serious Harold was in his love for Irene.

Harold had timed it perfectly. They both had felt so lonely — why not solve their mutual loneliness by being married? Then they could create a home for themselves where they would never be lonely again. It seemed like a logical solution, so Irene said yes.

Harold was not going to risk fate by waiting to seal this commitment! He suggested they be married that very day by a judge in the courthouse, there in Pocatello, Idaho. Harold was so persuasive, and their desire to be with one another was so great, that all other thoughts fled from their minds — their extended families, Irene's career, even the Temple marriage Irene had always *assumed* she would have, all seemed to fade into the background as they ran hand in hand to the courthouse to be married.

On February 23, 1926, at the age of nineteen, Irene was married to Harold by a justice of the peace. He asked Irene a lot of personal questions because he was *sure* she had eloped to get married without permission. Just to make sure they lived up to their promise to tell their parents, and without their knowledge, he called and put an announcement of Irene's marriage in the Salt Lake newspaper, which came out the next day. As fate would have it, one of Irene's sisters saw the notice in the paper about Irene's marriage to Harold and ran to tell her parents.

The next day, after their excitement and emotions had ebbed away, reality set in for both of them. What would Irene tell her family? Was she ready for the disappointment her family, and especially her father, would express after hearing the news? That night she wrote her parents a letter explaining her actions, but of course the letter would not reach her family until well after they read about the event in the paper. As for curing her loneliness and depression, at least for now, nothing would actually change. By the next day, Harold's car was fixed and he drove Irene back to Idaho Falls to resume work. Harold returned to Salt Lake to his own job, and to find a place to live for himself and his new bride.

Later in her life, as Irene reflected back on her decision to get married, she would say that if she could do it over again, she would *not* get married that way again! It was not right to get married so impulsively, and it was very hard on her parents to be left out of such an important event in her life. The only consolation for her parents was that they had met Harold before, so he was not a complete stranger to them. Irene and Harold had gone out together on and off for over a year. Irene said, "It was a spur-of-the-moment decision between two lonely people in love, and when you are young and alone, you are likely to do things you otherwise would not do." Irene would come to believe that her hasty decision to be married was a mixed blessing. She had married a good man, who became a kind and loving father. But later in life, while her passion for the gospel grew stronger, Harold's commitment to the Church remained lukewarm. Though always found worthy to enter the temple, Harold had a quiet way about him that seemed the opposite of Irene's exuberance and outgoing nature.

Irene's skyrocketing career was now over, but unknown to all but God, another, more fulfilling career awaited her in the future.

Early Married Life

About a month after her marriage, Irene's employer in Idaho Falls found someone to take her place and she was able to return to Salt Lake. By then, Harold had used up all of his money to rent a small one-room apartment with a Murphy bed that folded down from the wall. Harold was completely penniless, having not even the $2 deposit to turn on the lights.

But Harold always seemed to find a way to touch Irene's heart. Although the apartment was almost completely barren, he had the foresight to put a small bouquet of roses on the table. Until her death, it was the nicest bouquet of flowers Irene ever received! They had no lights, nothing to eat, and no gas for heat, but Irene had beautiful flowers to grace her table.

As Harold and Irene began to grow as a married couple, they naturally desired to secure an eternal future for themselves and their children. So, on December 13, 1928, almost two years after being married, Irene and Harold went to the temple to be sealed for time and all eternity. Though they both desired children, it would be four long years before they would have their first child.

Harold had worked for a local Piggly Wiggly as a store manager, but after the company was bought out by Safeway he was laid off, so he went to work at a Chevrolet dealership. Working on commission, Harold didn't make much money, but he finally found what he was good at—selling. Believing that he could make more money working for himself, in 1929 he took $500 and started a used car business on Main Street in Salt Lake City. What perilous timing—starting a business just before the great depression! But Harold was a good businessman, and by working long hours he was able to make it work.

After Irene was married, she went back to work just as she had done before, designing and making hats. She got a new job at a wholesale millinery company, where she worked until her first child, a daughter they named Shirley, was born on March 24, 1930.

After Shirley was born they decided an apartment was no place to raise a child so they bought their first home on Princeton Ave. With her skills Irene was able to demand and get high wages, and by being frugal with her money they were able to pay cash for their new home. During the depression, few people had much money. They paid only $2,500 for the home they moved into on Memorial Day, 1930. Irene's other three children—MaryAnn, John, and Richard—were born while they lived on Princeton Avenue.

Irene Discovers Service

Not long after Shirley was born Irene took a two-year break from her millinery career. This permitted her, for the first time as an adult, to become fully active in church activities. It was during this time, in the LeGrand Ward, finally settled into a home with a family, that Irene began to use her many talents for the benefit of the Church. During this period she would write many plays, songs, and other entertainments for the benefit of her ward and stake.

Her first church calling was as the Primary[6] Activity Director. Faithfully fulfilling this calling led to other callings.

At this time the Church began a pilot program in the Le-Grand Ward called "Junior Genealogy." Irene was called to be the teacher. As part of this calling, she wrote a play which was put on in the ward, called *Why Junior Genealogy*, that included an original song.

In 1939, Irene was called as Ward Mutual[7] President for the young women. Irene created an original one-act play once a month, every class taking a turn, so everyone could participate. They charged every adult who came to the plays a dime, which covered expenses and helped with the ward budget.

One day Stake President Marion G. Romney[8] met Irene in a meeting and said, "Sister Staples, I understand that you are the most outstanding Mutual President in the stake. Congratulations, we appreciate your good work."

---

[6]Primary is the LDS Church organization for teaching small children up to the age of 12 years.
[7]Mutual is the name of the youth organization in the LDS Church for teenagers up to the age of 18.
[8]Marion G. Romney later became a counselor in the First Presidency.

Irene was Mutual President for two years, and was released when she became pregnant with her last child, Richard. A notice was placed in the ward paper:

> "YOUNG WOMEN LOSE THEIR LEADER: After two years of faithful and devoted service, Irene Staples resigns as President of the YWMIA.[9] Her labors have been outstanding. Her effort sincere and genuine in character. Each department increased in enrollment and developed spiritually under her leadership. We are also indebted to her for the fine programs furnished the Personal Culture Class during the season. The sacrifices a young mother makes to render a church service of this kind are almost innumerable. All the Ward joins with us in an expression of appreciation which we hope in a small way will signify our thanks."

Eventually Irene was forced by circumstances to return to work. Harold's used car business was still struggling, due to the great depression, and Harold's mother convinced him that he should let Irene return to work as Irene could earn much more than Harold (Irene had been making about $50 a week when she quit work, while most skilled workmen were making $30 a week). Harold's mother even arranged to have a girl from Kanosh come to Salt Lake to tend the children.

A "Short" Trip to the Country

In 1942 Harold decided the family should move out of the city to the Cottonwood area, a more rural part of the Salt Lake valley located several miles south. Irene did *not* want to move back to the country! She loved the excitement of city life, and the new home would be so isolated it would require a *big* adjustment moving where the majority of people were still farmers. However, Harold felt that in the country they could have a garden, fruit trees, a cow and chickens, etc., so they could have and grow their own food. Following the great depression and during World War II everything was expensive and many items could still be very scarce. By living on a small farm, their cost of living

---

[9]Young Women's Mutual Improvement Association.

could be reduced. The obvious problem was that Irene would be the one that had to bear the burden of all the additional work, as Harold was still working long hours at his used car business and was out of town much of the time buying and selling cars. Although she disagreed with the decision, Irene packed up her home and family and moved with Harold to Cottonwood.

Irene had always been a faithful member of the Church, but for some reason it was after this move to the country that Irene's religious passions really began to burn. Perhaps it was because of the burden of responsibility that was placed upon her, or perhaps it was the people who quickly welcomed her into their ward and their lives.

Irene did not have to wait long to be called to serve in her new ward. Over time she would serve as First Counselor in the Mutual organization, editor of the ward newspaper, and Primary President. This was followed by Mutual President for the second time, Relief Society[10] theology teacher, Relief Society Homemaking Leader, and First Counselor and then President of the Relief Society. She was eventually asked to serve on the Stake Board for the Relief Society. These were followed by stints as Sunday School Teacher and MIA Drama Director.

During her time as Primary President, Irene had many Primary parties and carnivals, and even formed a children's orchestra! She also arranged a trip to the Tabernacle, where the children were permitted to sit in the choir seats during an organ recital, followed by a trip to Farmington, where the first Primary was organized, to eat a picnic lunch. One of Irene's Primary parades was so successful they were asked to have some of their floats in the State 24th of July parade in Salt Lake City.

---

[10]Relief Society is the LDS Church organization for women.

As a result of her service as Mutual President of the Cotton-wood Ward, Irene was honored by the General Presidency of the YWMIA with the *Individual Leader Achievement Award.*

While Relief Society President she organized a sewing project to provide everyone in the ward their own temple clothing.

During all this time of activity for Irene, Harold remained quietly in the background. He was called to be a Seventy[11] and then Superintendent of the Sunday School, but was not able to devote much time to church activities due to the responsibilities of providing for his family. However, he, too, loved to put on parties, and joined Irene in preparing their large yard and barbeque area for ward socials and events.

Irene Becomes Active in Politics and Civic Affairs

With their large front lawn and secluded location, the Staples often held ward and civic parties at their home. One such event in 1949 was a part of the Welsh Mapping Festival, called the *Gymanfa Ganu* held in central locations, such as the Hotel Utah, the University of Utah, or the Tabernacle. The social highlight of this year was a garden party held at the home of Harold and Irene. Many, including Irene, dressed up in traditional Welsh costumes for the occasion.

At a similar event in celebration of *St. David's Day,*[12] Irene chaired a banquet and musical program for about 200 held at the Hotel Utah. One invited guest of Welsh descent was David O. McKay, President of the LDS Church.

Irene was always proud of her pioneer and Welsh ancestry. She often spoke and wrote about the accomplishments of the

---

[11]A Seventy is a local missionary for the LDS Church.

[12]St. David's Day, held on March 1ˢᵗ each year, is a day of national celebration for the Welsh. St. David is the Patron Saint of Wales, credited with securing the permanence of Christianity in Wales.

Welsh people. For example, among the signers of the Declaration of Independence were 17 men of Welsh descent. Seven presidents of the United States were Welsh. Howell Dda (Howell the Good) was a great Welsh king of the 10th century whose just laws became a part of the Magna Carta which was granted the English after the Battle of Runnemede in 1215. Later this charter was written into and became part of the U.S. Constitution. Irene's passion for her heritage led her to write an essay on *Mormonism in Wales* that was placed in a local publication.

It was while living in the Cottonwood area that Irene first became involved in civic affairs and politics by joining the Holladay Pageant of the Arts and the Women's Republican Club. One event Irene chaired was a Republican fundraiser and appreciation dinner for Michigan Governor George Romney. Held at the Hotel Utah, Irene provided decorations for 120 tables and entertainment.

Brother Jim Faust[13]

Harold and Irene were part of the first group to welcome James Faust and his family after they built their home in the Cottonwood area. When Jim Faust was made the Bishop of their ward, Harold became Bishop Faust's home teacher.[14]

Brother Faust described Harold's visits to his home in this way: "His coming to my family was more than a visit, it was an event! Harold would tell my children deer hunting stories, and they never seemed to tire of hearing the story told by Harold of how his noble father was spared by the Indians because he manifested such great courage."

Over the years, Harold befriended many in the ward, including Brother Faust, by sharing with them his great passion, hunting.

Brother Faust, speaking at Harold's funeral, said:

---

[13]James Faust would later become a counselor in the First Presidency.
[14]Each month priesthood holders visit members of the Church in their homes.

Like many of you...I have enjoyed sitting with Harold in a duck blind. Harold was a perfect host...in the early morning when it was cold, Harold, just at the right time, would produce some warm food.

At tithing settlement, I recall the great impression it made upon me when, at the appointed time, into the bishop's office came Harold and Irene, and each of their children, and their children's husbands, and their children's children. All of them! And when it was discussed what their contribution should be, over and above their regular tithes and offerings, I believe it was Irene who said, "We should contribute as we have been blessed, with great abundance." Harold's faith was quite sincere, but it was unparaded. He didn't want his quiet kindness known, and more often than in words...it was done quietly, left on the doorstep. He didn't want to be seen of men, but there was no end to his generosity.

During the time Brother Faust served as Bishop, Irene wrote several ward skits that included Bishop Faust. These skits were designed to make light-hearted fun of people in the ward, their callings and habits.

Harold and Irene Come to an Agreement

In 1954, after years of working at his used car lot, Harold had the opportunity to buy a Chevrolet dealership in Bountiful, Utah. He could move out of selling used cars, and into the "big time" through owning his own auto dealership. Irene saw an opportunity to move the family back into the city. Harold needed money in order to purchase the new car dealership. The family had been renting their Princeton Ave. home, which could be sold to get the money, but Irene would only agree to sell the home on one condition—that they move back to Salt Lake City. Besides, if Harold was going to work in Bountiful, a city north of Salt Lake, living in Salt Lake City would cut in half Harold's travel to work.

So in 1954, 12½ years after moving away, Irene finally persuaded Harold to move back to the city. They sold *both* their homes, used the proceeds from one to purchase the auto dealership and from the other to purchase a new home on Virginia Street in Salt Lake City. Irene was happy and Harold got his car dealership!

Once again Irene was back in her element: high society and an exciting urban life. She seemed able to recapture the carefree life of her youth! She and Harold started the Top Hatters Club, a dinner and dance club that organized dances and parties. Irene also joined the Classics Club and Ladies Literary Club, promoting good books, poetry reading, and plays. Irene wrote skits and small plays for these clubs.

Of course, she continued to serve in the Church within the Federal Heights Ward, as First Counselor in the MIA, Visiting Teacher[15] Message Leader, and, for six years, as the Mutual President.

Irene's excitement at moving into the city, and the fulfillment of Harold's dream of owning a car dealership, were to be short lived.

Harold's Death

In the fall of 1959 the entire family had been invited to Irene's for a family dinner to celebrate Harold's birthday. During the dinner, one of the grandchildren said something nice about the dinner or about Harold. Harold was so impressed, he offered to give the child a reward of a dollar. The other grandchildren were quick to pick up on this reward system, and soon Harold was overwhelmed with compliments and expression of love! Harold was suddenly obliged to give out $1 bills to any of the children or grandchildren who said thank you, said they loved him, or had a second helping of Irene's lima bean soup with ham (a soup the whole family loved). After the dinner was over, Harold had doled out over $50 dollars! It was a happy time—the last time for a long time the family would be happily united.

---

[15]LDS women visit the home of each woman in the ward once a month.

Just before Thanksgiving of that year Harold would fall ill and be sent to the hospital, in grave condition. On December 5, 1959, Harold died suddenly of a brain tumor. Less than three weeks earlier, he had complained of a severe headache, coming home early from work. When the typical "home remedies" didn't work, and the pain increased, he was hurried to the hospital.

Harold was diagnosed with a brain tumor and scheduled for an operation. Irene had complete faith that he would be cured. Not only had a blessing been given, promising a recovery, but she had already witnessed a miracle[16] of a similar kind with one of her grandchildren. But all her faith and prayers were to no avail. When they operated and saw that the tumor had spread throughout his brain, the doctors knew immediately that it was inoperable...and there was no hope. Harold *was* going to die.

Many people would have let a devastating event like this break their faith. But Irene would weather this storm of life, and somehow be able to put it in perspective. Had this event not occurred, would she have been placed in the position to serve the Lord as she did? It is doubtful that, with life's ebbs and flows, Irene's path could have stayed the same. This terrible crucible of death and pain was preparing her to serve God in an even greater capacity. However, these things can only be seen in hindsight.

Their longtime friend, James Faust, now a Stake President, spoke at Harold's funeral. As usual, he was able to give some timely wisdom and advice to those who attended the funeral, and specifically to the mourning family.

> There is too much that is meaningful and precious for us to lose by not rendering the obedience that is necessary. You children might observe something out of the fabric of your father's life. I counsel you with all my heart not to fail him. Hold true to that which he believed in and practiced, that which brought him and has brought your mother great and rich happiness.

[16]See Chapter 4, *A Legacy of Miracles.*

Preaching was not one of Harold's fortes in the conventional sense. While talking little and saying much, there is something more than talk. It was the communication of a sincere spirit and an understanding heart, of a great soul who did wonderful things for other people's children.

And if we who are here want this day to mean much more than it can in any other way, we should do as Harold did, do something for another man's son. *For God so loved the world that He gave his Only Begotten Son. And the king shall answer and say unto them, Inasmuch as ye have done it unto the least of these my brethren, ye have done it unto me.*

Irene's carefree life was, for the second time, gone in an instant. Irene would be kept busy: the new auto dealership had to be sold; children would be graduating from college, getting married, going on missions; she would have to find work to help with the bills; and yet there was still too much time to think, and to feel the loneliness surrounding her. She had felt this type of loneness and despair years before, in Idaho, and did not want to feel it again. So Irene determined she would fill her life with more and more service.

Irene's primary reaction to Harold's death was to keep herself so busy she did not have time to mull over her circumstances. By trying to continue her social activity, further expanding her Church service, and finding other things to keep busy, she was able to keep her mind off her problems.

Irene was appointed a member of the Utah State Fine Arts Commission and Symphony Board by Governor Clyde; became active in the Daughters of the Utah Pioneers, church study groups, and the Red Cross; became Vice Chairman of the Salt Lake County Cancer Drive and a delegate to the National Cancer Conference in Ohio. She also worked with the Heart, Polio, Community Chest, and other associations.

As time allowed, her political interests continued to expand also. She served as President of the Salt Lake Women's Republican Club, member of the Utah State Republican Central Committee and the Utah Federation of Republican Women's Board, a county and state delegate, and a delegate from Utah to the National Republican Convention. She also served as receptionist at the House of Representatives for the State Legislature.

In January, 1960, Irene sold Harold's share of the auto dealership. Soon afterwards, she started working for a flower shop in Foothill Village. She was so good at creating and selling flower arrangements, the owner asked her to manage the Hotel Utah Flower Shop. She continued working there for about one year.

However, no amount of work or service, it seemed, could dispel her loneliness. On the six month anniversary of Harold's death, Irene wrote: "Six months today Harold was buried. I wish he could just once come and say hello to me. I am so lonely."

Irene began her "costume career" by volunteering to design and make the costumes for the MIA production of *Our Heritage* held in Kingsbury Hall.

In July of that year she attended the Republican National Convention as a delegate from Utah, and saw President Eisenhower give his farewell speech and Richard Nixon receive the nomination.

She continued to make costumes for various MIA productions such as *An Evening in Social Hall*, the summer festival at the University of Utah, and MIA dance festivals.

As 1961 rolled around, she continued to be busy with MIA meetings, Literary Club meetings, luncheons, and, of course, still making costumes for MIA conferences and productions.

In April she began preparations for the Western Governors' Conference to be held in May. The conference was held at the

Hotel Utah for 500 people, including 15 governors. Irene was in charge of the entertainment committee which included all the table decorations and providing the entertainment.

The *Deseret News Women's Features, May 25, 1961,* described Irene's participation in the Governor's Conference and the upcoming *Promised Valley* in this way:

> "My greatest joy is in service to others—whether in the field of home and children, politics, or civic interests."
>
> These sentiments have motivated Mrs. Irene E. Staples, 23 Virginia St., for as long as she can remember.
>
> "I have always felt that a person must have a balanced life in all fields of endeavor to achieve his highest potential. This involves a willingness to help others."
>
> This philosophy, says Mrs. Staples, "I've always preached to my children."
>
> And Mrs. Staples is one person who practices what she preaches, for her busy life is filled with an assortment of fascinating, worthwhile activities that involve, above all else, service to others.
>
> **Arranged Entertainment**
> Just such an activity ended this past week for Mrs. Staples. It was she who had charge of all the entertainment for the Western Governors Conference—banquets, programs, decorations—and her only compensation was the "joy of doing something for others." She hoped her efforts would contribute to an enjoyable stay for out-of-state visitors—so that "they would leave with a kindly feeling toward Utah."
>
> Mrs. Staples was a full month preparing for the convention entertainment. She worked out every detail with meticulous care, including the elaborate décor at the state dinner. For this event, among other things, she made by hand (for the head table) a 50-foot tablecloth of American Beauty satin brocade with silver underskirt.
>
> With the Governors Conference over, her time is consumed now with designing and making the costumes for "Promised Valley", to be presented June 6-10 under direction of the MIA at Kingsbury Hall. One room in her home is devoted entirely to this project at the moment—complete with cutting table, sewing machine, fabrics of every color. Again, her compensation is her joy in helping others.

During LDS conference sessions in April, Mrs. Staples conducted a work-
shop to show stake MIA workers from throughout the Church how to cut,
make and adjust costumes for their own "Promised Valley" presentations.

All that spring Irene had been working on designing and
making the costumes for *Promised Valley*, a play put on by the
General Board of the MIA during a General MIA Conference
held in June. She personally designed and handmade over 200
costumes!

The production of *Promised Valley* was such a success that it
was decided it could and should be performed for wards and
stakes throughout the Church. After the first production was
over, the costumes were then "passed around" to any of the
wards and stakes from Canada to Mexico that wanted them, so
they, too, could put on this pioneer production. For months,
Irene shipped out the costumes for the play to stakes and wards
around the country, and when the costumes were returned she
repaired them, cleaned them, and shipped them out to the next
group performing the play. By charging a small fee of 25 cents to
$1 for the rental of each costume, she was able to cover the cost
of their cleaning.

Among her thousands of friends in the Mutual Improvement
Association she is fondly known as "the woman who has sewed
for miles and miles." Her trusty sewing machine has provided
the power to bring her creative costume ideas to reality.

Her friends on the MIA General Board recall that, at the time,
Irene went far beyond the call of duty:

> Irene had designed and made hundreds of beautiful costumes for
> the presentation. After conference, letters started coming asking how
> wards and stakes could get costumes for their own productions, said
> one board member.
>
> As a board, we had no way of supplying costumes. But Irene was
> so anxious to help those people of the wards and stakes she started her

own rental service, charging just enough for maintenance of the costumes. She kept them cleaned, mended and on the go all over the country. All on her own time.

After the need for the costumes was over, Irene came into the board offices and left a check in the amount of all the rentals. We cannot begin to describe the invaluable service she performed at this time and many other times for MIA.

Irene did indeed report to the General Board of the MIA on the costumes she had been renting out for the church. She had rented 1,675 costumes to more than 60 stakes and wards. Irene presented them with $1,000 from the rentals.

In September of that year, Irene was presented with the *Service to Youth* award, a desk plaque of wood and bronze with the MIA emblem and the inscription: "Irene Edwards Staples: Beautiful example of selfless, loving and dedicated service to the MIA, Promised Valley, and the youth of the church. MIA Executives and General Boards, September 20, 1961." It was the first such award to be given to anyone outside the MIA General Board.

In August, Irene became a hostess for the Beehive House, giving tours several times a week. In a way, this was Irene's first introduction to being a hostess for the LDS Church. During this first exposure to acting as a tour guide, she would become intimately acquainted with Temple Square, the Lion House, and the Beehive House, all essential parts of the tours that would become an integral part of her later work as the Official Hostess for the Church.

In October, she was asked by the Governor to take charge of a reception at the State Capitol for the wife of the Foreign Minister of Indonesia. She also worked on a program for the upcoming General Conference of the Church.

In 1962, Irene's hectic pace continued. In March she was appointed to the Institute of Fine Arts by Utah Governor George Clyde. In February, she decorated the Republicans' Lincoln Day banquet in the Terrace ballroom for about 1,500 people. In June, she was made President of the Republican Women's Club. In July, she helped in the MIA production of *Papa and the Playhouse* at Kingsbury Hall. The rest of the year was spent attending meetings, luncheons, working, and sewing MIA costumes.

Then the other shoe dropped for Irene. It had been lonely for Irene when Harold died, but she still had a child at home to take care of, and she could busy herself with work and service. Now, the last of her children was about to leave home on a mission. The news was greeted by Irene with mixed emotions. On the one hand, Richard would be the only one of her children to serve a full-time mission, and for this she was immensely proud and grateful. On the other hand, it meant that her feelings of loneliness would increase, as she now would live in an "empty nest."

On December 3rd, Richard left on a mission to Switzerland, and then it was Christmas. Although she would share this holiday season with her married children and grandchildren, Irene could not seem to escape the feelings of loneliness and depression that would come flooding over her when she returned home to an empty house.

Irene began 1963 just as the previous year, filling her time with hostess duties at the State Capitol for the Governor, making costumes for MIA productions, working at the flower shop every day, giving tours at the Beehive House, and performing various ward callings...furiously working to dispel the feelings of loneliness and depression that seemed to have camped around her since Harold's death.

The Golden Gleaner Award

Irene's work and service did not go unnoticed. It led to her being given the Church's highest honor, the *Golden Gleaner Award*. The award was to be given at an elaborate dinner and celebration in June. This was truly a great honor, and was quite a surprise to Irene. Like many who focus on "service above self," she had not kept track of all she had accomplished. But others had!

According to Irene, she had not planned to attend the awards ceremony at all (the award was kept secret until announced). However, Irene's neighbor and home teacher had asked her to attend the ceremony with him. Irene accepted, not knowing that *she* would be one of the people receiving the award! It was quite the joke for those sitting at Irene's table because, as the speaker droned on and on about all the things 'the recipient' had done over the years, Irene was openly expressing her awe at how accomplished this person *must* be to have been able to get all of that work done! To her surprise and embarrassment, they then announced Irene's name! *She* had been the one they had been talking about all along! Those at the table roared with laughter and clapped loudly as Irene wended her way to the podium to accept her award.

In the fall of 1963, Irene received an offer to direct volunteer services at LDS Hospital. It was a full-time job managing the "Pink Ladies," that paid about $400 a month. She would stay at this job until leaving for her life's real work as a missionary and hostess to the world.

Just as the two previous years, 1964 began by preparing decorations for a state dinner for the Republican State Committee at the Terrace ballroom. In Irene's mind, other than the constant feelings of loneliness and depression, nothing had changed. Life went on as usual, filling her time with work and service to drive out the loneliness and give her a purpose in life. But things *were* about to change. Yet another decision awaited Irene that would change her life immeasurably!

Irene herself fully admitted that she had not always made the best decisions. She would often look back and wonder what kind of life she would have experienced had she chosen differently at critical times in her life. Now she was about to face another life changing decision that would eventually propel her into the upper echelon of Church service.

A Legacy of Miracles

Many people think of miracles as something uncanny, something not natural. Since we do not understand how they are performed, we are naturally inclined to feel that way. But if our minds were more enlightened, and we had only a small part of the wisdom and understanding that God has, we would know that these miracles are only natural happenings.

All nature is founded on system and order within certain governing laws. God, with His great knowledge and power, understands these laws and knows how to use them, just as we know that by putting a small seed in the ground a tree will grow. And so it is with God. He knows that under certain conditions, certain things happen in a perfectly natural way, but to us who do not understand, they are miracles.

The Lord has come to the aid of His people many times with miracles. The story of the plagues that were brought upon the Pharaoh and his people for keeping the Israelites in bondage, and then the dividing of the Red Sea while the Israelites walked on dry ground, were all miracles. Many people do not believe them, and say the writers just put in these stories to make it interesting, but that things like that are impossible.

But we Mormons know that nothing is impossible with God.

When our pioneers' fields were infested with crickets eating their crops, and the Lord sent the seagulls to their aid, this was truly a modern miracle.

So until we have greater knowledge, let us always remember that these miracles are perfectly natural with God, and let us never question their possibility.

Miracles are possible in our modern times just as in the past. As long as we are a righteous people, the Lord will come to our aid with His blessings, and even miracles if need be.

As we read the scriptures and hear of the miracles which transpired in ancient days, we begin to think miracles happened only in the past. Just as outsiders say the day of revelation is past, and God no longer appears or gives revelation.

You remember the story of Moses, when he led the people into the wilderness, where they soon began complaining, saying it would have been better to have stayed in Egypt than to come out into the wilderness to starve to death.

Moses called upon God for help and the Lord in His mercy sent manna each morning and flocks of quail came in the evening so the people had food. I am sure many of us think a miracle like that cannot happen today, but it can! The Lord is with His people today just as much as He was in ancient times, and practically the same miracle transpired with our pioneers.

When the pioneers were forced from Nauvoo they fled across the river to Iowa. There were hundreds of them camped along the shore. Their plight was pitiful. There in the scorching sun they were racked with sickness, fevers, and starvation. They cried to the Lord to come to their aid and help them. The Lord heard their prayers, just as He had heard the prayer of Moses, and He sent clouds of quail to those starving pioneers.

They came in droves upon the saints. They entered the tents, flew into the wagons, rested on the wagon wheels and yokes and tongues, and even the little children could catch them. There was plenty of food for everyone.

Thus a modern miracle was performed. If we live righteous lives, pleasing unto our Father in Heaven, the Lord will always come to our aid, yes even with miracles if it be necessary.

Irene

Over the years Irene had developed a desire and talent for service. It was as a result of that service that Irene became a witness to many events she considered miraculous. She came to recognize two things about miracles: first, that it was through service to others that true miracles were performed, and, second, that most miracles occurred through and/or with the help of natural, human means. Here are just a few of the stories that Irene would often relate concerning the miracles that had blessed her life.

A Miracle Blessing to the Cottonwood Ward*

The Cottonwood Ward had just been divided. It was depression days and the Ward was destitute. We even had to borrow the Sacrament Service[1] from another Ward, as we could not afford to buy one.

As Primary President, I asked Bishop Faust what we could do to help him. He said we might be able to raise a few dollars to help buy a Sacrament set.

With my 18 officers and teachers, we decided to have a Ward carnival. We worked very hard, but that was in the day when ice cream cones were 5 cents. Yes, and a quart of milk or loaf of bread was also only 5 cents! Yet with so many people out of work, there was no money to buy anything no matter how cheap it was.

When the carnival was over, we gathered up our nickels and dimes, which totaled $93.10. When we gave the money to the Bishop he looked at the money and asked us if we knew how much the sacrament service cost.

---

*These stories are taken directly from Irene's journal.
[1]The trays that carry the sacrament to members of the congregation.

"No" we replied, "but hoped this would help to buy one." As tears came to his eyes, he handed me the bill. The cost of the Sacrament Service was exactly $93. We had made 10 cents over!

A righteous desire is of great importance in the sight of the Lord, even if it is only a simple little Primary project! It was an act of love we held for Him and His church.

The Clawson's Miracle Baby

After my daughter Shirley was married and became pregnant, she found out that her blood was RH negative and [her husband] Kingsley's was positive. This often causes problems with children.

There was no problem when Kraig (their first child) was born, but when she was pregnant with Kevan,[2] the trouble started. The doctor was supposed to watch her closely. Harold and I were there when she went to the hospital for this second birth, September 25, 1952.

At about 10:00 pm, the doctor came out and said we had a fine young grandson. Shirley and the baby were just fine, and the nurse showed us the baby. But as we left, I told Harold that I was concerned because the baby did not have a good color. But Harold insisted that the doctor said everything was fine.

That night I lay awake worrying about Shirley and the baby. All of a sudden the phone rang…Harold was blessed with being able to sleep regardless of phone, or no matter what, for he said he went to bed *to sleep*. It was about 1:00 am, and I *knew* it was the doctor. Yes, it was, and he said, "Irene, I thought I had better call you tonight and tell you that Shirley's baby will not live. He is very bad with the RH factor and jaundice. I have had a specialist, a good pediatrician, Dr. Robert Rothwell, and he has done everything he can, but the child does not respond."

---

[2]The child in this story is the author of this book.

"When he tried to change the blood [a common practice at that time for RH babies] he was too weak and could not take the shock. It is too bad, but nothing more can he done."

I told him we would come right up, but he said, "No, do not come in now, I have told Shirley and Kingsley. They understand that it is better for it to go now than later. I have given Shirley medication and she is resting. They have taken it very good, but I thought I should let you know tonight."

I told him I still felt that we should come in, but again he said, "No, do not come in now. The baby will be dead before you get here, or he possibly is already. You will be needed in the morning instead."

I ran to the bedroom and woke Harold up. I told him what the doctor said, and that I felt we should go in regardless of what the doctor said. I told him I would quickly call Bishop James Faust, which I did, who said he would be ready by the time we got there, in about 10 minutes. It was quite a long way to the LDS Hospital, about 13 miles at least.[3]

We went directly to the nursery and asked to see the baby. The nurse said that the baby was *dead*, but if we wanted to see him we could. The Bishop and Harold put on hospital gowns and went in. I stayed outside and only prayed.

The baby lay there with no sign of life, no pulse, no sign of breathing—a sad looking little spirit. They anointed the baby with consecrated oil and laid their hands upon him. As Bishop Faust gave the child a special blessing, the Bishop distinctly felt a quiver of life come into that little body!

I felt good and had a comforting feeling come over me. So after checking on Shirley, we came home. Always with a prayer

---

[3]They were living in the Cottonwood home at the time, south of the city and hospital.

that the Dear Lord would continue to bless that little spirit with the blessings it stood in need of at this time.

There is no question in my mind, that through the power of the priesthood...that child which the doctors had pronounced dead, as did the nurse, was blessed according to the will of the Lord...and the spirit of that child returned to that little body!

I know this is true, I have a deep witness within my self: I KNOW WHAT HAPPENED!

We went to the hospital early the next morning. The nurse said it was unbelievable, but the baby was alive! She said, "This morning when the doctor came in I told him the baby was alive." He said, "It can't be, it didn't have a chance. It was dead before I left last night."

But after checking himself, he turned to me and said, "What happened last night?" I told him the child's grandfather and the Bishop came in and gave the baby a special blessing, and after, I checked the baby and I felt there were signs of life. The doctor only shook his head, as he knew it was not medical science which restored life into that child!

As this miracle happened... I knew that the Dear Lord would continue to bless him for a special mission in life, and I express my most sincere and humble thanks and appreciation to the Dear Lord for this great blessing. And may it be a testimony to the family and those who witnessed this miracle!

Day by day and week by week we watched and prayed for the welfare of this little child. He was so very ill that he did not open his eyes for over a week. And when they showed him to us through the glass enclosure, he looked like a new little bird fallen out of the nest, so sick and scrawny looking, with such a horrible jaundice color.

I, of course, put his name in the temple, and when we would ask the doctor about him, he would only say, "All I can say is that he is still alive."

I remember that after he had been in the hospital for several weeks I went with Shirley to bring him home. The doctor was there, and Shirley thanked him and said how much they appreciated what he did. As I stood there he said, "Don't thank me, for as far as medical science is concerned that baby should be dead. All I can say is that someone's prayers were answered."

I remember the medical school made a case history and investigation. They came and tested the blood of we grandparents, on both sides, and asked many questions. They wanted to know what happened, that the child was able to live. Little did they know the power of the priesthood and the miracle blessing that had come to this child.

I also remember when Shirley and I went to the hospital to bring him home. The doctor told Shirley that within six months the baby would possibly be in convulsions. Yet when he was 5 months old, after taking him to the doctor so faithfully, Dr. Rothwell said, "Shirley, I would not tell you this unless I was completely sure. After making all the tests, this baby is completely normal and well in every way. You will not have any problems with him whatever."

I remember I used to say, "If Kevan was any more normal than he is... he would not be normal."

Now Kevan is grown, he filled an honorable mission, and is married and the father of five beautiful children. Yes, his life was a Divine Miracle!

The Miracle Costume

One of my most memorable design jobs involved a single gown. After spending *weeks* preparing elegant Old English costumes for an MIA production to be presented at a General Conference, I was just exhausted!

Then one night around 11 p.m., a woman who was involved in a companion production came to the door with material under her arm and a request that I please, please, design a dress for one of the cast members in her play.

She didn't have the measurements—nothing. She just desperately needed the dress for a young woman who was going to the university. They'd tried three times to fit her and hadn't succeeded. They needed the dress *the following day* and the young woman had to be in school.

I commenced work on the costume with a prayer in my heart. Guided purely by inspiration, I started with only the material and my own imagination to work with. I didn't even know the size of the young lady who was to wear the costume! I stayed up all night making the dress, a colonial style with several layers of skirts and handmade roses.

By 7 a.m., I had it done, zipper, hem and all. I called the girl and persuaded her to come in for just five minutes before her first class. When the young girl came in she was still afraid she could not be in the show for not having a costume. When we slipped it on and zipped it up, neither one of us could believe it. It fit perfectly! I couldn't have taken it in an eighth of an inch. She was so thrilled she just shrieked. I will never forget her exclamation, "Sister Staples, it fits! And I'm so hard to fit! How did you know the size?" And then we both cried, overwhelmed with thankfulness. We both knew that the Lord had guided my hands!

The Mormon Pavilion/Eastern States Mission

To bring out the thought that our Heavenly Father is always right, I wish to tell a story.

Once there was a widow with only one son, her whole pride and joy. He was suddenly killed while working on a building. This widowed mother could not be comforted, and felt there was no justice. She condemned the Lord and said He had no right to take away her only loved one, whom she had raised to manhood to be a comfort to her in her old age.

But one night she had a dream. She dreamt that when her son had come to the time of his life that he was out for himself, and was forced out into this world of temptation and snares, he weakened. He was not strong enough to say NO. He began harkening to temptations and his life ended in horror and disgrace.

So the Lord, knowing this boy's weakness, had taken him home to save the destruction of his soul. The mother awoke, fell on her knees, and pleaded with the Lord to forgive her for complaining, and for not putting her trust in Him and His wisdom. She thanked Him for sparing her son the life that might have been his, and that now he was safe under his Heavenly Father's care.

> Let us always remember that if we are humble, prayerful, and live righteous lives, the Lord will watch over us and will give us the blessings we need. That we may always say..."Not my will, but Thine be done."
>
> Irene

The Mission Call

One has to wonder what really went through Irene's mind that Sunday morning in early January of 1964, when she first discovered her Bishop was planning to send her on a mission. Even when reading Irene's own words, we can only imagine the shock:

> This morning as I went into the office of the Bishop of the Federal Heights Ward, to give him my envelope of tithing and fast offering, he was busy filling out a large sheet of paper.
>
> As I turned to leave, he said, "Wait just a minute Irene, I would like you to sign this."
>
> "I have always been taught to read what I sign," I said.
>
> "Well it won't make any difference, you'll sign it anyway," he replied.
>
> When I picked it up to look at it, I discovered that it was a missionary call. I was so surprised I nearly fainted and exclaimed, "Bishop, do you know what you are doing? This is a mission application!"
>
> "I have never been more sure of anything in my life," the Bishop said in earnest. "I can't get you there fast enough. I know the Lord has a special work for you to do."
>
> I was surprised and shocked, for my son Richard was already on his mission to Switzerland and had been gone about 13 months. I wanted to go home and talk to someone—like Harold or my father or mother—but it seemed like there was no one to talk it over with. That is one of the heartaches of being alone.

> I accepted the call, for I have never turned down a calling
> from the Church, and I hope I never will.

Irene received her *official* call from David O. McKay February 20, 1964, at the age of 57. She had requested to be sent to the Hill Cumorah Pageant, where she could use her well known skills in making costumes and putting on plays and shows. So it came as a surprise when she was called to the Eastern States Mission.

As soon as she received her mission call it seemed that all hell combined to stop her from leaving. A series of bizarre accidents and incidents occurred that frustrated her efforts to put her things in order before she left. Like all senior missionaries, Irene had to find someone to rent her home, secure finances for herself and her son, who was already on a mission, decide what to do with her car, clothes, and furniture, etc., etc.

As Irene herself put it after *two* car crashes and her house being damaged by a large tree falling on it in a wind storm… "My theme song should be *Who's On the Lord's Side, Who?*"

Irene's farewell was held at her ward on Sunday April 12, 1964. She left directly for the mission home in Salt Lake City the next day. She viewed the many compliments given her at her farewell rather humorously:

> My farewell tonight was a wonderful experience. I felt that it
> was my obituary...I won't need to be here at my funeral, I
> have heard it tonight! I feel very humble for the many wonder-
> ful tributes paid to me. I hope my parents and Harold are
> close by. This has been a terribly hard effort. Sometimes I felt
> I could not go through with it. But of course I did what the
> Bishop wanted me to do.

Irene only stayed at the mission home in Salt Lake for two days before departing for her assignment at the New York Worlds Fair. While at the mission home, Irene immediately showed her natural leadership ability by gathering together the

other sister missionaries for a little skit and song she prepared
for a Family Home Evening. The song not only shows Irene's
sense of humor, but also her competitive nature and belief in the
equality of women:

(Sung to the tune of "This is the way we wash our hands")
Now we are the lady missionaries who come from far and near
We've come to do a special job, which the Elders can't do with their pride
We'll work much harder than they will, we'll teach the gospel too
We'll get so many converts, that they'll have nothing to do but baptize

This is the way we'll knock on the door, knock on the door, knock on the
door,
This is the way we'll knock on the door, so early in the morning

This is the way we'll smile so nice, smile so nice, smile so nice
This is the way we'll smile so nice, to have them ask us right in the house

This is the way we'll go out to tract, go out to tract, go out to tract,
This is the way we'll go out to tract, at five o clock in the morning

This is the way we'll teach the gospel, teach the gospel, teach the gospel,
This is the way we'll teach the gospel, until they ask for baptism.

This is the way we'll bring them in, bring them in, bring them in,
This is the way we'll bring them in, for you Elders to baptize.

The Flying 43

On April 13, 1964, there were 143 missionaries who entered
the Salt Lake City Mission Home. Ordinarily missionaries are
kept there about a week. But with the pressure of the New
York World's Fair opening in April, they only kept us there
two days.

We were sent out immediately. This was such a special group
that we were called the "FLYING 43." Others had gone on
the train and other transportation, but it was such an emergency to get us there that we all flew together to New York.

At the Kennedy Airport we were met by some of the Missionaries from the Mission Home. On the way in from the Airport, we passed the New York World's Fair, and in the distance we could see the spires of the Mormon Pavilion. What a

thrilling sight. They stood up above all other Pavilions, and made us real excited and anxious to become part of this wonderful Fair.

Being the Missionary Group was sort of special. With a very special call to be assigned to the Pavilion, we felt that we should organize a missionary group and call it "THE FLYING 43."

Ten of the group were from Salt Lake City and 30 from close areas, nearby. They were a great group and proved to be some of the very best missionaries in the Eastern States Mission.

A Short History of the Mormon Pavilion
(From notes, letters, and journals of those who served)

The creation of the Mormon Pavilion was a seminal moment in the history of the Mormon Church. Not only was it a monumental leap forward in the Church's attitude towards public relations, it became the *prototype* for every visitors center erected around the world for years to come. Each decision made about how the pavilion would look, what would be presented, and who and how the Mormon message would be delivered to the public would have a ripple-effect down through the years, leading to the conversion of *thousands* of people from around the world.

The Vision

In 1961, G. Stanley McAllister was President of the New York Stake. It would be his inspiration that would lead the Church to build a pavilion at the New York World's Fair. One morning, while reading the paper, President McAllister became interested in an article describing a great World's Fair to be held in New York in 1964 and 1965.

Many years earlier, when Brother McAllister was a missionary in the Eastern States Mission, he had longed for *something* in the eastern part of the United States that he could point to with pride and say, "This belongs to the Mormon Church." At that time there were not many Mormon chapels in the east, and the beautiful Washington Temple was still more than a decade away from being built. Most people living on the east coast knew little about the Mormon Church. In fact, the Church was commonly thought of as just another odd cult or sect.

The feeling that the Church needed a stronger presence in the East never left this young missionary, and years later when he read the announcement about the World's Fair the realization came to him with great force that *this* was the opportunity for which he had been looking. *This* was the event the Church could use to gain wide recognition and acceptance — not only in the East, but around the world. By building a beautiful pavilion at the World's Fair, *millions* from all over the world could learn about the Mormons!

President McAllister had many contacts within the Church that could help bring this vision to reality. One was the association he had with David W. Evans, who was working with the Church Information Service. This "publicity department" was under the direction of the Apostle Mark E. Peterson. During the previous four or five years, Brother Evans had been to New York a number of times, and on several of those occasions President McAllister had promoted the idea of the Church participating in the Fair. Brother Evans had agreed with him and had even begun developing a budget to present to the Church. However, after realizing the size and complexity of the project, it was decided the proposal should be taken directly to the First Presidency, with whom President McAllister had a good rapport.

President McAllister wrote to the First Presidency and suggested the Church participate in the New York World's Fair. He detailed the great advantages the Fair would give to the Church — not only the general publicity and recognition it would receive by attracting millions of people from all over the world, but also the great *missionary* enterprise it would be!

A short time later the World's Fair Organization sent a formal invitation to the Church to become one of the "Religions of America" represented at the Fair. The Church was pleased with the invitation, agreed that it would be a wonderful opportunity, and assigned Elders Harold B. Lee, Mark E. Petersen, and Richard L. Evans to investigate the possibilities of such an endeavor.

During the following months, a great deal of lively debate ensued as suggestions were given as to what extent the Church should extend itself in this venture. Initially, it was proposed that the Church simply have a booth in one of the buildings. This was the "safe" decision—the decision that had been made many times in the past when opportunities of this kind had arisen. Not only were the Brethren reluctant to spend an exorbitant amount of sacred tithing monies on "advertising," but they simply did not have the personnel and expertise to move forward with anything extravagant.

As the Church began to look for booth space in various pavilions, they ran into problems. Most pavilions would be noisy venues, with booths selling various products or food—not a proper atmosphere to share information about the Church in a way that was conducive to the spirit of God. So the Brethren began to move toward President McAllister's vision of having their own pavilion at the Fair.

The Fair officials had proposed the Church join with other Protestant churches and place a booth in the building that had been set aside for world religions. This had been the original basis for their invitation to the Fair. President McAllister had to explain that Mormons were not Protestants, and that the Protestants themselves would not welcome sharing a building with them. When he pointed out to Fair officials that the Catholics, and later the Christian Scientists, had been allotted space for separate pavilions, the Fair officials offered a separate space to the Church.

In the meantime, President McAllister, not satisfied with the direction the Church committee was taking, persisted in trying to convince the Church they should have a *separate* pavilion in which they could present a more appropriate vision of the Church. Having never received a firm answer, President McAllister wired the First Presidency directly, but still he received no reply. Finally, as time for final contract signing was about run out, and in desperation, he phoned Brother Evans to see what could be done. Brother Evans reported everything to the Church Information Service. Elder Mark E. Petersen then made an appointment with the First Presidency, recommending that the Church participate.

In 1963, the Church was still relatively small, with little more than two million members around the world. Many of the Brethren opposed the idea of building a pavilion at the Fair. They just didn't think the Church should spend the amount of money it would take to make this "vision" of President McAllister's possible. Conservative estimates had come in at upwards of *one million* dollars. This was an incredible amount of money, especially for an organization that had *no* experience in such a large project. The Church was used to small booths and outdoor pageants, not massive buildings and international promotions! It became clear that there was only *one person* that could make this decision—the Prophet himself.

It was decision time. After many months of investigation, planning, and many, many phone calls, a decision had to be made. Most assumed the Church would back away from this huge commitment of time and money. Everyone was surprised when President David O. McKay not only made the decision to go forward with the pavilion, but emphasized that this would be a *total* commitment to the project—cost would be no consideration!

An Executive Committee in Salt Lake and a New York committee were appointed to carry out the work of actually designing and building the pavilion. It was a complex and massive undertaking. The design, the architect, the builders, the theme, the displays and all the other many, many decisions that would go into such a project were mind-boggling!

The Publicity

The Church needed a dependable company with national contacts to handle all major publicity. Earl Minderman of Robert Mullin, Inc. based in New York City, represented the Church and the pavilion. This same company had worked with the Church before in handling special events in the east, including the *Hill Cumorah Pageant.*

The Church also had recently purchased a New York radio station. This gave them the opportunity to broadcast information about the Church's participation in the Fair as well as send programs and information concerning the Fair and the Mormon Pavilion to many foreign countries, especially in South America, where the Church was just beginning to find great success. Many people coming to the Fair from South American countries became interested in the Church.

Through the publicity generated by the World's Fair in the press, TV, and radio, the Mormon Church was brought to the knowledge of many people. Many who had never heard of the Church were now very aware of it and its teachings, ultimately bringing in thousands of converts.

The Groundbreaking

Groundbreaking for this massive construction project was held on March 27, 1963. Many General Authorities and local dignitaries were on hand. Speeches were made and prayers said… the die was now cast. An enormous amount of money and manpower was about to be set in motion. Harold B. Lee, representing the First Presidency, said the following at this special occasion:

> It's my high privilege and great responsibility to lead the officials of the Church in the direction of what is to us a very momentous and important occasion. Because this is to be the center of our Church activities, you will understand why I chose some Scriptures to introduce remarks I shall make.
>
> In a great and meaningful Scripture, the Lord said: "Wherefore, as ye are agents, ye are on the Lord's errand; and whatever you do according to the will of the Lord is the Lord's business" [D&C 64:29]. We conceive of this, therefore, as something more than just a business venture. To us it's a significant, spiritual operation. We are on the Lord's errand today, and we are now engaged in His business. He said on another occasion, "Wherefore, be not weary in well-doing, for ye are laying the foundation of a great work. And out of small things proceedeth that which is great" [D&C 64:33]. I suppose that not even the architects who have conceived the image of what will rise on this ground know the greatness of that for which they plan. The builders themselves may not conceive to full extent the magnitude of what will be conducted here.
>
> Perhaps none of us know the far-reaching effects of what we are building. But in order for us to understand, something else was said: "Behold," He said, "the Lord requireth the heart and a willing mind; and the willing and obedient shall eat the good of the land of Zion in these last days" [D&C64:34].I might say to you gentlemen who are associated with us, and to whom we extend deep gratitude and appreciation for your cooperation, we feel that the more unselfish, unpaid, dedicated service we can put into this endeavor, from the

Church's standpoint, the more will be achieved in greatness. For thereon lies the foundation of the Church. The dedicated service of its thousands of people in unpaid ministerial activities and missionary work has made the Church what it is today.

We were very much intrigued by the theme that has been chosen for the Fair—the dramatization of the interrelations of peoples throughout the world and their hopes for peace through understanding. We have tried to capture that spirit in this exhibit for our more than two million people throughout the world. Our theme is based on the premise that the aim of all purposeful living should be the pursuit of happiness, as distinguished from mere pleasure, and appears as scripture: "...and men are that they might have joy" [2 Nephi 2:25].

I would like to take this opportunity to express our deep appreciation to those on the local committee, particularly President McAllister, President West, and their associates.

To all of you attending our ceremony today, we express our appreciation and trust that the turning of the shovels full of dirt which signal the official beginning of the structure will mean a happy relationship for the forthcoming years, 1964 and 1965.

May I, in closing, as representative for the President of the Church, David O. McKay, assure you of our complete cooperation towards the success of this great Fair—perhaps the greatest the world has ever known. Thank you and may peace be with you always.

The Theme

About the time the Church decided to participate in the World's Fair in New York, the Seattle World's Fair was drawing to a close. Brother Evans had an office in Seattle and knew people who were close to the President and Managing Director of the Seattle Fair. A group of brethren, including Brother Evans, Mark E. Petersen, Richard L. Evans, Delbert Stapley, Harold Burton, and the Church Architect, made a trip to Seattle to gather information.

After talking to the people who ran the Seattle World's Fair, two things stuck out in their minds: first, there had to be a simple but powerful *theme* to their pavilion; and second, they should stay away from any food courts or eateries (these tended to be loud, full of debris, and smelled — all negatives).

When the other brethren returned to Salt Lake, Brother Evans remained in Seattle to try to come up with a theme for the pavilion. During the next day or so, Brother Evans remained in his hotel room thinking, planning, writing, and praying. It was in that small hotel room in Seattle that the concept for the New York exhibit came to him: *Man's Search for Happiness.* Brother Evans stated:

> Behind the selection of this theme is the thought that the aim and the end of all purposeful living is, or should be, the pursuit of happiness—happiness as distinguished from pleasure—as expressed in this scriptural text: "Man is that he might have joy." The theme will be developed on these lines:
>
> Unaided by wisdom beyond his own experience, or misguided by purely finite forces, man's quest for complete happiness can never be fulfilled.
>
> Only through communication with Divine sources—continuous revelation from God to man—can man find safe and sure guidance to the ultimate goals;
>
> ...faith that God created and controls the world, and a reassurance that man was made in the image of his Father;
>
> ...acceptance of the fact that the universe is controlled by Divine law and that rewards and punishments follow the keeping and breaking of these laws;
>
> ...understanding that the "glory of God" is intelligence and that man can be saved no faster than he gains knowledge;
>
> ...confidence that the Church of God, guided by revelation and inspiration, should be, and is, concerned with the whole life of man: spiritual, intellectual, social, ethical and physical.

It is to improve and promote this eternal happiness that the revealed principles and inspired programs of the Church of Jesus Christ
of Latter-day Saints have been established. These principles and programs provide the basis of the Church's New York World's Fair
Exhibit.

In the spring of 1962, Elder Harold B. Lee, General Chairman
of the Executive Committee, and Elder Bernard Brockbank, who
had been appointed on-site director, joined together with the
New York committee (the people in charge of actually building
and operating the pavilion) for a start-up meeting in New York.
The theme of *Man's Search for Happiness* was unanimously
adopted and Brother Evans was made coordinator of the exhibit.

For the next five or six months, Brother Evans and the other
members of the New York committee created texts and proposed
ideas for paintings, dioramas, statues, film strips, motion pictures, brochures, etc., to enlarge and develop the theme of *Man's
Search for Happiness*. The committee found artists, display builders, color photo processors, diorama builders, and experts of
many kinds, both within and outside the Church, who were capable of creating and producing the displays needed. Renowned
men such as Harry Anderson, Robert Skemp, Alex Ross, Sydney
King, Edward Vebell, Alexander Rosenfeld, and others were
gathered from around the country to participate in this project.

The Movie

It was decided that the most important tool that would be
used to share the gospel message with the public would be a
short motion picture that explained the Plan of Salvation as
taught by the Mormon Church. In keeping with the theme of the
pavilion, the movie was called *Man's Search for Happiness*.

Just like the pavilion itself, this project was going to be a major leap of faith for those involved. Brigham Young University
had some experience in making films for the Church, but had

never before approached a project of this size. Due to this lack of experience, the Executive Committee's first inclination was to hire professionals in California to create the movie. However, because of the sensitive, spiritual nature of the film, direction came from the First Presidency that the film was to be produced by BYU.

Immediately after the script was written and approved, those making the movie ran into their first hurdle: how should they portray the pre-mortal life? What did people look like in the life before this? At that time, the Church had never produced a film depicting the pre-mortal life. In fact, they realized the entire film would have the same problem—how to share the important *doctrines* of the Gospel of Jesus in pictures rather than words. They had to create a true-to-life vision of what those doctrines represent. Working with the Brethren, they turned to the scriptures to solve questions as they came up. For example, the answer concerning how to portray men and women in the pre-mortal spirit world came from two scriptures:

> *For I, the Lord God, created all things, of which I have spoken, spiritually, before they were naturally upon the face of the earth. (Moses 3:5)*

> *Behold, this body, which ye now behold, is the body of my spirit; and man have I created after the body of my spirit; and even as I appear unto thee to be in the spirit will I appear unto my people in the flesh. (Ether 3:16)*

In the film *Man's Search for Happiness*, men and women in the pre-mortal life, living as spirit children of God, were portrayed *exactly* as they are in this life—with tangible bodies and clothes. They simply used artistic interpretation to present them living in a *spiritual* realm. By working carefully with the Brethren, and using the scriptures as a basis of their portrayal, the BYU group created one of the most beautiful and important gospel films ever produced. Even today, decades after the film was first introduced, it remains one of the most powerful gospel tools available to teach people the Plan of Salvation.

This film would be run every 15 minutes in alternating theaters, and would be the culmination of the visit to the Mormon Pavilion. Tissues were made available at the exit of each theater, as many would leave the theater with tears in their eyes.

The Pavilion Design

Another important decision was the design for the pavilion itself. It had to be something recognizable — something *everyone* would associate with the Mormon Church. One suggestion was that it be a replica of the Tabernacle organ. After much discussion and debate, it was decided that it should be built to replicate the eastern facade of the Salt Lake Temple — including the Angel Moroni.

The Manpower

Perhaps the most important decision made was regarding who would man the pavilion, and what approach would be used to present the Gospel message to the public. Some thought a "soft" approach should be used — that overt proselytizing should be avoided. However, the pavilion operation was under the direction of Brother Brockbank, just back from serving as mission president in Scotland, and Wilburn C. West, current president of the Eastern States Mission. Their *zeal* towards missionary work led directly to the decision to use the missionaries of the Eastern States Mission to provide the manpower for the pavilion. These missionaries would not only teach the Gospel of Jesus Christ to those who visited the Fair, they would openly and proudly invite them to further their interest in the Church by taking the missionary discussions! The decision to use the missionaries in the pavilion and to actively proselyte visitors would have a profound effect on the success of the pavilion and have a ripple effect that is still felt decades later. All of the Church's visitors centers still use missionary manpower to this day.

The Site

A number of studies and site visits were made of the fair-grounds, but it seemed there were always problems. Either the Fair Board would not let the Church build in certain places, or the larger companies did not want the "Mormon Pavilion" to be next to theirs, as they felt it would detract from their own pavilions. It turned out to be much more difficult than expected to find a location that would justify the Church putting up an expensive pavilion.

Due to the delay in getting a final decision to build the pavilion, time had run out on the opportunity to choose the best locations within the Fairgrounds. Only one or two locations were left, and it was doubtful the Fair Board would let the Church have *any* location, as it was getting very late in the process, and most locations had already been spoken for. President McAllister, feeling very anxious, felt prompted to call a personal friend on the Fair Board to intercede on the Church's behalf. At the time of his call, the gentleman just happened to be in the meeting to decide who should have the last locations at the Fair. President McAllister convinced him that they should let the Church have the site by the front gate.

Only after the decision was made did the Church find out there was a major drawback for this specific site: it sat next to the "International Food Pavilion." As learned from their visit to the Seattle World's Fair, the area around the food pavilion was the most *undesirable* site at a fair, with all kinds of food smells and overflowing garbage cans. Many were heartsick, but what could they do about it? At this point they were fortunate to get any site at the Fair!

The Lord would show His hand in this endeavor when a few months later the company in charge of the food pavilion was thrown out for breaking the Fair rules in the type of building they were erecting and failing to keep to the schedule. As it was too late to bring in another vendor, the Fair simply left the lot empty. Although the empty lot gave an unrestricted view of the Mormon Pavilion from the front gate, the lot had been left unfinished, with construction debris lying around.

Then a second miracle happened! When the pavilion workers arrived the day before the Fair was to open, they found that the Church's landscape gardeners, with men and bulldozers, had worked throughout the night to transform this lot into a garden. The whole corner had been leveled off, and a green lawn, shrubs, and large trees had been planted, making a beautiful park. A perfect setting for the front of the Mormon Pavilion!

The Mormon Pavilion site, once the most undesirable site in the Fair, became the *perfect* location! The *first thing* visitors would see as they entered the fairgrounds was the majestic spires of the beautiful Mormon Pavilion! Imagine...a lovely green lawn, with stately trees in the background, sunken gardens overflowing with flowers and plants, benches placed in the shade of the trees, and a large reflecting pool with "floating islands" of flowers! It formed a perfect setting for the *Lord's Pavilion*.

The Construction

The final design of the building was beautiful. It was an exact replica of the eastern facade of the Salt Lake Temple, rising 127' in the air, with a golden Angel Moroni glistening in the sun. But there were problems, always problems. For example, the construction was not always the best, as they had to rely on local unions to provide *all* the labor for the project. Elder Brockbank, the on-site representative, and a builder himself, continually faced

construction problems caused by the local labor unions sending
unqualified workers to the jobsite. Two of the biggest problems,
the roof and the air conditioning, caused constant headaches for
pavilion personnel. The building's roof leaked like a sieve and
the Elders working inside were constantly running around with
buckets to catch the water. One morning, after an especially
heavy rain during the night, they found the building completely
flooded. Elder Brockbank had even gone to the roof himself to
try to patch the holes. However, after much work and patience,
the many problems were corrected.

One of the most unique aspects of the construction of the pavilion was that the building materials could be re-used. It was a
great expense to build a massive pavilion, to be used for just two
years, and then torn down! But the Brethren were very frugal
and wise, and had the pavilion designed so it could easily be
taken down and re-used in constructing a new chapel. In addition, all the expensive artwork—the paintings, dioramas, statues,
etc., were to be re-used when the main Visitors Center in Salt
Lake City was built.

Labor problems were a real issue at the Mormon Pavilion, as
they were at all of the pavilions at the Fair. For example, just before the Fair opened, a special interest group made it known
through both press and radio that they were going to picket the
Fair, and were going to keep it from opening. They felt more mi-
norities should be hired. On opening day, everyone was on
guard and wondered what would happen. The City of New York
had police everywhere, but there was no serious trouble.

One humorous incident occurred at the Mormon Pavilion.
Members of one particular special interest group came into the
pavilion and demanded they be hired. They were told that they
would be hired immediately…*if* they were willing to work for
the same wages everyone else was being paid at the pavilion.
When they asked how much the pay would be, they were told

that everyone working at the pavilion were volunteers...no one was paid! They could hardly believe it, and were never heard from again!

During construction there was a constant battle between the union workers, who demanded that *any* and *all* work done at the pavilion had to go through them, and pavilion workers. For example, the Church had a small pick-up truck which they had been using to go into the city for supplies. It was also used to haul the waste paper and trash away from the office. The union would not allow this, and the pavilion was forced to hire them to haul the paper and garbage.

Once, Irene was doing touch-up painting on one of the wall exhibits that had been damaged. She was stopped and scolded by a union worker who told her if he saw her do it again the union would shut the project down! One day Irene heard some of the men talking during a lunch break. One said, "I really feel guilty, when I see all these fine young men working for free, donating their time, and here I am making the wages I am." "Yeah," replied the other, "It sort of gets to you, doesn't it?"

The beautiful marble statue "The Christus" was sculpted in Italy, and air-freighted to New York. Due to union restrictions, it cost more to have it delivered from the airport to the pavilion, than it did to ship it from Italy to New York!

Raising the Angel Moroni

The focal point of the pavilion was the front façade of three towers. Crowning the center tower, 12 stories off the ground, was the familiar gilded statue of the Angel Moroni. Placing the Angel Moroni on the highest spire of the Pavilion received more national publicity than any other single event of the Mormon Pavilion. Hundreds of newspapers around the country published the picture of "an angel flying through the air" with a related article, bringing enormous publicity to the Church.

Because it took such a large crane to lift the statue 130′ in the air, everyone working at the hundreds of pavilions at the Fair stopped to watch. There was a "standing room only" crowd, with press photographers taking hundreds of pictures. The publicity generated by this event created an image many visitors coming to the Fair remembered: everyone wanted to see the "Angel" at the World's Fair.

The Pavilion and Grounds

Everyone seemed to know about the Mormon Pavilion. The publicity generated during its construction, the beautiful gardens that beckoned visitors, and the recognizable facade of the Salt Lake Temple all added to the attraction. A person could see the spires from all over the Fair grounds, and knowing the pavilion was located near the main entrance made it a welcome landmark as to the direction one was going. Children loved it...they called it their "Fairy Castle" and *always* wanted to go in. They were probably expecting to see Cinderella or some fairy tale characters!

The facade that replicated the Salt Lake Temple stood out several feet from the rest of the pavilion. There was a door into the facade and several times people tried to open the door to get inside the "temple." When they found the door locked, they were heard to say, "I was told that the Mormons wouldn't let anyone into their temples!" The Elders quickly tried to explain that it wasn't a real temple, it was only a facade and there was nothing inside but storage. It only *represented* the famous temple in Salt Lake which everyone recognized.

There was a large reflecting pool in front of the pavilion. Flower "islands" were placed in the water, and it was lighted at night, giving the area a surreal, wonderland feeling. While cleaning the pool and setting new flowers, it was amazing how many pennies were collected from people making a wish and throwing them into the pool. The money was collected and sent to Primary Children's Hospital in Salt Lake City, as was the money collected at the Seagull Monument on Temple Square.

Behind the temple facade were twin halls containing 50,000 square feet of exhibition space. The walls, inset with golden glass, provided a sunny atmosphere in the interior. The twin exhibit halls housed galleries in which dioramas, statues, and paintings would tell the story of the Church, its beliefs, and its history. There were also two theaters with a capacity of 350 each which alternated motion picture showings to ensure all visitors would have an opportunity to see the new film: *Man's Search for Happiness.*

A shift of Elders was assigned to stay in the evening and clean the pavilion. They washed walls, cleaned the carpet, and performed other major jobs to keep the pavilion looking beautiful. As the workers were often complimented on how beautiful it looked, this extra work paid off. There was no trash lying around or spilled-over garbage as one found at many other pavilions. Of course, that was the way it should have been — in keeping with its conception as the *Lord's* pavilion!

The wonderful design of the building and the peaceful and beautiful landscaping worked hand-in-hand for the success of the pavilion, and in bringing happiness to many people who entered the door.

The Gardens

In the same way the spires and the Angel Moroni drew people to that area of the fairgrounds, the beautiful landscaping and reflecting pool drew people inside the pavilion! Almost everyone had been to a fair of one kind or another and was used to seeing a patchwork of buildings and venues that were not always the most presentable. Imagine yourself slogging around a busy fair. It's hot, you're tired, your feet ache, and more than anything you just want a quiet place to sit and rest! Suddenly, you turn the corner and there in front of you is a beautiful garden with large trees shading green grass and several benches. As you rest comfortably in the shade, you gaze upon a fountain with large exotic flower "islands" floating in the water. The sweet aroma of flowers cover the foul smells coming from other areas of the fair and you hear soft music playing in the background. Who would not stop to experience this oasis, and want to know *who* created this heaven on earth?

All of this came to pass through the dedication, the desire, and the hours of devoted service of the Church's landscape architect, Brother Irvin T. Nelson. His goal was to make the grounds of the Mormon Pavilion the most attractive of the entire Fair…to make it so beautiful that passers-by would feel compelled to stop and enjoy the beauty. Then they could be encouraged to come into the pavilion, where they would be told the story of the Restoration of the Gospel of Jesus Christ!

This goal was accomplished. Not only did these gardens bring millions of visitors into the pavilion, but Mr. Robert Moses, President of the New York World's Fair, said, "The Mormon Pavilion and its grounds is the beauty spot of the Fair!" Brother Nelson made a formal report of the landscaping project of the Fair, describing in detail the formal layout plan. Quoting in part from that report, Brother Nelson said:

> We are glad to report that our landscape layout is primarily responsible for the large attendance at the Pavilion. We had to date over a million more persons attend than we had anticipated. People have repeatedly told us that the attractiveness and beauty of our plantings, was what brought them into our building. They also have said that our seats in the shade, surrounded by flowers and moving water, prompted them to stop, rest and visit us.

A typical story of what was often heard by those working at the pavilion, was told by Brother Nelson: "A young man about 25 years of age stopped and spoke to us as we were doing some planting near our reflecting pool. He complimented us on what we were doing and added, 'I am one of the workmen here on the Fair Grounds, and go by this way every morning. I stopped to tell you that by vote of the regular workers here, your exhibit is declared the most beautiful of the entire Fair. We always slow up as we pass by on our way to work and get the inspiration and uplift that comes from seeing something very neat, really clean, and unusually beautiful. Your plantings are food for the soul!'"

The gardens surrounding the pavilion won First Place by the American Association of Nurserymen for the year 1965. This brought great honor to Brother Nelson and even more publicity for the Mormon Church.

Once all the work was completed in designing and installing the landscaping, it had to be maintained for two years as the Fair progressed. Peter Lassig, an assistant to Brother Nelson, and several "work missionaries" spent two summers at the Pavilion, keeping the gardens and grounds beautiful.

It was Peter who also designed the "floating islands" for the large reflecting pool in front of the pavilion. These islands were covered with grass, which made a bedding for hundreds of gorgeous begonia blossoms of every color, some measuring 10 inches in diameter! In the evenings, with the pool lit with indirect lighting and the flowers reflecting on the water, it made an enchanting spectacle of indescribable beauty.

The Message

The tour started with a statue of Adam and Eve, to show that Mormons believed that "man was created in the image of God." The next stop was the "Christus," the famous statue of Christ, illustrating that Mormons are Christians, and not "just another odd sect" of some sort. Then came the mural of Christ ordaining his Apostles to the Priesthood of God, which was used to stress the importance of having "authority from God" to perform religious ceremonies and rites.

Visitors then walked to the long mural of the ministry of Christ. Sidney King was the artist of this wonderful painting that was 110' long and covered the entire length of the center of the pavilion. It included scenes of Christ's baptism, the calling of Peter and Andrew, the Sermon on the Mount, the Garden of Gethsemane, the betrayal by Judas, the Crucifixion, the resurrection, and, finally, Christ's ascension into heaven. The purpose of this large mural was to show that Mormons believe in and follow Christ's teachings.

Visitors were then taken to see the movie *Man's Search for Happiness*. This inspired movie highlighted the doctrine that life is an eternal progression from our pre-mortal life, through this mortal life, and on throughout eternity. This doctrine was new to most people visiting the pavilion. Many were very moved by the idea that their loved ones, who had departed this life, were not only still alive in the spirit world, but that the time would come when they would be united with them again! Many left the theater with tears in their eyes, and reached for the tissues offered them.

After the movie, and at the end of the large mural depicting the life of Christ, visitors saw a picture of John the Revelator writing the Book of Revelation he received by inspiration on the Isle of Patmos, with the quote: "And I saw another angel fly in the midst of heaven, having the everlasting Gospel to preach unto them that dwell on the earth, and to every nation, and kindred, and tongue, and people" [Rev. 14:6]. After reading this prophecy, they then turned to the mural of the angel Moroni, with his trumpet, declaring to the world this message…Yes,

Moroni was the angel which John saw in the last days, restoring the Gospel!

Included in this area was a diorama about the great apostasy, showing how and why the teachings of Jesus were lost or changed over the centuries, and showing the need for the gospel to be restored to the earth in our day.

This concept was new to the visitors—they had never heard of such a thing before. It was at this point that many would realize that the Mormon Church is a *restored* Church...that it is not the Church of Joseph Smith or of Brigham Young, but the *restored Church of Jesus Christ* once again on the earth, and that was why it was called the Church of Jesus Christ of *Latter-day* Saints.

In a natural progression, they were taken to the sacred grove diorama, which had a model of Joseph Smith kneeling in the sacred grove, asking for wisdom to know which Church was right, and receiving the first vision. The missionary guide would *always* bear his testimony to the truthfulness of this vision and of the Prophet Joseph Smith being called as a latter-day prophet.

The visitors were then taken to a diorama of the Book of Mormon. This showed Christ before his ascension telling his followers, "And other sheep I have which are not of this fold: them also I must bring, and they shall hear my voice; and there shall be one fold and one shepherd" [John 10:16].

There was an adjoining diorama showing how Christ came to the western hemisphere, visited with the people there, and established His Church. It was also in this area that the statue of the Prophet Joseph Smith was placed, with a list of his accomplishments and the Articles of Faith.

The last stop on the tour was the "Plan of Life" mural. This mural was designed to reinforce the concepts taught in the movie they had seen. It depicted our life at the beginning as we left our

Heavenly Father's home; as a child with our earthly parents, our schooling, marriage, our life's work, old age, and as a grandparent with a little grandchild; then ended at death's bed with heavenly hands stretched out to welcome us back into our Heavenly Father's home.

At the end of the tour the visitors were taken to the Information Desk, where they were given pamphlets or could buy copies of the Book of Mormon. The missionaries would answer any questions about the Church (on the wall near the desk was a picture of the Prophet and General Authorities of the Church). As they exited the pavilion there was a Guest Register that visitors could sign and referral cards they could fill out so the missionaries could call on them at their home. These signed slips generated nearly *700,000* referrals!

Opening Day

The opening day of the pavilion was an exciting event. Elder Brockbank, President West, and the missionaries had worked and planned for weeks as to how to take care of pavilion visitors. Without any previous experience, it was difficult to decide exactly how to handle the crowds they hoped would engulf the pavilion.

The inside of the pavilion was very well designed. As people entered they would be met by a *greeter*, who would record the number of visitors with a mechanical hand counter. The tour guide would stand in the center of the entrance, facing visitors. He would use a short introduction, an "overview" of what they would see during the tour—whatever was needed to keep the group occupied until the next tour was ready to start. After he saw a group move away from the first stop along the tour, he would move his group forward. It was quite a juggling act trying to keep the groups from running into each other! Sometimes two or more groups would pile together, creating quite a traffic jam. However, the missionaries soon became quite professional at moving thousands of people through the pavilion without incident.

On opening day, the Elders were stationed at the various stations: at the statue of Adam and Eve, at the Christus, at the mural of Christ ordaining his Apostles, etc. As each Elder would finish the dialogue at his station, he would ask the group to move on to the next Elder. This however, did not work well at all: without a guide, the people tended to break away from the group and simply wander around. Each Elder seemed to have a different style of presentation, and it broke up the continuity of the tour.

It was soon decided that each group should move through the entire pavilion using *one* guide. Each visitor would be met at the front entrance by a missionary who would welcome them and ask them to wait until the group ahead of them had moved on. Then that same missionary would take them on a complete tour of the pavilion. After the tour, this same missionary thanked them as they moved through the exit to the fair grounds. It began to work like clockwork, enabling them to easily and professionally move *thousands* of visitors through the pavilion each day.

There were, during the two years the pavilion was open, many special events which took place, which demanded additional publicity and special arrangements. Events such as "Utah Day," the Mormon Tabernacle Choir singing at the Fair and also at Carnegie Hall in New York, the visit of the "Singing Mothers" of the Eastern States, the King Family, the Osmond Brothers, and many other prominent groups, all added to the exposure given to the Mormon Church while bringing additional pressure to bear on the missionaries and pavilion workers to create a friendly and relaxed atmosphere.

The Begonia Project

In April 1963, while attending Primary Conference in Salt Lake City, Bradley McDonald of Santa Cruz, California, read in the *Deseret News* about the work starting on the Mormon Pavilion at the New York World's Fair. Having just completed two historical wax museums he saw an opportunity to serve the Church, and desired to participate in this great missionary project. After meeting with Brother Brockbank and David Evans, an artist was commissioned to make a wax figure of the Prophet Joseph Smith. However, the Church Committee decided to go in another direction for the pavilion exhibits.

Still wanting to be involved in some way, Brother McDonald wrote to Elder Brockbank in September of that year and suggested the idea of using begonias at the pavilion. He then arranged to make a display of these flowers in the garden of the Santa Cruz Stake President. While waiting for the opportunity to "show off" the garden display, he shipped a small load of the begonias to float in the water at the base of the Sea Gull Monument in Temple Square for General Conference, in hopes the Fair Committee would see the beauty of the flower in the water.

"Operation Begonia" started to form soon after this. The Antonelli Brothers agreed to donate *all* the flowers that would be needed *if* the Church did the picking, packing, and shipping. The Santa Cruz Ward members were then told of the plan and asked if they could supply the labor needed. They agreed to help.

The next major problem was finding someone to actually ship the flowers across the country to the pavilion site in New York. In a stroke of luck, a close neighbor of Brother McDonald's had a son that was a Vice President of Tiger Airlines. After presenting the challenge to the company, their prayers were answered: the company agreed to air freight the flowers to the pavilion without any cost to the Church!

Brother McDonald had arranged to obtain thousands of free flowers, had persuaded ward members to pick, process, and deliver the flowers to the airport, and convinced Tiger Airlines to ship the flowers to the Fair! The only direct costs would be for the packaging. Used strawberry boxes were purchased from local supermarkets for 6 cents each, then the flowers were packed in damp cotton so they would retain their freshness.

Now that the arrangements and costs were in place, all that was needed was the final approval from Church Headquarters. Elder Brockbank gave them the green light to start shipment of the flowers the first part of July 1964. With the first shipment of flowers, the pavilion announced "Begonia Day," giving just one more reason for publicity at the Mormon Pavilion.

The Santa Cruz ward members were the backbone of this *two year* project. The youth and sisters of the ward would go into the fields early in the morning to select the blooms and pick them. Then they would pack them in wet cotton ready for shipment. At the end of each day they would be tired and wet to the knees. This work went on every week for two years!

The tremendous good Operation Begonia did in bringing beauty to the pavilion can never be completely realized. As soon as workers began putting the flowers out on the islands in the reflecting pool, people would stop and say, "My, it is so beautiful here! Let's go inside and see what it is like."

Irene's contribution to the World's Fair

As soon as Irene arrived, she was called on to help with many of the details required to get the pavilion ready to open the following week. Being creative by nature, she was called on to work with the displays and dioramas. The pavilion was very well thought out, and as Irene worked with the other artists and craftsmen to complete the work, she felt it was a great compliment and honor to serve the Church at the pavilion. The image the pavilion would portray in the name of the Mormon Church was going to be very impressive! Her original desire to work at the Hill Cumorah Pageant had become a distant memory.

There was always a strong spiritual feeling at the pavilion. Elder Brockbank would hold a short "prayer meeting" every morning and before every change in personnel shift during the day. This gave *everyone* a spiritual "spark" before they started their day's work. In addition to the prayer, someone would be assigned to give a short talk, which inspired everyone to do their best. Often Elder Brockbank himself would inspire the group by talking about the importance of their calling to serve at the pavilion.

The missionaries were always reminded what a great influence they had on the people that came to the pavilion...either for good or bad. In *one day* a missionary would have the opportunity to bear his testimony to more people than most missionaries would have during the whole two years of their mission! How important it was to make that impression a good one!

It was here that Irene's social talents served her the best, as she was able to comfortably talk with *anyone* who came to the pavilion. People of all tongues and nationalities from every corner of the earth were visiting the Mormon Pavilion every day, and Irene was able to make each one comfortable and welcome. A newspaper article captured Irene's attitude:

> "No matter where you go people are the same" Irene said as she paused at the information counter. "There are wonderful people everywhere, in New York as well as Salt Lake City...the only trouble is I wish I could speak 10 different languages!"

> "People are genuinely curious about the Mormon religion," Irene said. "This exhibit at the fair answers many of their questions and induces them to want to know more. Generally, comments about the exhibit and about the Church have been favorable."

Irene's first "unofficial" assignment was to help prepare the pavilion to open on time. Her first "official" assignment was to be in charge of the front desk and the registration books, where people would make comments and ask for referrals. But Irene was *never* satisfied with a simple assignment — she always found additional, interesting ways to serve and keep herself busy.

Beheading the Prophet Joseph

Irene's first introduction to the pavilion was rather startling. David Evans, who had charge of all the dioramas and displays for the pavilion, had called Irene after she arrived in New York and told her he had a "special job" for her. As she walked in the front door, there stood a poorly built mannequin of the Prophet Joseph Smith that was rather frightening! It had been placed at the front of the pavilion to be an *inspired* introduction to the Mormon Church! There was Joseph, the Prophet of the Restoration... with his head twisted at an odd angle, arms akimbo, his legs warped and lumpy, and to cap it off, the construction crew had removed the Bible from his hand and replaced it with a pack of cigarettes!

Brother Evans, standing with Irene as they both inspected the Prophet Joseph said, "Irene, something's wrong! What can you do with him?" Her first reaction was to say: "Nothing, send him back from whence he came."

The mannequin was so artificial looking! He had a hunchback look, a stiff rigid posture, and to top it off, he had a beatnik hair cut! His head was tilted up instead of downward in a more relaxed position, and he was standing awkwardly on a pedestal, giving him an unnatural stance. Adults would have been offended and children would have become frightened to see such a hideous man standing above them! Brother Evans didn't want to send it back if there was anything they could do with him. Irene said that she would try, but suggested that they order a "proper"

statue of the Prophet to replace him (which they eventually did).
But Irene would do the best she could for the time being.

The first thing Irene did was to take off all his clothes, and
shave his head! Boy, did that give her a funny feeling... Then,
she put the Prophet Joseph across two saw-horses and...cut off
his head! Thus, the other missionaries were introduced to Irene's
"talents" in this bizarre way: walking into the building to dis-
cover Irene straddling the prone and "naked" Joseph Smith with
a saw in her hand, cutting off the Prophet's head!

Once Irene lengthened and adjusted the neck, the head could
be tilted slightly forward in a much more natural looking position. Then she adjusted his arms and torso and got glass cloth
and glue to put his hair back on. She also padded his knees so
they would look more relaxed and bent. Finally, she put his
clothes back on and made a new cravat. After her tender care
and workmanship, Joseph actually looked presentable.

This whole procedure had given Irene and everyone watching a very strange feeling. Unfortunately, no pictures of Irene
were taken in the act of cutting off the Prophet Joseph's head...it
could have been used to blackmail her for years! Irene was sure
she was the only woman ever to saw off the head of a Prophet! I
am sure Joseph Smith himself would have been amused!

When she was done, the mannequin did look better...but still
looked unnatural. In the end, this cheap imitation would not do
justice to the handsome Prophet, Joseph Smith, who was so beloved. However they had to use this sorry representation of Joseph until they got a replacement. Finally, sometime later, a
proper statue of Joseph arrived at the pavilion. It had been cop-
ied from the one which stands on Temple Square.

When the statue arrived, Irene suggested that a blue drape be
put on the wall behind, giving the statue a soft background,
rather than a stark white wall. This suggestion was approved

and Irene was asked to follow through with the project, which she did. The statue is now in the Visitors Center on Temple Square, next to the diorama of the sacred grove.

As for the poor old mannequin, it was taken to the attic where they kept supplies. Many times the workers would be startled when they entered the semi-darkness of the supply room to suddenly see a freakish man staring at them!

The Prophet Joseph—a chain smoker?

Until the new statue of the Prophet Joseph arrived, Irene was constantly having problems with the union workers at the pavilion taking the Book of Mormon out of Prophet Joseph's hand, and putting a pack of cigarettes in its place. This was a great amusement and delight to all the workers, and even Irene had to admit that it was amusing in a startling way. It always caused a panic to good Mormons when they saw the Prophet Joseph indulging in this manner!

Guest Registration Sheets

One of Irene's proud moments on her mission was designing the registration sheets used at the pavilion to keep track of those attending so the missionaries could follow up on the names and addresses of those desiring to know more about the Church. The registration sheet Irene created could be easily cut into strips so the names and addresses of the visitors could be sent to LDS missions around the world.

In fact, the printer thought Irene's design so unique and original he offered her a job in the lay-out department of his printing company! Those same registration sheets were being used in Church visitors centers years later.

The comments written on the registration sheets by the people were very thrilling to read and almost always complimentary.

Very few were derogatory, and most of those were from teenagers or from people with such names as "Smokey the Bear."

Each week Irene made a copy of the most unusual comments, since they were so exciting to read. The pavilion workers had hoped the referrals would be followed up immediately while the visitors were still filled with the Spirit of Truth which they had felt in the pavilion. The problem was that there were *so* many referrals, and *so* much interest generated by the Mormon Pavilion, it was simply impossible to contact every one quickly. One gentleman came to Irene and said, "I have signed registers, filled out request cards, and asked for the missionaries, yet no one has contacted me. What do I have to do to learn more about this Church?"

Many were interested to know how many converts came as a result of the Fair. It is impossible to know, but it would run into the thousands. Even ten years later, Irene would meet new converts whose first contact with the Church was at the New York World's Fair. While the Fair was open, the New York, New Jersey and Cumorah stakes led the Church in baptisms!

The Flower Lady

Irene's experience in working with flowers and managing the Hotel Utah flower shop helped her with another project. The begonia project was a great success, and had a profound effect on visitors to the Fair in helping to bring them into the pavilion. Often many more flowers were shipped than were needed to maintain the "floating islands" in the reflecting pool. These extra flowers gave Irene the opportunity to magnify her calling as a missionary at the Fair.

As a public relations effort, Irene suggested to Elder Brockbank that she make flower arrangements to take to the different pavilions at the Fair. He thought it was a great idea, so Irene went to work. The begonias often measured 8 to 10 inches across, and came in every color imaginable. They were the most gorgeous flowers one could imagine. Each flower arrangement created by Irene was sent with an Articles of Faith card, and a pavilion card signed: "To our good neighbor, with sincere best wishes. THE MORMON PAVILION."

Irene would not only introduce herself and her flowers to each and every exhibit in the Fair, she would then invite anyone working at the exhibit to visit the Mormon Pavilion. Those who responded in a positive way would be visited again and again, and Irene would answer their questions about the Mormon Church. Eventually Irene became well acquainted with the personnel and managers of the other pavilions. She told them that when they were going to have special guests, or group dinners or luncheons, to let her know so she could make a centerpiece for them. She also offered to make a corsage for each of the women that would be attending these functions. Irene gave this description of one of these events:

> One day the Illinois Pavilion called and said they were having some special guests and could they please have some flowers and also a special corsage. When I took the flowers over, there stood Madam Chiang Kai Chek[1]. She was beautiful and had on a gorgeous dress, with a full length black broadcloth suit, and a large black fox collar. I happened to make a corsage of a Begonia with different shades of red, with green satin leaves and ribbon. It couldn't have been a better color, and as I pinned it on her, how thrilled she was. She thanked me most graciously and when I said it was from the Mormon Church Pavilion, she said that she had heard many good things about the Mormon Church, and thanked me again. With her shining black hair, and this stunning suit with the black fur collar, she really was a picture. She was taken all over the Fair grounds to the different pavilions, and everywhere she went, the Pavilions would recognize the special corsage she wore from the Mormon Pavilion!

---

[1]Chiang Kai Chek was the Chinese military and political leader of the Republic of China from 1928 to 1975. After fighting and losing to the communists in 1949, he fled to Taiwan.

There were many times Irene was asked to make special flower arrangements for the other pavilions. This created a very warm, friendly relationship between the "Mormons" and the rest of the Fair. Irene became known all over the fairgrounds as "the Flower Lady."

The flowers were so beautiful it became a special event and a feather in one's cap to be visited by the "Flower Lady." Many of the pavilions that had *not* been visited by Irene wondered when *they* would be visited and given flowers! One of the exhibits farthest away from the Mormon Pavilion, and one of the last to receive the blessing of Irene's flowers, was the Vatican exhibit of the Catholic Church. One Priest at the exhibit became very rude to Irene, scolding her for taking so much time getting around to giving *them* flowers, when everyone else had already received flowers! Irene tried to be pleasant, and tried to assure them that it had not been intentional, that she was just very busy. The incident showed how well known Irene had become, and how much *everyone* at the New York World's Fair waited to be able to get *their* flowers from the "Flower Lady."

One of the side benefits of Irene's efforts with the other pavilions occurred when she would take a special guest to visit the other pavilions. They would immediately take them in without having to wait in the one or two hour lines. Irene commented:

> I was called on to escort many special guests coming to our pavilion to other pavilions in the Fair, and when these pavilions saw me coming, they would immediately open the door, and welcome us, and say, "Oh, here comes the Flower Lady! What can we do for you?"

Corsages were made for *hundreds* of women and wives of VIPs, including the movie star Gloria Swanson, and Mrs. Walt Disney. Often corporate heads would arrive, such as the wife of the President of the DuPont Company, the wives of executives at

General Motors and Ford, and the wives of many, many other corporate executives who visited the Fair.

One group of executives from Columbia University came to the Fair as guests of a church member, Dr. Kenneth Beesley. Irene was asked to make corsages for all the ladies in the group. Dr. Beesley commented later that everywhere they went the personnel of the different pavilions recognized the flowers, and after commenting on them would say, "Oh, those flowers are from the Mormon Pavilion! They are such nice people over there. Their pavilion is so beautiful. We really have enjoyed the beautiful flowers they have sent over to us, etc...." He said the good will and public relations of the Mormon Pavilion, as expressed over and over again by the workers at the Fair, was a real thrill to him and also made a definite impression on the VIPs that were with him.

The goodwill Irene created with the other pavilions was tremendous. It brought great recognition and fostered good feelings towards the Mormon Church. They all recognized the Mormon Pavilion from the flowers. If someone was wearing a corsage, they would say, "You've been to the Mormon Pavilion!"

The Missionaries

After all the debate concerning who should staff the pavilion, the missionaries turned out to be the greatest asset the pavilion had. Other pavilions in the Fair had beautiful murals, dioramas, interesting displays, etc., but there was only one pavilion which had the personnel that the Mormon Pavilion had! With their "clean-cut" image, there was something different about these young men.

In the first place, they did not serve for wages, as did personnel in other pavilions; they volunteered their time for two years, and were set-apart for this special calling to serve the Lord. This, with the Priesthood which they held, made them "stand out" from other personnel at the Fair. Irene said with pride that this was the only pavilion in the Fair which had been dedicated to the Lord, with the authority to preach the true Gospel of Jesus Christ. *They* had the advantage of everyone else in any pavilion on the Fair grounds. About 250 missionaries served at different times at the pavilion during the two years it was open. They did a wonderful job.

Irene felt especially close to the young missionaries working at the Fair. They reminded her of her own son, Richard, who was then serving a full-time mission in Switzerland. She often desired to know more about what he was doing and experiencing on his mission. This gave her the idea to interview each Elder, write a small article about his experiences, and then, along with his picture, send them to his "home town" paper — all without the knowledge of the parents or the missionary! What a thrill it must have been for parents to read those articles and see pictures of their sons in the local paper! Papers seemed anxious to use these write–ups, and it was a good way to generate additional news about the pavilion. According to Irene, every paper to which she sent articles published them.

The missionaries were called on to do many different jobs while serving at the pavilion. One of these was carrying in and storing the 15 million pamphlets and many cases of the Book of Mormon that were distributed to the visitors coming to the pavilion. In addition, they acted as a "clean-up" crew in giving the pavilion a real housecleaning. The pavilion literally would shine when they got through! They were also called on to do special gardening jobs as well as many, many other assignments. They were essential to the operation and success of the pavilion.

Even on the "breaks" during their shift, the missionaries were asked to put together Joseph Smith and World's Fair pamphlets so they could be passed out to visitors as they left. The missionaries would often change from working in their "grubbies" to their conventional white shirts, ties, and dark suits. It didn't take them long to "transform" from one type of worker to another — from laborer to Teacher of the Gospel of Jesus Christ. However, no matter what they were called on to do — it was still the Lord's work — and they met the challenge!

Mother to the Missionaries

Part of Irene's calling at the pavilion was to be a "surrogate mother" to the many young Elders serving there. They felt the motherly influence Irene had for them because of her age and willingness to help them. She sincerely loved each one, because they were such fine young men, and reminded her of Richard. Often her heart went out to them because they were there under very difficult circumstances. The Elders seemed to rely on her for many things, including consoling them when they received a "Dear John" letter from their sweetheart back home.

Irene often discovered that the Elder was the only member of the Church in his family, and that someone in their ward back home was keeping him on his mission, or that he himself had earned and saved his own money. She noticed how carefully they watched the few dollars they had left for food for the week. To help them, Irene would treat the Elders to breakfast.

Irene discovered that the missionaries *loved* hot scones, so every Monday morning, on their diversion day, she would invite all the Elders — about 35 of them — to her apartment early in the morning for hot scones. Each one would bring their own quart of milk, plate, knife, and spoon. At first Irene furnished the milk also, but with the *gallons* they were drinking, she soon decided they would have to bring their own!

Irene furnished the scones, honey and jam, butter, and a large platter of fresh fruit. Irene noted:

> Unless someone has been out in the mission field, they will
> never know just how many hot scones an Elder can eat! I had
> two large kettles on the stove frying scones, and one would
> never be able to count the hundreds of scones it seemed like
> one Elder could eat. I always had a whole pound of butter on
> the table and large bowls of fresh strawberry jam and a big
> bowl of honey. With their milk and all the fresh fruit they
> could eat—it was a breakfast to remember. There was no limit
> as to how many they could have—they ate until they could not
> eat another one! I am sure it helped the wonderful Elders
> more mentally than it even did physically. For they seemed to
> relax and have a change from their cooking, which wasn't al-
> ways the best, as one could imagine.

One of the more tragic things Irene experienced concerning
the Elders was finding out that some never heard from home,
even on special occasions. Irene never forgot one Elder from
Montana who had *never* received a letter from home and had
been in the mission field for a year and a half. Christmas had
passed, and she knew that his birthday was coming soon. As a
surprise to him, she invited the Elders in his district to her apartment for dinner and baked a birthday cake as a surprise for him.
He was truly surprised and delighted, but she could see he was
still heartsick because, even on his birthday, he never heard from
home! Irene wrote:

> The sweet Elder would always say, "It's all right, I know my
> parents are so very busy." Could any parent ever be too busy
> to write to their son away from home, doing such a wonderful
> work? I often prayed for a special blessing on this wonderful
> young man.

A Special Pavilion Birthday

One day, as was her custom, Irene took a flower arrangement
to the Montana Pavilion. During the ensuing conversation, one
of the personnel remarked that in a few days their manager, Mr.
Ott Tschache, was having a birthday, and mentioned the date.
Irene wrote down the date so she would not forget.

When the day arrived, Irene wrote a special birthday poem and took the poem and a beautiful arrangement of begonias to Mr. Tschache for his birthday. He was *very* surprised that Irene knew it was his birthday, and incredibly moved that she would write such a beautiful birthday tribute to him. After thanking her, Irene and Mr. Tschache had their picture taken in front of the pavilion.

Ten years later, Irene was hosting some friends around Temple Square in Salt Lake City. When they were finished with the tour, they said:

> Irene, we have been meaning to tell you! We were at a National Convention back east, and a man we met asked us if we happened to know Irene Staples. When we informed him that we did, and that you were a good friend of ours, he reached in his brief case, took out an envelope and handed it to us to read. It was a birthday poem and tribute you had written to him over 10 years ago, when you were at the Mormon Pavilion at the New York World's Fair! The gentleman told us, "I always carry it with me. I have read it many, many, times. It has meant more to me than anything else I have. I treasure it!"

This is a lesson Irene would learn over and over again: we never know what affect we might have on those we meet, especially because of some little act of kindness we stop to do along the way. Irene assumed that her little poem had been thrown away long ago. In fact, she had completely forgotten the incident herself.

Irene returned home and went through her notes taken while at the pavilion...and there, written in a little book, she read the entry:

> Sept. 12, 1964. I took a large begonia arrangement to the Montana Pavilion and wrote a birthday poem to their manager Mr. Ott Tschache. A picture was taken outside in front of the pavilion. He seemed pleased.

An Embarrassing Moment

One day Irene was in the office when one of the Elders, a farm boy from Idaho, came running in, looking embarrassed. Irene could tell that something was wrong because he had the biggest brown eyes of anyone she have ever seen, and those eyes were now as wide open as saucers. In a most terrified voice he said:

"Sister Staples, what do you do when the seat of your pants pops out, right when you are with a group of people in the pavilion?"

"Well," Irene replied, trying to keep her giggles to herself, "don't worry. If you stand straight and tall and look them right in the eye, you will have them so entranced with your testimony that they won't know whether you have pants on or not! Then if you bring them over to my apartment tonight, I will be happy to mend them for you."

The Elder felt much better, and dashed back into the pavilion, then stood very carefully with his back against the wall while he spoke, and finished his shift for the day. Several months later, after having been transferred to another area, this Elder returned to the Fair (the day the Fair closed, all the missionaries who had worked there were permitted to return to say goodbye). He came into the office with a big grin on his face and said, "Sister Staples, I just thought that I would tell you, that I am still wearing the same pants that you mended several months ago! Thank you again, so much."

Joseph climbed a tree... and had a vision?

Humorous experiences were very common while working with the Elders. Irene told about an Elder from Ogden who told her the following experience: He had been assigned to the sacred grove diorama, and was in front of a large group of people telling them the story of Joseph Smith's first vision. As he turned to the side and pointed to the Sacred Grove, he discovered that there was a little boy climbing up one of the trees in the exhibit. It startled him so much he forgot what he was saying, and, without realizing it, said, "And the young man Joseph Smith, climbed the tree, to see which Church was right." Everyone in the group saw his confused face, and burst out laughing.

The Post Office

Whenever Irene went to the post office, the personnel would all run to the window to see what they could do for her, many times leaving the people who were patiently waiting, wondering "Just who is she, to get such attention!"

The manager, Fred Rinaldi, had a buddy in World War II who was "about the greatest fellow I ever knew." His friend had been a Mormon, so anything Mr. Rinaldi could do for the Mormons was a privilege and a pleasure.

The post office workers often came to the pavilion, and Irene would always make a special recognition of them. They were a great group of men, and she enjoyed her association with them. Irene would go to the post office to cash personal checks either for supplies or just for cash. No one else would cash personal checks from a bank in Utah!

One of the postmen was a Russian Jew named Ike. He had been a great help during the war hiding American flyers shot down, so they would not be captured by the Germans. President Eisenhower rewarded him with U.S. citizenship and a permanent government job in the Post Office. He was a very fine gentleman and was always smiling.

One day Irene went to the post office and could tell there was something wrong. When she asked Ike what was bothering him, he replied, "Oh, Sister Staples, I am so worried. My wife has had to go to the hospital and I have no one to tend my two little girls!" She asked him if he had called Social Services and he said,

"Yes, but they have so much red-tape I cannot wait that long."
Irene suggested he contact his Church, which he said he did—
but they too turned him down and said that they had no means
for tending any children.

"Well, Ike," Irene replied, "you just belong to the wrong
Church! I will have someone at your home tonight to help you!"

On her way back to the pavilion, it struck her: "Why did I tell
him that? I didn't know a soul in New York to call. Well, I had to
say one of my very special little prayers for the Dear Lord to help
me." Irene called the Bishop of the Manhattan Ward to get the
Relief Society President's name. He informed her that she had
moved to Utah and the Relief Society was disorganized, but he
could give her the name of another sister who might help her.

She called, but was given another name to try. It went on this
way for some time until finally Irene called one sister, and when
she told the woman what she wanted, the woman started to cry.
Irene asked her what was wrong, and asked if she could help.

The woman explained that she was a new convert. She was
not too well educated, especially concerning the Church, and she
had become despondent. That very morning she had been on her
knees asking God to open the way that there might be *something*
that she could do to show her great appreciation for the blessings
she had received since accepting the Gospel. Not long after closing her prayer Irene had called!

The woman lived in the Brooklyn area, and, in fact, even
knew the street this postman lived on! She told Irene she would
be happy to go over that very night to make arrangements to
tend the children...

We can only imagine how thankful Irene was that her prayer
had been answered. Not only would Ike's family be helped, this
humble sister had found a place where she was needed and
could serve others!

Several days later Irene returned to the post office and asked Ike how he and the children were getting along. He replied, "Wonderful! The woman is so good to the children, they love her so much. She was teaching them about Jesus, and they were learning to pray and always asked a blessing on the food. She was teaching them so many things that the children were saying, 'Daddy, we don't need mother to come home, we like this lady to take care of us!'"

Irene became convinced that the Lord needs each one of us, in one way or another. No one is insignificant or useless in the sight of the Lord. Humble and inexperienced as one may feel they are, there is a special work for each of us to do.

The Members

Many members of the Church visited the World's Fair, and Irene wanted to make their time at the Fair a pleasant one. She would often call and make arrangements for them to be able to go in through VIP entrances, without waiting in line. Irene would tell the other pavilions that she had an "Elder" of the Church at the Fair and ask if they could please give her VIP tickets. They never turned her down. However, one time, one of them did ask, "Mrs. Staples, just how many Elders do you have in your Church?"

From then on, Irene would call the brethren who visited the Fair by the priesthood office they held: a High Priest, a Bishop, or whatever his priesthood might be. Even a "Deacon" sounded very important to other people! She was careful not to say anything which was not true—she felt that would be wrong—she merely stated their office in the priesthood. The pavilions always accommodated her, and in return Irene was careful never to take advantage of their hospitality. She would always take over *another* special arrangement of begonias, to show appreciation for their kindness.

The Catholic Bishop

Some of the most interesting observations Irene wrote about concerned how other ministers of religion reacted when they came into the pavilion, especially if they were Catholic. It seems that at that time Catholics were not allowed to investigate or even enter another Church. For many, this was the first time they had the opportunity to learn what the Mormons were like and what they believed.

One day a Catholic Bishop came into the pavilion and had a very long visit with Irene, asking many questions concerning the Church. Finally she said "I will be happy to present you a copy of the Book of Mormon, on one condition, that you read it!"

He was delighted and said that he most certainly would read the book; he said he had always wanted to know more about the Mormon Church. As he turned to go, a large group of nuns and Catholic priests came into the pavilion. He dropped the book immediately and said, "I'm sorry, I cannot take it. I couldn't possibly let anyone see me carrying a copy of the Book of Mormon out...but do you have some pamphlets and brochures that I could put on the inside of my coat, so that they won't be seen?" Irene loaded him up with everything he would take. She laughed as he turned to leave...he certainly had a different shape than he had when he came in! Just as he was going out the door, Irene ran to catch up with him and said, "Excuse me, but who have I been speaking to?" "Oh, excuse me," he said. He turned and handed her his card. "You know, Mrs. Staples, the Catholic Church isn't true...any more than any other Christian church. There isn't any of them who is following the true teachings of Jesus Christ. And as far as I am concerned, it is only a job!"

Irene stood in stunned disbelief as he turned and left. She studied the card he had given her as the words he said rang in her ears: "It is only a job!"

How tragic! Each Sunday this Bishop was getting up before his congregation, preaching the "truths" of his religion, yet within himself, he knew what he was saying was not true! Irene wondered, "What did the Dear Lord say about hypocrites? How thankful we can be that we do have the truth, and our leaders are not preaching false doctrine!"

One Lost Shoe

It was a question for the ages: someone lost *one* shoe…who did it belong to? It was a custom after each showing of the film, Man's Search for Happiness, that the Elders would ask the group to carefully look around them and be sure they had not left anything behind. Yet here came an Elder, holding one women's shoe…wondering who it might belong to. Irene could understand a woman with tired, aching feet slipping off her shoes…it felt so good, she just didn't realize she no longer had her shoes on when she left! But *one* shoe? Who leaves *one* shoe and doesn't notice it gone? She could just picture it…sometime, hours later, the woman would look down at her feet and wonder: "Where in the world did I leave my shoe?" Then, being too tired to go back and look for it, she simply went home? It was a wonderful puzzle for the workers at the pavilion. They even wondered if there was a person that only went around on one foot, to save the wear and tear on their shoes! It was a constant game that was played with the many odd things that were left in the theaters.

Darkness Covered the Earth

The Fair was not all work and no play. Here is another humorous event shared with Irene by a missionary:

> One evening, as an Elder was explaining the doctrine of the apostasy to a group of visitors, he said, "And the time came when there was a great darkness which covered the earth." Suddenly the lights went out

in the pavilion. The people were quite startled, and then realized what happened... a thunderstorm had caused the power to go out. All got quite a chuckle out of it.

President McKay... Isn't Going Anywhere!

On May 9, 1965, Hugh B. Brown, while visiting the pavilion, spoke to the missionaries one morning and told a funny story about the Prophet David O McKay:

> After meeting with some of the "younger" General Authorities, like Elder Hanks, Elder Monson, and Elder Hinckley, Hugh B. Brown (he being in his 80s and President McKay 92) turned to President McKay and said, "After hearing of the vigorous young vitality and testimony of these young men, I'm sure the church will go on after we are gone."
>
> "Gone?" answered President McKay, "I'm not going any place, where are you going?" President McKay added, "I wish I could live another 50 years. For the great things that are going to happen in the next 50 years are beyond our faintest dream."

Richard

Irene received a temporary release from her duties at the pavilion to pick up her son Richard from his mission in Switzerland. In June, 1965, Irene flew to England and met Richard in London. They had the opportunity to tour the city. They visited the old Edwards farm where John Edwards, Irene's grandfather, had lived—this was the home their "friends and neighbors" had raided of its contents while the family watched from their wagon.

Irene discovered that serving a mission at the same time as her son Richard had actually "brought a closeness between mother and son," rather than making the separation more difficult.

By July, Irene was back at the pavilion and preparing for "Utah Day", held at the Waldorf Astoria Hotel in New York. A luncheon was held and President Hugh B. Brown spoke. Of course, Irene was assigned to make all the decorations. All of the stakes along the Atlantic seaboard were invited to come. Visiting General Authorities and Utah dignitaries, such as the Governor, also attended.

When the time came for Richard to return from his mission in Switzerland, the Church felt he should not return to an empty home (his mother being on a mission also). Irene would either have to be released to go home with him, or he could stay in New York and work for the summer so they could go home together in the fall when the Fair was over. Richard decided to stay at the Fair with Irene and try to get a job for the summer. Getting a job as a Mormon missionary was a unique experience for Irene's son. It turned out to be an *advantage* to be a returned missionary if you wanted to find a job in New York, or many other places.

Richard applied everywhere—at stores, employment agencies, etc.—wherever he thought he could find work, but it seemed no one had work. Schools had been out just long enough for students to obtain all the summer jobs, and it seemed like no jobs were available. He felt very discouraged.

Finally, one day he went to yet another employment agency inquiring about work, but again they turned him down. They told him they didn't even want him to fill out an application because they simply had no jobs. As he turned to go, the gentleman hesitated and then asked Richard where he had been. Richard told him he had been in Switzerland for two and a half years. When asked what he had been doing in Switzerland, Richard told him he had been a missionary for his church. "Which church?" inquired the man. "The Mormon Church," replied Richard. Whereupon the man quickly asked, "Are you a Mormon missionary?" "Yes," replied Richard.

The man quickly held out his hand and said, "Here are six jobs, which one do you want? Why didn't you tell me that you were a Mormon missionary? We can put them in jobs anytime! Everyone wants them!'

Irene wrote:

> What a tribute to the missionaries of our Church! There has always been something different about Mormon missionaries—they have matured beyond their years and are dependable. They are honest, and know what life is all about. They know where they are going in life, and they are able to take care of themselves. There were many companies in the United States which required a college education for all their employees...except a Mormon missionary. They accepted their "schooling" in the mission to be more than equal to a college education.

Testimonies from the Pavilion

Volumes could be written about the faith promoting experiences that occurred at the Mormon Pavilion. Thousands were converted, new wards were organized on the Eastern seaboard, and stakes divided. Chapels were built because of the increased membership, and "Mormonism" really began to make itself known, not only in the east but throughout the whole United States. Irene heard of many converts, even as far away as California, as a result of the Fair referrals, which she would send to the missions.

Irene began collecting the comments of visitors who would write their impressions and reactions as they signed the registration books before leaving the pavilion. When the missionaries and other personnel would read them it would fill them with enthusiasm, and "recharge their batteries" to put greater effort in their work. Here are a few:

Pennsylvania
"I had previously regarded Mormons as a rather fanatical sect, but I am now impressed as to the intelligence, logic, and open-mindedness which these guides have shown. I am going to investigate further."

New York
"Beautifully done, a soul lifting experience, the only honest attempt to teach true religion at the fair."

New Jersey
"I am just completing a world tour, this is the greatest thing I have seen on my trip."

Canada
"I know this is the word of the Lord and His Prophets, I am going to look into your religion further."

Brazil
"God inspired, please send me literature on how to join your church."

Illinois
"You certainly have inspiring dedicated guides, I am very impressed with their caliber. There is hope for our country with people like that."

New York
"Wonderful, it shows the true meaning of God. My Mormon friends are industrious, honest and sincere. I am going to investigate your church."

England
"I sensed a feeling of peace and tranquility, a beacon of light in the dark. Maybe this is the religion I have been searching for."

Irene's Mormon Pavilion experience truly developed her desire to do missionary work:

> These comments and experiences have proved to me that people are in search of truth. That they are wandering to and fro—as the scriptures tell us—searching for peace and hope for the future. What they see portrayed here in this great Mormon Pavilion, is truly inspired of God, as hundreds testify who visit here.
>
> Therefore it becomes our obligation to heed the admonition of our Prophet when he said for every member to be a missionary. That we may through our efforts further the cause of

> the slogan of the World's Fair: "Peace Through Understanding."
>
> We know that only through understanding and living the Gospel of Jesus Christ will peace come to the world.

Conversions

The "Tired Feet" Conversion Method

One day after Irene returned home to Salt Lake, she met a good friend who had received a letter from a non-Mormon friend back East, telling her about an experience she had at the Mormon Pavilion.

One day while at the World's Fair, she had been so weary and her feet ached so badly from walking for many hours, she simply wanted a place to rest. She looked in the distance and saw the Mormon Pavilion. The gardens looked so inviting she hobbled there, went inside, and sat down. She immediately slipped off her shoes, and began to rub her feet. Soon a woman came up to her and said, "My, your feet are so swollen, please come with me and I will help you." The woman took her to a small room in the back of the Pavilion, and said, "Now you lay down on this couch and rest, I will lock the door from the outside, so you won't be disturbed. You can stay here as long as you like, and have a good rest."

This woman was so appreciative of the concern shown her, she expressed the thought: "If there is a Church that is this concerned with a woman with aching feet, it must be a very special Church!" When the Elders called on her sometime later, she welcomed them with open arms, and soon was learning about the Gospel.

The friend said to Irene, "Irene, I wrote to my friend in the east, and told her that I knew who the lady was that helped you! It was my friend from Salt Lake. Irene, when I heard her story, I just knew it was you." Irene *did* remember this woman, but much like the Birthday Card story noted above, she had long forgotten such a small act of kindness. Irene was often amused and surprised at the many ways people are brought into the Church!

The Miracle

One day as Irene was at the Information desk, she saw across from her a middle-aged couple with their backs towards her, looking at the pictures of the Prophet and other General Authorities of the Church.

She was impressed with them for some, reason—even just seeing them from behind—and felt strongly that they were a very special couple that the Lord needed in His Church. Irene thought, "Well, I might as well just go and tell them so."

She did go over and introduce herself, and had a stirring conversation with them. They seemed very interested. They visited for about an hour, and afterward Irene told them that she would be happy to come to their home some evening and explain more of the Gospel to them. They said they would be happy to have her, but that they were going on a world cruise. However, when they returned, they would be happy to have her come. Irene explained that by that time, she would be back in Salt Lake, but she would arrange to have the missionaries contact them.

They thanked her and handed her a business card so the missionaries would have their contact information. Irene thanked them again for visiting the Pavilion, and added, "I hope the next time that I see you, it will be Brother and Sister Tippy!" They again thanked Irene and, almost as an afterthought, asked her for a favor: "When you return to Salt Lake, would you please call your Mr. Tanner[2] and give him our best regards." It seemed that they had known him in Canada.

---

[2]Elder Nathan Eldon Tanner was a member of the First Presidency of the Church.

As Irene looked at the business card she had been given, a feeling of wonderment came over her. Mr. Tippy was the President of a large co-operative in the Commonwealth of Canada, with offices on Park Avenue in New York City, and here was little Sister Staples going up to them, telling them that the Lord wanted them to join the Church, and that He had a *special mission* for them!

Irene wrote a letter to President Tanner, telling him of her experience with his friends. He wrote back and thanked her for her letter, but explained that in Mr. Tippy's important business position, it was not very likely that he would take time to even investigate the Church. It would truly be a miracle if they joined!

Some time after Irene returned home President Tanner called and said, "Sister Staples, I wanted to call and tell you that I just received a letter from Brother and Sister Tippy. They have joined the Church! I also received a letter from the Bishop of Manhattan Ward that talked about what an outstanding couple they were. Brother Tippy was a powerful executive, yet so humble, that he was passing the Sacrament with the young Deacons. And Sister Tippy was active in the Relief Society."

Irene writes that after receiving the phone call, she closed the door to her office, knelt down, and with tears streaming down her face thanked the Dear Lord for this miracle conversion.

A year later Irene happened to run into the Tippys in the Hotel Utah. They remembered Irene and gave her a big hug. They visited for a short time and Irene discovered that they had been sealed for eternity in the Hawaii Temple. They mentioned that they had an appointment with President Tanner later that day.

Some time later it came out in the Church News that Brother Tippy had been called to go to the Hawaii Islands as the Executive Assistant at the church college there! He had given up his position in New York to work for the Lord at the church college. Irene had been right...they *did* have a special mission waiting for them!

The "It" Factor

A young couple tell of their experience in their own words:

We attended the World's Fair and somehow found ourselves resting in front of the Mormon Pavilion. We had heard some of Mormonism and we said to each other, "'Let's find out what these people have to say."

We entered the Pavilion, and saw your beautiful displays, and since the movie was about to begin, we entered the theatre and saw the movie. For about half an hour after we left the theatre, we hardly spoke to each other. We did buy a copy of The Book of Mormon.

After the period of silence, my wife broke the silence by asking: "Can you believe it?" I knew what she meant by "it." "It" referred to your Gospel and the message we got from the movie. My response was, "Yes, I can believe it, and it is a wonderful thing to believe."

The subsequent events were anti-climatic. I called the local Ward, talked briefly with the Bishop on the telephone, and promised to attend Sunday School within the next two weeks, which I did. I went alone since my wife, who is a nurse, was busy on a case. When she came home that Sunday afternoon, her first question was, "What did you find out in Sunday School?"

We discussed the matter further. Then two missionaries visited us and taught us about the Gospel. We believed and we were baptized. We are doing our best to live up to the teachings. Difficult? Yes, it is very difficult, but we are convinced of its value and we are happy we have made the decision.

Our next object is to go to Salt Lake City, and be married to each other, forever and all eternity.

The Lutz Family[3]

On October 22, 1964, the World's Fair closed for the winter. Over 3½ million people had come through the pavilion. Thousands of referrals had been received and passed on to missionaries around the world. Irene was ecstatic about the success of the pavilion:

> I feel that it is the beginning of a new Church era in bringing the gospel to people in a more dynamic way than by knocking on doors. Here thousands hear the gospel every day—more than an Elder could reach by knocking on doors for many years.

From October 24, 1964 to March 1, 1965, Irene served in Levittown, Pennsylvania (the Trenton Ward). During that winter Irene would perform more "normal" missionary work, with an assigned companion. It was during this first winter, working in New Jersey, that Irene was able to participate in her first "missionary" baptism.

A family living in the Trenton Ward by the name of Lutz came to the attention of Irene. This active family with eight children was, in fact, a part-member family, the father not being a member at the time. Irene decided she would focus her missionary efforts on this family.

Speaking of the Lutz family, Irene said,

> When I learned that he was not a member of the Church I was heart-sick, and said to myself, "There is a man waiting for someone to really open his heart to the Gospel. He must join this Church!"

Soon afterward, a situation arose that permitted Irene to come in contact with the family. Sister Lutz was rushed to the hospital, and the family was in need of someone to take care of

---

[3]As related to Brother Franklin D. Richards in a letter dated 12/7/64 and his response dated 7/5/65.

their children while Brother Lutz also went to the hospital. Irene had her opening, and offered her services to the family. This provided an opportunity for her to get to know the family and to befriend them.

On a subsequent Sunday, Irene worked up the courage to ask Brother Lutz to come to the Mission Home to talk with her (she had tried to talk about the gospel during visits to the Lutz home, but, with eight children, the chaos always seemed to interrupt any gospel discussion). She felt that if he would be willing to come to a quiet setting, the Spirit would have an opportunity to work. To her surprise, he agreed to meet with her the next Wednesday.

That day was a day of fasting and prayer for Irene and her companion. To their surprise, they received a phone call from Sister Lutz. She, too, would be fasting and praying that this meeting would touch her husband's heart. Irene felt a great burden placed upon her...she had to be successful! She prayed harder and longer, preparing for the discussion that evening.

The Lord did not let Irene down.

> For an hour and a half, if ever I taught with the spirit of the Holy Ghost, I did then, for it seemed as though the words came to my mind faster than I could speak them.

There were no commitments made that evening, and Irene was left to ponder whether she had done any good at all. Irene did not have long to ponder her effectiveness. The next day was a Mission Conference, where Franklin D. Richards was to speak. At this conference a remarkable thing happened: as President Richards spoke, Irene heard almost word for word the discussion she had taught Brother Lutz the night before!

> In our mission conference (Brother Richards) repeated almost word for word everything I had told (Brother Lutz) the

> night before. It sounded as though I was listening to a recording of my talk—speaking through a different voice. I turned to my companion and said, "Sister Stevens, something is happening! President Richards is saying almost word for word, everything that I told Brother Lutz last night!" A most unusual feeling came over me...for now I knew that this was a witness to me that what I had told Brother Lutz last night were truly the words given me under divine inspiration!

A few weeks later, in a letter written to Irene by Brother Richards, he spoke of the inspiration that had come upon him at that conference:

> I clearly felt the spirit lead me in speaking as I did to the missionaries in the Short Hills Ward in early December. We pray for inspiration and direction and on this occasion I was led to change the theme I had intended to follow.

When Irene spoke to President Richards after the conference, and told him about the unusual experience, he had only one thing to say, "Did you set a baptismal date?" Fortunately, Irene *had* set a date for him—a tentative date—that very Saturday! But Brother Lutz had not yet made a firm commitment. That night Irene returned to the Lutz home to speak one more time with Brother Lutz. She again testified to him about the truthfulness of the gospel, and asked him again if he would be baptized Saturday. He told her he would give her an answer the next day.

At seven o'clock the next morning, Sister Lutz came running in the door and exclaimed, "Sister Staples, Sister Staples, my husband said to tell you that he is going to be baptized on Saturday!" Tears flowed freely as these two sisters wept for joy at the success their prayer and fasting had brought them. Irene noted in her diary that he was baptized on the anniversary of Harold's death.

What a touching scene awaited those that attended the baptism that Saturday: to see a mother and eight little children, standing around the edge of the baptismal font, watching their father be baptized. A goal was set to go to a temple of the Lord and be sealed as a family. That goal was kept one year later.

Irene would be involved in 10 baptisms, through the pavilion and direct missionary efforts in the wards in which she served.

The Close of the Pavilion

Unlike many fairs that see attendance drop as the fair nears the end, the Mormon Pavilion continued to receive higher and higher attendance as people were determined not to miss this spectacular exhibit. Irene's brief remarks in her journal give a hint of the effort the missionaries put forth at the close of the fair:

> Sept. 5, 1965 largest attendance so far this year: 20-26,000; sold 493 Book of Mormons.
>
> Sept 22, 1965 three men came into the pavilion to scope out the building—in preparation to tear it down. Irene was curious and talked to them. When she heard why they were there, she said, "You won't have to tear it down...it will be washed down with tears!" The toughest of the three men said, "Well, you know, this building has got to me. I don't know whether I could destroy it or not—there is something here that is different. It's got me in here (putting his hand on his chest). I don't know whether I could take this job or not."
>
> Sept 25, 1965 the biggest day ever in attendance, Book of Mormon sold, referrals, etc.
>
> October 9, 1965 largest day at the fair: 35,000; Book of Mormon sold 1,165; referrals, etc., the Saturday before the fair closes.
>
> Oct 16, 1965 biggest day ever: 40,000; 1,665 Book of Mormon; 6,432 referrals.
>
> Oct 17, 1965 Sunday, pavilion closes, people still came until 10pm!

Irene was very proud of her participation in the New York World's Fair. She firmly believed that the Mormon Pavilion was a turning point in the Church's expansion into a worldwide organization:

> The Mormon Pavilion at the World's Fair is the greatest tool the Church has ever had to promote the Gospel. People came from all over the world. Here they found their first contact with and information about the Mormon Church. Here they found out that it is not some "odd sect," but is an established worldwide church, and that we are Christians!

It was very difficult for many to see the Mormon Pavilion torn down. Everyone knew that the building had been *designed* to be torn down and re-used to build a local chapel, but to the missionaries who had served in the pavilion it had become a living edifice with a soul, representing the glorious truths of the restored Gospel of Jesus Christ. To these selfless workers, it was more than a mere building, it became a dear friend, and a true servant of the Lord.

The pavilion had been made of pre-cast stone shipped from Salt Lake City. After the fair was over, most of the building materials, such as windows, electrical fixtures, the stone slabs and many other building materials were carefully taken down and used to build a new chapel in Uniondale, New York.

Moroni...Becomes a Catholic?

Knowing that all the pavilions would soon be torn down, the Church received a request for another church to purchase the "Angel Moroni". There was a new Catholic Church that was being built in the New York area, and the many Catholic visitors to the Fair, having seen the beautiful angel atop the Mormon Pavilion, had admired it so much they wanted to know if they could have or buy it to put on the top spire of *their* church!

Everyone felt it was a nice compliment to Moroni...but they were not sure that *Moroni* would appreciate the opportunity to stand on top of a Catholic Church! The message he had for the world probably would not be appropriate for other churches... so the request was denied.

A Final Impression

The Mormon Pavilion not only served as a powerful missionary tool, but because of its success it became the prototype for all the visitors centers built by the Church in the years to come. The beautiful murals, statues, and paintings that were created for the Mormon Pavilion were brought to Salt Lake, and are now an integral part of the visitors center on Temple Square. The Christus from the Pavilion was sent to Los Angeles to be used at the visitors center there (the much larger Christus in the Salt Lake visitors center was ordered at the same time).

The experience and knowledge learned at the Pavilion helped develop completely new ways of bringing the Gospel to a much larger number of people. The Church learned that *all* people are interested in religion—even at a fair. Who would have thought that people would come into a religious pavilion, when there were so many other exciting places and events at the New York World's Fair? Who could have imagined that nearly *six million* people would enter the doors, and, on leaving, many thousands would leave asking for more!

It truly was a miracle! Since this experience, the lessons learned have been put into use at pavilions in many other locations, such as fairs in Canada, Seattle, Texas, and Japan. In addition, the pavilion was the model for many visitors centers all over the United States, special historical places, and at temples throughout the world.

The experiences and lessons learned at the Mormon Pavilion at the New York World's Fair will perhaps never be fully recognized. Since then, the Church has grown faster, has accomplished more, and made greater strides than at any time in the Church's history.

In the year before the World's Fair opened there were only *six* adult convert baptisms in that portion of the Eastern States Mission. In the first full year after the Fair opened, there were more than *one thousand* baptisms. In the second year, there were another thousand. And in succeeding years, there were six to eight hundred per year. This, of course, did not include the many uncounted baptisms which occurred throughout the world from the pool of people who visited the Mormon Pavilion in its two half-year showings in 1964 and 1965.

At the conclusion of the Fair, President David O. McKay issued the following statement:

> With the recent closing of the New York World's Fair, the Church completed one of the most unique and effective missionary efforts in its history.

A Hint to Irene's Future

Irene's mission call and experience at the Mormon Pavilion was a turning point in her life. It seemed to heal old wounds and lift her spirit. Irene had always been active in church and civic affairs, but for all her service she had never found fulfillment. She would always return home feeling alone and despondent. But this had been different! Using her many talents directly in the service of the Lord was a healing balm to the pain she had held in her heart from past mistakes and life's cruel events. Each day at the pavilion, as she magnified her calling, Irene grew spiritually and emotionally. She had become a force for good and a great tool in the hand of God.

In August, as the World's Fair was coming to a close, Brother Brockbank, President of the pavilion, was put in charge of the Bureau of Information for the Church (a position previously held by Mark E. Peterson). He assigned Irene to compile a complete history of the Mormon Pavilion,[4] and suggested that Irene *might* join him on the committee upon her release from her mission...

Fair Information

The Executive Committee: Elder Harold B. Lee, Elder Delbert L. Stapley, Elder Richard L. Evans, Elder Bernard P. Brockbank (President of the Mormon Pavilion), and Wilburn C. West (President of the Eastern States Mission).

The New York Committee: President G. Stanley McAllister (President of the New York Stake), President George H. Mortimer (President of the New Jersey Stake), Brother Kenneth H. Beesley, Isaac M. Stewart (Vice President of Union Carbide Corp. and President of the Tabernacle Choir), David W. Burton (Church Architect), David W. Evans (Church Information Service), and Robert N. Sears (Vice President, Phillips Petroleum Company).

Architects: Fordyce & Hamby Associates, New York, and Harold E. Burton, Salt Lake City, Supervising Church Architect.

Builder: George A. Fuller Company, New York.

Coordinator of Exhibits: David W. Evans, Salt Lake City.

Public Relations: Robert Mullen, Inc., 200 Park Avenue, New York.

Church Landscape Architect: Brother Irvin T. Nelson; and Harris Grand Inc.: landscape architects hired to work with Brother Nelson.

---

[4]Much of the information in this chapter came from the history Irene put together for the Church.

Articles Sold at the Pavilion

The pavilion sold very few items; mostly the Book of Mormon, postal cards, and slides of the pavilion and the gardens. There was a great demand for Tabernacle Choir records, and many other books, such as a History of the Mormons by school children who needed information to write history papers (they had been assigned to write about the Mormons settling the west).

However, sales of any kind were kept to a minimum. The Church did not want the pavilion to look commercialized like other pavilions, such as the Vatican, which was just the opposite—they charged for everything and had boxes for contributions everywhere.

The Mormon Pavilion had many people offer contributions, but they were refused, and told that while the Mormons did take contributions in our churches, the pavilion was free, and most of the literature was free for the taking. The items that were sold to the public were sold at cost:

The Book of Mormon	50 cents
Postal cards (both large and small)	5 & 10 cents
35 mm slides of the pavilion and grounds	$1.00 per set
"A Marvelous Work and A Wonder"	50 cents
Large illustrated copies of the Book of Mormon	$2.50
Picture print of "Peace Be Still," by Arnold Freiberg	

Articles given away at the Pavilion

Text of the Film: "Man's Search for Happiness"
Articles of Faith cards
Book of Mormon, New York World's Fair covers
Pamphlets on all Church subjects

Statistics

Mormon Pavilion attendance	5,769,835
Referral cards & guest register referrals	930,489
Joseph Smith's Testimony pamphlets	2,508,035
Mormon Pavilion colored folders	2,137,278
Other tracts & pamphlets distributed	270,800
Book of Mormons sold	97,385
Number of missionaries serving	360
Referrals	689,271
Number of baptisms?	(MANY THOUSANDS)

Records were not kept for the month of April, 1964, or for two weeks in April, 1965. These totals are *conservative*, for in one day, the last day of the Fair, it can be verified that there were 1,556 copies of the Book of Mormon sold!

The true count of baptisms generated by the Mormon Pavilion will never be known. Referrals were sent to Missions throughout the United States and Canada, and even many Foreign Missions. Even ten years later, baptisms were coming in whose first contact with the Church was at the New York World's Fair.

The Gardens

Trees: Many large specimen trees were planted, 28' to 30' high enclosing the gardens.

Shrubs: Approximately 400 shrubs were used to fill in areas between the trees, giving it a green carpet effect.

Flowers: Spring: 5,000 tulip bulbs from Holland, in a wide variety of colors, with hyacinths, were used for the early spring planting. Summer: geraniums, 12 to 14 varieties of annuals such as petunias, snapdragons, azaleas, etc. Using thousands of these plants, it made a garden of a mass of color. <u>Fall</u>: Great masses of chrysanthemums in a great variety of colors were used.

Pottery: 112 pieces of ceramic and fiberglass planters were used.

The Begonia Project

Number of flowers sent:	40,000
Number of boxes sent	3,200 (6 tons!)
Air miles by Tiger Air Lines	250,000

Official Church Hostess

> "Now let every man learn his duty...He that is slothful shall
> not be counted worthy to stand." [D&C 107:99-100]
>
> If we are not willing to work for the Church, we should not be
> entitled to hold its membership or to receive its blessings.
>
> We want the Lord to give us the bounties of the earth and yet
> are we willing to give to the Lord our time, talents, and all that
> we possess as the Law of Consecration asks us to do?
>
> Let us keep giving...until the Lord quits giving to us!
>
> Irene

After Irene's Mission

At the close of the World's Fair in October, 1965, Irene went
home to Salt Lake City and back to a simple life, revolving
around her friends, her ward, and her family. She immediately
began to be invited to wards and stakes to speak about her mission.

As Irene and Richard had come home together from their
missions, the Bishop decided to hold their homecoming at the
same time. Just as Irene and Richard had served their missions at
the same time, they were able to celebrate the successful completion of their missions together.

Irene Staples: Hostess to the World

In November, 1965, Irene was instrumental in developing and implementing the very first installation of Christmas lights on Temple Square. She volunteered to host tours of Temple Square and the Beehive House, just as she had prior to her mission. As Christmas approached, Irene noticed the contrast between the emptiness of the temple grounds and the gaiety of the city surrounding the temple, with its colorful Christmas lights. The following story is taken from an article written by Irene about this inspiring event. The first year more than 100,000 visitors would travel to Temple Square to see these spectacular Christmas lights.

CHRISTMAS ON TEMPLE SQUARE by Irene Staples

In early November of 1965, the Salt Lake City streets and store windows were decorated with all the gaiety of the Christmas season. Even the proverbial Santa Claus was there ringing his bell by the kettle, in hopes the passerby would drop in an extra coin, so others could have a "Merry Christmas."

As an official Temple Square Guide, I spent much time on Temple Square. I noticed that while the whole city seemed filled with lights, music, and the Spirit of Christmas.... here our own special Temple Square was dark and quiet, as if it was at peace and resting for "a long winters nap!" It just did not seem right!

One day, while visiting with Earl Hawkes, Publisher of the Deseret News, I wondered why Temple Square could not be decorated, honoring the Christmas season. He immediately agreed and wondered why not do something about it?! He explained that in Boston they had a square that the City always decorated, and it added so much to the festivities of the season.

Knowing that we would have to get permission, I called and made an appointment with President David O. McKay, to get his reaction to the idea.

President McKay listened intently as we explained our motive to decorate Temple Square, not in a garish design, but with reverence, dignity, and beauty. Of course we would have music, for what would Christmas be without music! We also explained that we would be very conservative, and do much of the work ourselves, in order to cut expenses.

President McKay hesitated and then, with the usual twinkle in his eye he got when something seemed to please him very much, he said, "Well, the only thing wrong with it is...why haven't we done it before?" As he clasped

136

our hands he said, 'Thank you for coming in with such a beautiful suggestion. It will be a great way to honor Christ and a contribution to the city. I know that you will do a good job. The Dear Lord bless you!"

How thrilled and delighted we were! We immediately got a committee together that included David W. Evans, and some of his staff (including Richard Marshall, Tom Lasko, and others) to have charge of the lighting design, with the cooperation of the Church electrician, Ned Huntsman (who did the actual work). They did a wonderful job. Ned and his crew worked early and late, under pressure of time, putting hundreds of strands of colored lights, beautifully arranged, on trees, bushes, and paths. In addition, they artistically arranged floodlights on the buildings.

The lights changed the whole area of Temple Square into a beautiful and breath-taking scene, bringing many "Oh's" and "Ah's" from those visiting. To see such a glorious sight...one can hardly describe!

Tom Lasko, who had charge of displays and dioramas on Temple Square, had the project of placing a beautiful, life size, nativity scene on the grounds between the Tabernacle and the North Visitors Center. It was very effective, especially with the "Nativity Story" broadcast, along with the music of "O Holy Night". This gave one the spiritual, true meaning of Christmas: expressing love and glory to our "New Born King!"

We asked Brother Les Goates, who worked for the Church Information Service, to be in charge of the music...what would Christmas be without music! He, too, did a great service, for he had the inspiration to ask the city high schools combined choirs to give concerts in the Tabernacle. The schools were very co-operative, and most delighted to have the opportunity to participate. The young people loved this special activity. For many, it was their first time to even be in the Tabernacle!

Many came to see and hear all of those wonderful young people (who filled not only the choir seats, but the adjoining half-sides of the balcony) sing with enthusiasm and feeling—it was a very emotional occasion. Yes, they sounded like they were in close harmony with the Heavenly choirs themselves!

Also, "Amahl and the Night Visitors" was presented. It was a beautiful musical and spiritual production, which added to the spirituality of the evening. Also, between these activities, how appropriate it was for our Tabernacle Choir to sing, the music to be broadcast over the Temple grounds. Yes, even the air was filled with glorious music!

An original log cabin, built in 1847, sat in the southeast corner of Temple Square, quite alone, and forlorn looking. I suggested that we should refurbish and fix up this little cabin, to show a typical pioneer home as it might look at Christmas time. The Committee was delighted with the idea, and said, "Great, Irene, that is your project."

The little cabin had a dirt floor, but this was soon replaced with old wood and, after the cob webs were brushed down, the walls were 'white washed'—as they were in pioneer days, and even for many years after.

With a white, ruffled, tie-back curtain at the window, several rag rugs on the floor, and a table with a red and white checked table cloth, set with original dishes, the little home seemed to come alive again—not even forgetting the little washstand, with its home-made soap!

But the room needed one more piece of furniture—an original pioneer bed! This was very difficult to find, but then, there one was...just waiting for us to put it in the little pioneer house!

I made a "tick", as it was called, for the mattress, filled with straw. In pioneer days and for many years afterward, during the threshing season, the father would gather up all the "ticks" from the beds and take them to the grain field where the farmers were threshing their grain, to have the ticks filled with fresh new straw.

What a delight it was for the children to climb up on the balloon-like beds. No, there was no coaxing at bed time, for they had fun on the nice bouncy beds. By the time the next threshing season arrived, the straw had become completely flattened and offered very little comfort. I was able to get an original "patch-work" quilt, and with an embroidered "Sham" to cover the pillows the little cabin was quite complete.

Now for the pioneer family themselves! Discarded and repaired mannequins (remember the Prophet Joseph!) were found consisting of a father, a mother, a 16 year old daughter, a 12 year old son, and an 8 year old daughter, with a baby in the cradle!

What a delight it was to design and make the pioneer clothes for the mother and the two girls. But the father and the son were very difficult. Where could one find jackets or coats with buttons, instead of the modern zippers?! I went to all the second-hand stores, and Deseret Industries, but to no avail. I finally went to Willard, Utah, where my family still lived and many pioneers had settled. Sure enough, there in the attics, I found the needed clothing, even to the boots and the broad rimmed hat; except, I could not find long woolen pants for the father.

I was desperate, until I saw tall Ted Cannon walk into the office, the only man with extra long woolen trousers! I pleaded my problem with him. Ted laughed and asked me if I needed them "right now!" "Well ... no," I said, "but if you had an old discarded pair ... I would surely appreciate it." He did, and donated them to the cause. He even said the family had an original baby cradle I could borrow. With a baby doll, this completed the family for most every home in that day had a baby in the home.

Now, for the Christmas tree and the decorations! My little grandchildren Cristopher, Stephanie and Gretchen Clements were delighted to learn how to make green and red paper chains, to string popcorn, and polish red apples to hang on the tree with, of course, fancy cookies to eat later and even a yellow star for the top of the tree. It looked very special standing by the fireplace.

This little cabin turned out to be a highlight on Temple Square, especially for the little children, to see a real pioneer home and how they decorated it for Christmas. Many children had their pictures taken in front of the cabin as a remembrance of their trip to "Christmas on Temple Square" with their parents!

The first year, everyone on the committee, with Earl Hawkes checking every detail, put their hearts into this project, to make it a success. If the people in the city were not too thrilled with it, and did not support it, of course it would not be repeated the next year.

We all hoped and prayed for guidance and inspiration that it would be a success, if for no other reason than for our beloved President McKay's sake, for he was kind enough, and had the inspiration and foresight, to give us permission to do it. We could not let him down!

It was, to our great joy and happiness, a great success. We received hundreds of calls and letters, complimenting us on how wonderful it was—especially as a place for a family activity where the whole family could come together and see Temple Square!

Since then, many people from out of the city have written or called, asking when the lights would be on at Temple Square. They wanted to schedule their vacation time so they would be in Salt Lake to see our beautiful Temple Square that they had heard all about!

After several years of this responsibility by the committee, the Christmas project on Temple Square was turned over to the Physical Facilities Department of the Church, with Peter Lassig, our Church Landscape Gardener in complete charge...and what a wonderful job Peter does! In the summer he has charge of the beautiful flower gardens on Temple Square, and in the winter he replaces the flowers with the beauty of the "Lights of Christ", as they are often referred to.

Many other areas of the Church, from Washington to California, have now established a similar Christmas project, with great success.

139

Through the years, this beautiful, spiritual event has taken place, bringing millions of visitors to stop in Temple Square and ponder the most important time of the year... wherein we truly honor our King of Kings and Lord of Lords, by the inspiration of having: CHRISTMAS ON TEMPLE SQUARE with LIGHTS OF CHRIST.

Official Church Hostess

As did many other years, 1966 began with Irene seeking to fill her time with friends, social and civic opportunities, and, of course, service. In January, Irene was invited to join the Classics Club. She also took a trip to California to see relatives, and on the way stopped in Las Vegas to see the show "Hello Dolly."

When she returned from her trip, her brief "vacation" was over. Soon after Irene returned she was called by Elder Mark E. Peterson and Elder Richard L. Evans and offered what would be both a job and a calling: to become the *Official Hostess for The Church of Jesus Christ of Latter-day Saints.*

On February 1, Irene began working for the Church Information Service with Brother Kenneth Bennion as head. She made $350 a week. As usual, her labors began even before "officially" starting work.

On January 31, Irene was given her first assignment: hosting the *International School Teachers:* women from Yugoslavia, Japan, Argentina, Haiti, and India. Her first official tour was an all-out extravaganza that would be the standard for Irene throughout her years as a hostess. Her personal tour included Temple Square, an organ recital, and a visit to the Beehive House, which she knew well, having hosted numerous tours prior to her mission.

Then it was lunch at the University of Utah, a tour of Salt Lake City, and a visit to the University of Utah Medical School. The day concluded with dinner at Irene's home in the evening.

Irene never confined her activities to just hosting. Just as on her mission and the other callings and jobs she had held in the past, Irene was never content to do the minimum required. Through all her years as Official Church Hostess, Irene continued to find other activities to fill her free time, and to serve in other venues.

In July, Irene was asked to be a Judge at the Pioneer Day Parade held in Salt Lake City.

In September, Irene was privileged to go through the Salt Lake Temple with the Lutz family, as they were sealed together as a family for time and eternity.[1]

Irene spent 1966 perfecting her abilities as a host. On the practical side, she memorized facts and figures for her tour and developed even more contacts with both Church and State officials. She created a network with businesses, hotels, restaurants, transportation companies, and translation facilities, etc. — anyone and everyone that could help her host her special guests in a more professional and efficient manner. On the spiritual side, she spent time reading the scriptures and in prayer, pondering how she might better touch those with whom she came into contact. Towards the end of the year, everything began to come together and she was now ready for perhaps the most important endeavor she would participate in as Church Hostess: developing a relationship with the State of Israel.

And so began Irene's tenure as the Official Church Hostess. Through the upcoming years her service would expand, her tour would be perfected, and her ability to touch people's hearts with her simple testimony of the Gospel would become profound.

---

[1] This is the family Irene worked with on her mission, while the Fair was closed for the winter.

Irene Staples: Hostess to the World

Highlights of 1966

January

31   The International School Teachers

February

7   Gregory Peck (movie actor)
25   The Ambassador from Greece
26   Edward Nelson (movie actor)

March

4   Art Linkletter and wife (television and radio star)
9   Two members of the New Zealand Parliament
10   Major General Francis Greenleaf

April

6   Tennessee Ernie Ford (famous singer)
        At the organ recital he sang *The Lord's Prayer*
18   Jimmy Dean (famous singer and sausage king)

June

13   Archbishop John Wendland
        Head of the Russian Orthodox Church of North and
        South America
28   A German soccer team
29   Billy and Shirley Casper (professional golfer)
        Irene became good friends with the Caspers, and attended
        the temple with them several times.

July

11   The King Family singers

August

7   Brigadier General Thurston T. Paul Jr.

September

9   Richard L. Evans and family

November

3   Major General Charles Easterbrook and Lieutenant
        General Charles Dodge

Statistics for 1966:

Total visitors hosted	9,813
Foreign visitors	663
Countries represented	125

Note: In 1965, prior to Irene being called as the Official Church Hostess, the total number of individual and VIP guests was 1,391, including 341 foreign visitors from 114 countries.

Irene Staples: Hostess to the World

Israel, O Israel

There are two thoughts that I would like to bring out. The first one is: Don't feel that the smallest duties aren't worth making the effort to do, and instead seek positions which seem more important or might receive more notoriety.

I remember years ago a man moved into our ward who was on the general board of a Church organization. When the bishop asked him to be a ward teacher, the man told him he really didn't have time. Hardly a week had passed when the stake president called him to be on the stake high council—which position he immediately accepted. And then it seemed as though the Lord wanted to teach him a lesson for the Stake President asked him to take charge of the ward teaching! He was now in a position where he was asking others to do something which he had refused to do.

When President Clark was moved from 1st counselor to 2nd counselor, it really showed his greatness when he said:

"It matters not where you serve in the Church, but how."

That is a lesson for all of us.

The second thought which I would like to leave with you is: After we have accepted a position, let us fill that position to the best of our ability.

I remember, years ago, when I was working in the Mutual, trying to get the Young Men's President to cooperate in getting a project done. He said to me:

145

> "Oh, Irene, why work so hard? I've found out that if you sort of follow the line of least resistance you get along just as well. The Mutual seems to go on just the same."
>
> It is following the line of least resistance that makes rivers and men crooked.
>
> Let us follow a straight course. How many blessings do we lose by following the line of least resistance and not putting forth every effort we can to accomplish that which the Lord has asked us to do?
>
> We are working for the Lord, not for the bishop or the Relief Society president. Of course, we work to help them too, but if this is Heavenly Father's Church, aren't we working for Him?
>
> We always have time to do the things we want to do—let us want to work for the Lord.
>
> "Let us pray as though everything depended on the Lord, and let us work as though everything depended on us."
>
> Irene

The year 1967 would turn out to be a momentous year for Irene. She began to come into her own, truly magnifying her calling as Church Hostess as she entertained every type of VIP from royalty to high government officials, military commanders, world renowned choirs, boy scouts, and, as always, just plain folks. More importantly, the year would begin what would become her most important accomplishment during her service for the Church: the development of a close relationship with officials of the State of Israel.

In early 1967, Irene continued to enjoy the relationship she had developed with Sidney King, of Virginia, the artist who painted the long mural of the Life of Christ in the Mormon Pavilion. He was in Salt Lake City, commissioned to paint the universe on the dome of the Visitors Center. It is the background for the large Christus that would be one of the highlights of the tour in the newly built Visitors Center on Temple Square.

One of Irene's favorite stories is her claim that all of the "pink" in the painting of the universe above the Christus was a suggestion to the artist by Irene. She explained that, one day, while visiting the building during construction, she stood and watched Sidney King painting the dome. After a few moments hesitation, Irene "suggested" that he needed a little more color in the painting. She told him a bright pink would be just the right touch (of course, Irene's favorite color just happened to be pink). When she returned several days later, she noticed bright touches of pink in the clouds surrounding the painting. Her thrill at his acting on her suggestion was voiced on almost every tour…as she concluded her tour at the statue of the Christus, she would often tell people the story, and conclude: "Whenever you return to the Visitors Center and see the pink in the clouds, just remember Irene!"

Another highlight of Irene's career as Church Hostess was the opportunity to host Princess Irene of Greece in January of 1967. The Mormon Church had been developing a close relationship with the people of Greece for many years. For example, on November 29, 1954, President David O. McKay was given the Cross of Commander of the Royal Order of the Phoenix, the highest honor given by the country of Greece, for the aid given Greece by the LDS Church after a devastating earthquake in the Ionian Islands in 1953. The Church's donation had been the largest single contribution to the Greece Relief Fund in the whole world. Then in 1962 Archbishop Iakovos the head of the Greek Orthodox Church in both North and South America visited President McKay. Over the years they would become good friends. This visit by Princess Irene was the culmination of those efforts.

Now, here were "Irene and Irene" together, arm in arm, touring the sights and sounds of Temple Square! Her Royal Highness Princess Irene of Greece, and youngest sister of King Constantine of the Hellenes, played the Tabernacle organ after having heard the regular broadcast of the Mormon Tabernacle Choir. Included in this prestigious group with Princess Irene were Consul General Anthony Protonotarious, Her Majesty Queen Frederica, Queen Mother of the Hellenes, and Emmanuel Pavlakis of the Archdiocesan Council.

Irene began to be noticed for the great work she was doing for the Church, for the City of Salt Lake, and for the State of Utah. During 1967 several articles were published about her work as Church Hostess. Here is one example from the Salt Lake Tribune:

Red Carpet Given to Visitors by Church Hostess
by Stephen W. Gibson, February 1967

Rolling out the red carpet for visitors in Salt Lake City has almost become a tradition.

In order to help this tradition grow and as an aid to tourism, the Church has a Hosting Department and a full-time Church hostess.

Irene E. Staples, Church hostess, explained her office has the responsibility of helping dignitaries and VIPs see the many Church attractions in the Salt Lake area.

Last week, the hostess arranged special treatment for the Vienna Choir Boys. The 22 boys from Vienna, Austria, sang for Pres. David O. McKay, swam in Deseret gym, saw Temple Square, and ate lunch at the Lion House.

Having arranged thousands of itineraries for royalty, military leaders, governors, ambassadors and many other leaders, both industrial and professional, the Church hostess still hesitates to label one person a VIP and not another.

"We treat all guests of the Church and city as VIPs. After all, who is to say one individual is more important than another."

Work for the Hosting Department, which was established four years ago, often starts with a letter sent to the Church offices inquiring about what the Church has to offer the tourist in Salt Lake City.

"Letters of this type are forwarded to me," explained Mrs. Staples. "We send a personal letter to the letter writer inviting them to the city and telling them of all the wonderful things to see here."

Hotel managers, city and state officials, and leaders in the business community also let Mrs. Staples know when "special" people are coming to the city.

The office then arranges special tours of Church attractions to fit visitors' schedules.

"Most people who come to Salt Lake want to see Temple Square, the Tabernacle Choir, and the Great Salt Lake," Mrs. Staples said.

The hosting department also arranges for convention visitors to tour church attractions here.

"More than one convention chairman has told me they wouldn't have their convention here if it wasn't for the Mormon landmarks," said the Hostess.

Last year the hosting department helped more than 15,700 visitors enjoy the city. This included international visitors from 63 foreign countries.

The Hosting Office maintains a list of international clubs in Salt Lake City, so visitors from foreign countries can meet fellow countrymen now living here.

This enables visitors to have guides that speak their own language which, according to the Church hostess, makes them feel more at home.

Mrs. Staples also has a list of leaders in several different professions who have shown a desire to meet and guide visitors of the same profession through the city.

Many of the visitors receive a bound booklet about the Church with their name embossed in gold on the cover.

"This helps them remember their visit and also serves as a missionary tool. Many visitors have told me about their friends who have visited Temple Square and shown them one of the bound booklets we have given them," the hostess said.

"In the summer, the production *Promised Valley* is a great way for the visitors to spend an evening in Salt Lake. It also gives me a chance to show them our beautiful city at night after the play.

"In the case of international visitors, many want to see an American home, so after the play they often come to my home for snacks."

The Church hostess said personnel at Temple Square have been most helpful in arranging special tours for the Hosting Department.

She said the General Authorities of the Church also are very hospitable when it comes to greeting visitors.

Although not designed or intended as a direct missionary tool, the Hosting Department does provide thousands of referrals each year.

"Whenever we feel the visitors would welcome missionaries, we send a referral to the mission home in their area," said the hostess.

One returned missionary recently told the hostess he baptized three families on his mission from referrals received from the Hosting Department.

"This year we sent out several thousand Christmas cards to people who have visited Salt Lake City as a guest of the Hosting Department."

"Many wrote back, saying they were surprised to be remembered among the many thousand visitors who see Temple Square each year."

Probably one of the most faith-promoting stories to come from the Hosting Department is one about a town in Germany which welcomed the missionaries following a visit by its local soccer team.

"Prior to the visit here by the Patterborn soccer team, the missionaries couldn't even get a hall to meet in. After we hosted the team, the whole town seemed to open up," the Church hostess said.

Mrs. Staples feels the Salt Palace, now under construction, will attract thousands more to the "world capital of Mormonism."

Future groups which will see Mormon attractions under the direction of the Hosting Department include students from Yonsei University, Korea, Sons of the American Revolution, and the International American Conference of the Partners of the Alliance."

Irene's Introduction to Israel

Irene had many Jewish friends and had heard a rumor that a Consul from Israel would be visiting Utah. He would be coming to visit the local Jewish community, who had recently built a new community center and had given generously to the cause of Israel. At the moment she heard of the visit, her mind began to race…had she *ever* hosted someone from Israel? The answer was unsettling: in all the time she had been hosting VIPs on Temple Square and for the State of Utah, she had not met a single person from Israel! This just felt wrong to Irene. The Mormons—more than any other religion or people on the earth—were tied to the Jews and to Israel. In every sense of the word, the Mormons and Israel were brothers. Israel was the Tribe of Judah; the Mormons were the Tribe of Joseph. They not only had the same religious roots, they were, in fact, brothers by blood. Irene *had* to do something about this…and she did. From the Jewish Community Center she obtained the name and address of Moshe Yegar, the Consul of the Western States. She wrote a carefully worded letter to the Consul, who was stationed in Los Angeles, inviting him to visit Temple Square while in Utah.

In a letter dated January 25, 1967, addressed to Moshe Yegar, Consulate General of Israel, Irene extended the following invitation:

> We are very happy to hear you are planning a visit to Salt Lake City. We extend to you a very sincere welcome!
>
> We in the Hosting Service of the Church of Jesus Christ of Latter-day Saints are most anxious to extend our complimentary services to you. I personally will be happy to make arrangements for you to see special places of interest, including our renowned Temple Square with its famous Temple, Tabernacle and great Choir.
>
> I will also make arrangements for you to meet both State, City and Church Officials. The State Legislature is in session now, and I will be happy to have you be presented to them.
>
> I hope you will be able to arrange your schedule so you may be here on a Sunday morning to hear the national broadcast of our 375-voice Tabernacle Choir at 9:30 a.m. It is a rich spiritual experience.

> If there are any special arrangements or appointments that I
> can make for you, I will be happy to do so. We want your trip
> to Salt Lake City to be a memorable one for we are happy that
> your itinerary includes our city.
>
> Once again—welcome! If we can be of service to you, please
> let us know. It will be a privilege and a pleasure to host you.
>
> Most Sincerely, Irene E. Staples

Anyone can see from this letter how the abilities of Irene as a
hostess had begun to shine. It was a gracious invitation and yet
directly to the point: when you come to Salt Lake, you come to
see the Mormons, the temple, and yes, to have a *spiritual experience!* In addition to the emotional and spiritual hook, she also
offered to introduce him to the powerbrokers of Church and
State—a promise she could and did fulfill!

Within days the Consul wrote back and thanked Irene for her
offer, saying that he was looking forward to visiting *all* the places
she suggested, and especially the opportunity to hear the Tabernacle Choir. He said he would be in Salt Lake the following
week, but for just three days. Irene wondered if he was just being
courteous and whether he would have the time to visit Temple
Square. Little did she know that at just the *mention* of the Tabernacle Choir the Consul had already decided he would not, could
not refuse Irene's offer!

Although the stage was set, the introduction of the Nation of
Israel to the Mormon Church and the Gospel of Jesus Christ was
not going to be easy! As the visit of the Consul neared and Irene
had not heard directly from the Consul's staff about his visit, she
anxiously contacted the Jewish Community Center for information. Her hopes were soon dashed. The Consul's office had already arranged for a local member of the Jewish community to
act as a guide and host for the Consul during his visit to Salt
Lake. After all, it was the Jewish community that the Consul was

coming to see, not the Mormons! When Irene contacted the man who would be the Consul's host during his trip to Utah, and offered her services, she was told in no uncertain terms that the Consul was "all booked up." He would be speaking at the University of Utah, holding a TV interview, a luncheon, and a dinner, and so forth, so Irene's services would *not* be needed!

This just felt wrong to Irene, especially since the letter she had received directly from the Consul himself had stated how much he was looking forward to learning about the Mormon Church. Irene *always* followed her feelings, knowing that God often communicated to her that way, and her feelings were telling her that she was to introduce Moshe Yegar to the Mormon Church! But try as she might, she just didn't know what else she could do...

When the time for the Consul's visit arrived, Irene had not heard from the Consul or his staff and assumed her opportunity to introduce him to the Church had been lost. But suddenly, very early on a Wednesday morning, Irene received a phone call from the Consul's host, asking if it was possible for Irene to meet with the Consul and take him to the places she had suggested in her letter! The Consul had been *very* disappointed in the schedule that had been laid out for him, and *demanded* that the remainder of his schedule be altered so he could tour the Mormon sites with Irene. What an astonishing turn of events! Irene left at once for the Hotel Utah, where the Consul was staying.

Irene met Moshe Yegar and his local host at 8 a.m. and, as promised, took the Consul to the Legislature where both the House and Senate were currently in session at the Utah State Capitol building. By using her numerous contacts, Irene was able to arrange to have the Consul formally presented to the Senate and the House of Representatives, where he was asked to give a short talk.

Irene tells how the Consul received everything he had been
promised, and much, much more:

> Consul Moshe Yegar was a very fine personable gentleman.
> After meeting and getting acquainted, I suggested that, in the
> interest of time, we go to the Capitol immediately, which we
> did. Once there I took him to meet Governor Rampton, who
> cordially welcomed him, and presented him with a book
> about Utah. I then took him to the House and the Senate
> Chambers, where he was given a very warm welcome. After
> giving a short talk, he was given a standing ovation by both
> Houses. He was very impressed with the reception he had
> received!
>
> As we left the Capitol, I suggested that we just had time to go
> to the organ recital, on Temple Square. Moshe said he loved
> music and would be delighted to go. At this point the Consul's
> host hesitated, and then said, "Well, I can see, that I am not
> needed." And he left in his own car!
>
> It was a miracle that I found a parking place right by the Tem-
> ple Square gate, just in time to take Moshe to the Choir seats,
> located right behind Dr. Alex Schreiner, the organist, to watch
> him play this marvelous instrument. Alex was most gracious to
> him: playing a special number for him, and explaining the
> mechanics of this great organ.
>
> After the recital, I started taking Moshe on a tour of Temple
> Square. The first thing he saw was the Star of David on the
> Assembly Hall. He was very excited and exclaimed, "Irene,
> the Star of David on your Church! What does it mean?"
>
> I told him that it showed that we both were from the House of
> Israel. He was from Judah, and I was from Joseph. "SO
> WELCOME TO ZION, COUSIN!" I said as I shook his
> hand in welcome! I explained that we have a natural love for
> the Jewish people.
>
> I have never seen anyone more excited and emotionally
> moved than he was, to hear that statement!
>
> I took Moshe to Welfare Square, which to some extent com-
> pares to the Kibbutz in Israel. People and places were so very

different and new to Moshe, and he seemed to enjoy seeing and learning wherever we went. Our people welcomed him most warmly!

At the end of the day, Moshe said, "Irene, could you possibly meet me tomorrow? I have had such a wonderful day I want to learn more of your Church and your people."

"Yes, of course," I replied, "I will be most happy to meet with you, anytime."

I found out that Moshe was very interested in genealogy. So I got special permission to take him out to the granite mountain vaults, 20 miles from Salt Lake, up in the mountain. It is completely bomb and earthquake proof, the safest place in the world to store records. It is 700' below the surface of the mountain, and all solid granite!

When Moshe saw the large map of the world (while inside the vaults), with red tacks on the nations where the Church had microfilmed vital records, he excitedly exclaimed, "Poland, Poland, that is where my people lived. They all died in the Holocaust! But maybe I could find their records in your Genealogical Library. I surely hope so, they were so very dear to me!"

As we returned to the city, we passed This Is The Place Monument and other sights of the city, including the University of Utah. I told him how it was started only 3 years after the Mormon pioneers arrived in this barren desert, and that the Church stressed education.

I expressed my wish that he could have stayed over Sunday, so he could have heard the Mormon Tabernacle Choir broadcast on Sunday morning. Immediately he turned to me and said, "Irene, does that Choir belong to your Church? Let me tell you of an experience I had with them years ago."

As he finished the story, which was most interesting, I felt the Choir should hear it also, so I suggested that after dinner he go to the Choir rehearsal, which he was very anxious to do.

We sat on the first row in the Tabernacle. I explained that it was just a rehearsal, with stopping and starting, so we could leave whenever he would like to. His reply was, "Irene, I love this beautiful music. My host is going to pick me up at 8:30, to catch the plane at 9:30, can we stay until then?"

"Yes, of course, as long as you want," I replied. Then I had the inspiration: If Richard Condie, the Director, had a 10 minute break just before 8:30, I would take Moshe up and have him tell the Choir this lovely story. So I watched the clock...8:25 — 8:30 — 8:35...Richard was not going to have the break, so I had to do something about it.

Yes, once again, as I often had to do, I silently said a prayer, "That if the Dear Lord so desired, would He please impress on Richard to just have a 10 minute break, so the Choir could hear this lovely story." Then I just relaxed, and waited.

As usual Richard was vigorously directing the Choir when, all of a sudden, he stopped, and not to the Choir, but turning to the audience and looking right down to us, said, "All right, all right, a ten minute break!"

What happened? How did he know? I was shocked, I could not believe my prayer was heard so quickly! I grabbed Moshe by the arm and said, "Come, Moshe, I want you to tell the Choir the story you told me."

After introducing him to Richard Condie and the Choir, I explained that he had a most interesting experience concerning the Choir, I wanted him to tell them. As they settled down to listen he said:

"Several years ago, I was in the Far East with a group from Israel. We were very homesick because it was the time of year to celebrate our Jewish holiday, "Hanukkah". Part of the reason we were so despondent was that we had no music to help in our celebration. How could we celebrate this special holiday without a Jewish choir singing anthems...it is so much a part of who we are and how we celebrate this joyous holiday. We received some hope of obtaining this music when one of the men said he was traveling to New York. He would get a recording and return in time for us to use it for our celebration. We were all uplifted, knowing we would have music after all!

"On the appointed day, as we gathered for the celebration, I was handed the recording to play. As I looked at it, I was shocked! The record was by the Mormon Tabernacle Choir! Who were they? We knew of no other choir that could sing the anthems like our own Jewish choirs. Although I was completely heartbroken, it was all we had, so I assumed that it would be better than nothing."

The entire group was in for a surprise! The recording was the most beautiful interpretation of these anthems we had ever heard! It was beautiful beyond words, and the most uplifting, spiritual feeling came over all of us. The music sounded like angels singing, and we knew that we were not alone: God was with us!

"After the recording ended, I got up before the group and said, 'If God is willing, I hope someday I can go wherever that Choir is and personally thank them for what they have done for us this night!'

As he raised his arms to the Choir, he said, "Tonight, God has given me that privilege. From the bottom of my heart, I want to thank you, and express my most sincere appreciation for what you did for us those many years ago!" He was filled with emotion as the Choir gave him a standing ovation!

As the Choir President, Isaac Stewart, presented him with the newest Choir album, the Consul said, "For me, a Jew, you are giving me a gift?" "Yes, of course," President Stewart said, "with our love and friendship, as brothers!" And they truly embraced as brothers.

One cannot describe the beautiful feeling that was there, except to say that many tears were shed! We had completely lost track of time. When I glanced at the clock it was 9:00 o'clock! Dan, who was to pick him up at 8:30 to take him to the Airport was pacing back and forth at door #6!

I quickly suggested that we had better leave, but the Consul seemed unconcerned whether he met or missed his plane. The emotions he was feeling were so strong! He was impressed: what he felt was different from anything he had ever experienced before and he did not want to leave!

> Finally, as we left the Tabernacle, Moshe said, "Irene, I cannot express what these two days have meant to me. All I can say is, "Next to Jerusalem and my own people, Salt Lake City and the Mormon people are the greatest in the world!"
>
> Then, hesitating, he again turned to me and said, "Irene, will you do something for me?" "Yes, of course. What can I do for you?" Then he said, "Irene, I know your prayers are always answered. Will you please pray to the God you have told me about and ask Him to open the way, that I will be able to come back and bring my wife Edna so she can see and hear what I have experienced. Will you do that for me?"
>
> I assured him that I would be glad to, and said, "Moshe, I promise you, that if the Lord wants you to come back, you will be here!" He kissed me on the cheek and said, "Goodbye," and left, waving as the car hurriedly went up the street.

Within days, Irene received a letter from Moshe thanking her for an experience he would never forget. He also sent letters to LeGrand Richards, thanking him for sending a copy of his book *A Marvelous Work and a Wonder,* and to Isaac Stewart, President of the Tabernacle Choir, thanking them for the experience they shared and promising that when he returned he would make a point to come to *both* the Thursday rehearsal and the Sunday broadcast.

Due to Irene's inspiration, Moshe Yegar had been touched by the spirit of God. He would return to Utah again and again to relive the experience. That same spirit and influence would begin to grow and spread throughout the Jewish community and eventually the State of Israel. Soon *many* Israeli government officials and businessmen visiting the United States were going out of their way to stop in Utah to meet the Mormons! As they came to Utah, met with Irene, and experienced the now perfected "Temple Square Tour," even the most hardened were touched.

On May 4, 1967, Irene hosted Monica Dickens, the grand-daughter of Charles Dickens. Irene couldn't wait to share with her the story of her grandmother Gwennie's connection with Charles Dickens, and how they had met on the ship Amazon just prior to coming to America. "Little would Grandmother Edwards and Charles Dickens dream that their two granddaughters would meet in Utah 104 years later!"

On May 7, 1967, Irene hosted Samuel Krakow, the head of International Affairs for the American Red Cross. Due to her numerous and varied volunteer work over the years, Irene almost always had a connection of some kind with the guests she hosted. In this case, her connection was that she had worked as a volunteer for the local Red Cross organization.

Irene had a wonderful talent for sensing others' needs. Often she would find a way to touch a guest in a way that only the Spirit could have shown her. For example, after watching an organ recital, and at Irene's suggestion, Roy Darly, the Tabernacle organist, asked Mr. Krakow if he would like to play the organ himself...

> He nearly exploded with ecstasy—just like a little child at Christmas! He played and Roy pulled the stops as he played. When he finished, he was so overjoyed he almost wept. He shook Roy's hand and was overcome with happiness and appreciation. He said, "Now I am ready to die. I have accomplished my life's ambition—to play the Tabernacle organ. I feel like I am up in the clouds and I never want to come down."

Irene had a picture taken of Mr. Krakow at the organ as a memento of the occasion. Yes, Irene always seemed to know what people desired and how to touch the deepest part of their heart. It was one of the reasons why her testimony of the Gospel became so powerful and touched so many people.

In June another article was written about Irene's work as a hostess:

Official LDS Hostess Enjoying Role; Escorts Visitors, Explains Religion
By Judy B. Rollins, Church Writer, *Salt Lake Tribune*, June 24, 1967

Mrs. Irene Staples is truly a hostess with the mostest.

For Mrs. Staples, official hostess for the Church of Jesus Christ of Latter-day Saints, makes meeting visitors to Temple Square and making them feel at home her special responsibility.

"I love my work," Mrs. Staples said. "I enjoy it most because it involves working with people. It is amazing to see a visitor's reaction to Temple Square, in particular, and Salt Lake City, in general, and to tell them about the LDS religion. I have yet to have any person say they are disappointed in the city or its sights."

Mrs. Staples began her special task for the LDS Church after working for two years in a similar capacity at the Mormon Pavilion at the New York World's Fair.

Her work is a full-time job, seven-days a week and more than eight hours a day. And guests to the city don't stop with bad weather, Mrs. Staples said she performs her duties just as readily whether it's snowing or the sun is shining.

Most popular sights around the city and surrounding communities are Temple Square and concerts or rehearsals of the Mormon Tabernacle Choir, she said.

The hostess has found that most persons come to the city with misconceptions about the founding and development of the LDS Church.

"Many persons come knowing little about the city or the Church. Some have heard nothing of the Church except Brigham Young and polygamy," she said.

Mrs. Staples assists only non-members of the LDS Church in tours of the city and she has greeted persons from around the world. Special treatment for visitors includes a bound story of the Church with the guest's name embossed on the cover.

"My goal is to give these visitors an understanding and to make their visit a pleasant experience. My tours are both educational and enjoyable," she said.

She selects what she shows according to the age and interests of the guests. Foreign languages have proven no barrier since interpreters are available and can assist her with communication.

One of her fondest recollections is of Tennessee Ernie Ford's visit to Temple Square and the Tabernacle where he heard an organ recital. Following the recital, Mrs. Staples asked him if he wouldn't like to test the acoustics in the building. With Alexander Schreiner as his accompanist, Mr. Ford sang "The Lord's Prayer."

Recalls royal Visit
Another guest she remembers well is Her Royal Highness, Princess Irene of Greece who said she was interested in the LDS religion and would like to know more about it.

Mrs. Staples' contacts come from referrals by General Authorities of the Church who usually cannot find time to escort guests themselves.

But her efforts to make guests feel at home do not end with her official duties. Many times she meets people and invites them to her house to take a peek at the way an American home functions.

By now Irene's talents were becoming well known among the Brethren of the Church. Many of them had become aware of Irene because of her involvement over the years in civic and social activities, others through her design and construction of hundreds of costumes for the MIA pageants, and, of course, others had heard about the wonderful success she had while serving her mission at the Mormon Pavilion. But now that Irene was working on Temple Square, and *all* of her many talents were on display, the General Authorities began using Irene more and more to host high profile guests and personal friends. An August 22, 1967, letter from Sterling W. Sill to Elder Mark E. Peterson[1] about Irene's work as Hostess showed the respect he had for her:

> I mentioned to you the other day what a great job I think Irene Staples is doing with the visitors that she visits with while they are in Salt Lake City. I am enclosing herewith a file on one of the latest of the ministers that she has discussed the Church with. I thought you might like to see it.

---

[1]See Appendix I, *Comments About Irene.*

161

I am familiar with other cases where she has done an equally good job. I think if we all did our work as well as Irene does the Church would be in pretty good shape.

Whenever people of other religions visited Utah, it was always Irene that would be given the assignment. This was due to her tolerance of other's beliefs, and because she had become so adept at answering questions that might come up.

In June of 1967, Irene hosted Reverend and Mrs. D. Austin Bowen of England. Once again Irene had a connection. Irene had first met the Reverend while visiting Wales when she went to England with her son Richard after his mission to Switzerland. It turned out that the Reverend was the great-grandson of Titus and Mary Bowen Davis, Irene's great-grandparents! This is Irene's own report of hosting the Reverend and Mrs. D. Austin Bowen:

> They came in June, during the MIA June Conference, with all the activities. I not only took them all over the valley, but I also took them to the beautiful dance festival which was held in the University of Utah football stadium where over 8,000 young people from all over the Church, in bright costumes, went through an evening of all types of dances from folk to ballroom. It was a breath-taking event. They were quite overwhelmed with what they saw. I had special reserved seats and also introduced them to many General Authorities. I also took them to the Tabernacle where 3,000 young people gave a musical concert. Never had they seen anything like this before!
>
> I also took them to the Tabernacle Choir broadcast on Sunday morning, and had their names announced as special guests from Wales. I took them to Willard so they could see where their relatives and where great grandfather came and settled.
>
> I took them to the Federal Heights sacrament service. Afterward, there was no special comment from them, and I wondered what they thought of it, which is so much different from their church services.

After Church I invited all the relatives from Willard and cousins in Salt Lake to my home for a buffet dinner as a farewell in their honor. At the close of the evening, I stood and expressed my appreciation for the privilege of having these cousins with us, the first ever to come from Wales. And then I said, "What a special blessing it has been to have our cousins with us, and in appreciation of them coming, and of the many blessings we all have, let us sing, COUNT YOUR MANY BLESSINGS. This we did with all the true feeling of love and appreciation for our many blessings.

When we were through Reverend Austin stood up and said, "Irene, can I say a word or two?" "Of course," I replied. Then he stood there and told of all the wonderful places they had seen and the wonderful youth conference, with the activities they had seen. Then he said how very impressed he was with the church service they had attended, commenting that each one who gave talks were just members from the congregation. How unusual that was and how very good each one was. The beautiful music furnished also by members of the congregation. No paid clergy. No paid choir. Everyone participating. This was a real revelation, for here it was the people's Church, each one taking their part in it.

And then he added, "In Wales, we have not even considered Mormons as true Christians, but I want you relatives to know that I have found more Christianity here in one week than I have found in Wales in my whole lifetime. I am going back to Wales and tell them the truth about the Mormons, that you are true Christians in not only your Church attendance ... but also in your way of life. I cannot express the beautiful feeling I have here."

Then he turned to me and said, "And to you Irene, our special thanks, for if it hadn't been for you we wouldn't have been here and had this most wonderful experience. We want to thank you for your kind hospitality, and all the many things you have done for us. All this, Irene, is because of you and I cannot express my gratitude and how much it has meant to us," and...he broke down with emotion and wept!

I walked over to his side and putting my arm around his shoulders, thanked him for his kindness. He, in turn, embraced me, and with great emotion, could only say...

"God bless you, God bless you. God bless you wonderful people!"

Yes, they could not help but feel the friendship and love we have through the teachings of our Gospel. They felt the Spirit here, for many times his wife, Brands, would say, "Austin, I think I will let you go back to Wales and I will stay here." And then one day she said, "Austin, why do you wear that garb anyway?" (meaning his clergy clothes).

Whereupon he turned to me and said, "Irene, why do I wear these clothes, do you know?" What a shock it was to have him ask me!

I immediately told him that it was only one of the many changes which had come into the Church after Christ had established it. How, when the Lord spoke to the Prophet Joseph Smith, He said, "They have a form of godliness, intermingled with the teaching of men!" And surely that is true, for many things have been changed since the Savior established His Church, and Ministers wearing special dress was one of the changes, for how did Christ dress...like the most humble of all men in that day! "Oh," he replied, and said no more.

He was escorted through the Genealogical Library, and was overwhelmed with all that he saw. He was also told by one of the Library officials that if the time came that he would decide to join the Church, there was always a position waiting for him here in the Library!

What a blessing that would be, not only for his help in the Library, but also a great blessing to them and their family to belong to the True Church of Jesus Christ.

Back in Wales, he was a great help when a Genealogical Library official was there. He opened the way for many church records to be microfilmed. Most churches in Wales will not allow the Library this privilege, but through the kindness of Austin, and having been here...he opened up the way for many records to be microfilmed.

Yes, it was a real blessing to have the great grandson of Titus and Mary Bowen Davis here in Salt lake City, so he could see for himself – why his great grandfather made such a sacrifice to come here, and why he accepted the truths of this new religion ... the true CHURCH OF JESUS CHRIST OF LATTER-DAY SAINTS!

May the time come when... other blessings will come from their desire to come here to learn more about the Mormons. I am sure in the Dear Lord's own due time ... these blessings will come, to them and their loved ones.

Highlights of 1967

January

25	Irene's letter to the Israeli Consul in Los Angeles

February

9	The Vienna Boys Choir
14	The Ambassador from Denmark

March

3	First visit of Moshe Yegar, Israel Consul General
21	Vera Miles (stage and movie star)

April

14	Jack Benny (comedian and actor)
20	Brigadier General William R. Porter
21	Illinois Congressman John B. Anderson
30	150 World War I veterans

May

2	Major General Edwin Chess
4	Monica Dickens, great-granddaughter of Charles Dickens
5	A group of college student body presidents

8	Major General William H. Baumer
9	Robert Goulet (singer, actor)
11	The Supreme Court Judges of 3 western States
15	Dr. Yona Malachy, Ministry for Religious Affairs, Jerusalem

June

7	Brigadier General Steve A. Chappuis
9	Major General N.B. Edwards
16	A German soccer team
29	The Japanese Prime Minister
30	A Baptist youth tour

July

26	Judge Julian E. Hughes

August

5	A group of German scout leaders
9	Reverend Gerald Leo Tierney
14	A group of Japanese boy scouts
31	Dugway Proving Grounds Military Tour

September

13	The Utah State Medical Association
23	Lord and Lady James Netherthorpe

October

2	Father Gerard Leo Tierney, a special guest of the Prophet David O. McKay, during General Conference

November

9	General Harold K. Johnson
18	Premier and Prince, Pousima Afe'ahi, Tonga

December

3   Mr. and Mrs. A. Ben Ari, government head of Israel tourism industry

14   Paul Harvey (radio commentator)

Statistics for 1967:

Total visitors hosted	12,772
Foreign visitors	739
Countries represented	57

The year 1968 started off badly for Irene. For the first time in years she was forced to take time off work due to a fall on the steps of her home. In February, Irene had her foot operated on and was laid up for several weeks. Then she went right back to what seemed like a 24 hour a day, 7 days a week schedule.

On March 25, Irene once again had the opportunity to host the Consul from Israel, Moshe Yegar. This time Irene introduced him to many of the General Authorities of the Church, including President Nathan Eldon Tanner and Elders Ezra Taft Benson, Richard L. Evans and Howard W. Hunter. As chance would have it, Elder Benson, while serving as United States Secretary of Agriculture, became very well acquainted with General Moshe Dayan, who at that time was also Secretary of Agriculture for Israel, so they had much in common.

Since her last visit with the Yegars, Irene had entertained hundreds of the Israeli people who were beginning to visit Salt Lake City. They were always impressed with what they saw and heard. Irene wrote:

> I have never met anyone who was not thrilled with their visit. Often they would say to me: Irene, what is it...what is the feeling I have here? I feel like I belong here!" And others would say: "I feel like I am at home. It is so different here...there is

167

> this wonderful feeling among the Mormons, a feeling I have
> never felt before!

Irene continued to receive compliments about her work as Official Hostess for the Church. In November of 1968, while eating lunch at the Lion House with a friend, Elder Spencer W. Kimball came by and stopped to visit with Irene. He turned to Irene's friend, and pointing directly at Irene, said, "There is the Church's greatest missionary!"

This statement was not far from the truth! Each week Irene would send referrals to missions around the world, and every month she would receive letters from the mission field describing the conversions that had come from her referrals. If one was to add up all the referrals over all of the years…the mind struggles to fully comprehend the impact this one woman has had on the spread of the Gospel around the world!

Highlights of 1968

January

19	General James H. Woolbough and Brigadier General John G. Appel

March

12	Dr. Hillgenberg, the German Consul
25	Second visit of Moshe Yegar, Israel Consul General

April

30	Miss USA, Cheryl Ann Palton

May

12	Jerry West (professional basketball player)
18	Major General and Mrs. J.F. Franklin, Jr.

June

10	White Rock, Texas Methodist church group
27	A German soccer team

July

7	The President of Bolivia
30	Lieutenant General W.B. Bunker

August

1	Reverend Gerald Leo Tierney

December

19	Archbishop Iakovos of the Greek Orthodox Church

Statistics for 1968:

Total visitors hosted	15,798
Foreign visitors	663
Countries represented	60

Irene Staples: Hostess to the World

The Return of Friends

> Self control means one must be able to control his temper
> and not give way to anger. Self control means that when you
> are tempted to do things wrong—to break the laws of the
> Church or the laws of the land—you can turn away and say
> NO.
>
> Irene

The year 1969 was filled with the "return of friends." Many
of the people Irene had hosted over the years returned to Salt
Lake, and specifically to see Irene. Their experience the previous
visit had been so powerful—so *spiritual*—they just had to return.
There was *something* about the Mormon Church, *something* about
Salt Lake City, and most importantly, *something* about their
friend Irene.

In February, Irene once again hosted Her Royal Highness
Princess Irene and guests, and organized a luncheon in their
honor. After the visit, Irene wrote a letter to Her Majesty Queen
Mother Frederica of the Hellenes, the mother of Princess Irene of
Greece, expressing her gratitude and love for the Princess.

Also in February, Irene received another letter from Moshe
Yegar telling her that he would finally be bringing his wife,
Edna, to Utah. During Moshe's first trip to Salt Lake he had re-
quested that Irene say a special prayer to help him bring his wife

to Utah. It seems that a short time later Irene's prayer had been answered!

Prior to his being transferred to Philadelphia following a promotion to Consul General, the Jewish community in Los Angeles wanted to give Moshe and his wife the farewell gift of a week vacation for him and his wife to *any* place they desired. They all assumed they would pick some exotic location like Hawaii, but they were in for a surprise!

Moshe had replied, "There is no decision to make—Salt Lake City."

"Salt Lake City?" they asked, "What is in Salt Lake, surely nothing for you!"

"Salt Lake is the greatest city in the whole United States," he replied. "You have no idea what there is there, and that is where we want to go!"

So, in March, on the third visit of Consul General Moshe Yegar, he brought with him his beloved wife so she, too, could have the "Mormon experience."

When Moshe arrived with his wife they met with President Nathan Eldon Tanner (a member of the First Presidency of the Church), Elders Ezra Taft Benson, Howard W. Hunter, Richard L. Evans (members of the Quorum of the Twelve Apostles), Sister Belle Spafford (the Relief Society president), and Cleon Skousen (a noted professor at BYU). When they attended the choir rehearsal, the choir sang *God Be With You* especially for them. Pictures were taken of them and Elder Benson, and also Moshe and his wife in front of the famous Tabernacle organ. In the evening Irene held a private dinner at her home where they met with the Skousens.

The next day, while touring BYU, they were introduced to the Orson Hyde Club—a group of students that were studying the Hebrew culture. Included were classes in the Hebrew language, programs for Hebrew dancing and learning Jewish songs—all under the direction of a Jewish convert! They were simply overwhelmed with what they saw, and said, "What is there that I can tell the Mormons? It is like talking to the converted—they are already our friends!" Irene wrote about the experience:

> I arranged special activities, including a trip to the BYU, where President Ernest L. Wilkinson and several BYU officials entertained us at a special luncheon in their honor. I had contacted the BYU Israeli organization to entertain us. They had a wonderful program, with Israeli songs and dances. It was a wonderful afternoon, and the Yegars were quite overwhelmed with the reception they received.
>
> I also entertained them at my home at a dinner party with, as special guests, some Jewish people who had joined the Church and others, including the Mayor of our city!
>
> The highlight of their trip was when I again took them to the Thursday Choir practice, where Richard Condie, Isaac Stewart, and the Choir welcomed them, for they all remembered them. Richard Condie had the Choir sing a special number in their honor.
>
> As Moshe Yegar got up to thank them, he said, "No words can express our most sincere appreciation for the wonderful reception we have received." The only thing he could say was ... "May God bless you, that you may continue singing!"
>
> The next day, on our way to the airport, Moshe said to his wife, "Edna, isn't it like I told you, isn't it wonderful here?" "No, it isn't," she replied ... as my heart sank! Until she said, "It is far greater! I thought you were just exaggerating. It has been a most wonderful trip!" Then they said "Goodbye" with an embrace, saying it was a week they would never forget!

During this visit the *Deseret News* wrote an article about Moshe Yegar. After he returned home, he wrote a letter to the *Deseret News* complaining about the article. It seems as though they left out an important part of the interview:

> It was very kind of the *Deseret News* to honor me with the nice write up. My only regret is that one thing that I discussed with the reporter who interviewed me, was omitted, and this was the special tribute I paid to Mrs. Irene Staples. Mrs. Staples is worthy of very high praise, and thanks to her our visit to Salt Lake City has left such a deep impression.

In addition, Moshe wrote Irene directly to thank her for the wonderful experience he and his wife had shared in Utah:

> Honestly, Edna and I don't even know how to begin to thank you for all that you did for us. I enjoyed your hospitality twice before, but this last visit undoubtedly was the most memorable one. It was quite difficult for both Edna and I to go to the airport, knowing the friendship, kindness and hospitality we left behind. Namely, Irene Staples.
>
> Because of you Salt Lake City will ever be a treasured part of our memories. You are indeed <u>VERY SPECIAL</u> and will always be so for us.

Moshe then gave Irene his personal contact information and invited her to come visit them in Philadelphia at any time—and better yet, in Israel!

Sometime later, when Irene flew east to attend the baptism of a family of five that she had hosted on Temple Square, she stopped in Philadelphia for a few days to visit with the Yegars, who still had fond memories of Salt Lake. Irene wrote:

> Upon an invitation from the Consul and his wife, I was a house guest for three days in their Philadelphia home. Here the Consul invited leading Jews of the city to meet me, and have me explain the Book of Mormon and our relationship as a Church with the Jewish people. It was a most interesting and unusual experience.
>
> There at the Consulate, when special Government officials came from Israel, Moshe would immediately tell them about Salt Lake City, and of his wonderful experience here with the Mormons! That it was the "ZION OF UTAH", and that they had to go there, giving them my name and phone number, saying, "You just call Irene. She will take care of you!"

By this time the word about the Mormons was getting around Jewish communities within the United States, as well as Israel. Many of those coming to Salt Lake discovered the Spirit of God for the very first time — and were converted. One such conversion took place about this time, as Irene records:

> THE CONVERSION OF ALVIN MOELING: A JEWISH CONVERT
>
> I was called by Brother Cleon Skousen and asked if I would meet a Jewish couple he had met while on a speaking engagement in California. He informed me that she had joined the Church four months previously, and that the husband was here in Salt Lake to find out more about the Church.
>
> When I met Alvin and Elissa Moeling, Alvin immediately told me that his wife let the missionaries come to their home four years ago. He was very upset and didn't approve. However when he heard her say that she did believe in Jesus Christ, he went white with anger and said that he would rather have seen her drop dead than to hear her make such a statement!
>
> Finally, after four years, he gave her permission to join, and now, after four months, he came to Salt Lake to really find out the truth about Mormonism.
>
> As I began taking them on a tour of Temple Square and the buildings, I naturally brought much of our doctrine into the conversation. He stopped me and said, "Mrs. Staples! I know all the beliefs and doctrines of your Church; you don't have to tell me anything. I came here for one purpose only and that is to know whether President McKay is a Prophet or not. If he is—the Church is true. If he isn't—it is false! It is just that simple. I want to go see President McKay and I will know whether he is a Prophet or not".
>
> I immediately told him that it would be impossible to see President McKay. In the first place, President McKay was very ill; in fact, he wasn't going to be able to attend April Conference. And second, it would be wrong to gain a testimony that way —just by seeing a man, and deciding whether he was a

Prophet or not, and upon that snap judgment know whether the Church was true or not.

He immediately became very belligerent and hostile, and demanded that he see President McKay, regardless of the situation.

I began reasoning with him, that he could not get a testimony simply by looking at a sick man, and also that doctors orders were that he should not be disturbed by anyone. It would be an injustice to President McKay, as well as Mr. Moeling himself.

And then I said, "Al, remember the gates of Heaven are built so low that you have to get on your knees to enter. You will never get a testimony unless you humble yourself through faith, repentance, and prayer!"

It seemed like that was the worst thing I could have said, for immediately he became so belligerent and so filled with evil that he could hardly contain himself. He became so enraged that he wanted me to know that I or no one else could keep him from seeing whom he wanted. I was just putting him off. He wasn't going to start at the bottom — he was going to the very top and get what he wanted!

Finally, I suggested that we go over to President McKay's office and talk to his secretary, which we did. As we entered, I told Sister Middlemiss that this gentleman was very desirous of seeing President McKay.

She immediately tried to tell him how very ill the President was and that doctor's orders were that no one, not even those from foreign countries could see him. She showed him pictures and gave him a book on President McKay's life and tried in every way to satisfy his desires. But again, the more either she or I talked to him, the more belligerent and angry he became, until he became so enraged that no one could talk or reason with him.

The most horrible feeling filled the room. I felt that it was filled with evil spirits—that the walls were closing in on me and I was going to collapse unless I got out of there!

His sweet little wife stood silently by with tears streaming down her face. I finally suggested that we go over to the Lion House and I would buy them lunch. He didn't want to go and insisted that he was going to stay there until he saw President McKay—he was going to the doctor himself and tell him so. He was even going to bribe the bell-hops at the Hotel Utah to find out which apartment was President McKay's, as neither Clare nor myself would tell him.

Finally, when I could stand it no longer and was being overcome with this terrible feeling, I grabbed him by the arm and simply rushed him out of the room, exclaiming that we had to leave immediately!

As I turned to close the door behind me, Sister Middlemiss collapsed at her desk. She was overcome with the same terrible feelings and the strain of being with such an irrational and demanding person.

As we hurriedly walked through the Church Offices I silently prayed so very hard: "Dear Lord, I need your help! I have done all I can do with this man. He is so filled with bitterness that I need thy help. Please Heavenly Father, I need the Priesthood to cast out the evil feeling that is within this man. Please help me."

When we entered the Lion House it was ten minutes to two. It was empty, since it normally closed at two o'clock. We got our trays, and as I walked into one of the dining rooms, followed by Al and his wife, another man came through the door from the opposite direction. He and Al abruptly met face to face.

After a second's pause, the other gentleman said, "Hello", and Al answered, "Hello...where have I seen you before?"

Whereupon the stranger answered, "You have never seen me before, but I know why I am here. May I sit at your table?"

I immediately spoke up and said, "Certainly."

As we sat down, the gentleman, whom I had never seen before, spoke up and said, "My name is Sherman Young. My office is just across the street. I had the impression and feeling that I was needed in the Lion House. So I cancelled my appointments, locked my office door and here I am. What can I do for you?"

I immediately introduced myself and Mr. & Mrs. Moeling to Brother Young, and then he said, "I was set apart by Elder LeGrand Richards as a special missionary for the preaching of the Gospel to the Jews. Forget about wanting to see President McKay. Get that out of your mind and I will be glad to help you."

Immediately Al calmed down, and there was a peaceful, quiet feeling among us, as Brother Young began to talk to them. Sherman was kind enough to say that he would spend the rest of the day with them.

I was very thankful for this turn of events because I was completely drained of every ounce of strength I had.

Of the many, many times I have been in the Lion House to eat, as does Brother Young, I had never met or even remember seeing him there before. And yet at closing time, here he was walking through the dining room in order to meet Al Moeling!

My prayers had certainly been answered—the Lord had sent the Priesthood to cast out the evil, belligerent feeling which so possessed this man. Through the efforts of Brother Young and other contacts, Al spent the next few days either in Salt Lake or in Provo. I also met with him again during this time; once at April Conference and once at a Jewish entertainment program. The program was put on by the Orson Hyde Club of the Brigham Young University.

The following Thursday I met Al in front of the Church Offices. He was standing there as if waiting for me. As soon as he saw me, he came up, threw his arms around me, and said, "Do you mind if I kiss you? I am so happy! I am going to be baptized Saturday."

What a change had come over him! No longer was he the arrogant, belligerent person he had been a few days ago, but was filled with humility and had a strong testimony of the Gospel. Yes, he had been seeking a testimony, but without the right spirit!

178

When I asked him what had happened, he told me this story: He said, "I had been invited to attend a meeting of the welfare workers. I wasn't anxious about going, but somehow I went. As I sat there, I looked over the audience. They were crippled, blind, and aged. Then I heard the Bishop say, "We have a special guest here this morning, a Mr. Moeling...we would like to have him say a few words".

I was so startled—what could I say to these people, and especially people in their circumstances? But there I was starting to speak. As I looked over the audience, no longer did they look old, crippled, and blind—they were CHILDREN OF GOD!...and I was one of them.

A feeling came over me, and I found myself telling of the truths of the Gospel. I turned to see who was saying the words I was hearing—there was no one there except me. And then, overcome with emotion, I heard myself say, "I want to be baptized!" I knew it was the Holy Ghost bearing witness to me of the truthfulness of the Gospel.

Irene, it was as you said, I couldn't go to the top for my answer—I had to humble myself and go to the very lowly, the humble. I had to get on my knees in humility in order to go through the gates of the Gospel! It was very hard—but now I know for sure."

That Saturday in the Tabernacle baptismal font this fine gentleman was baptized by Elder Cleon Skousen, and confirmed by Elder Sherman Young, whom the Lord had sent in answer to my prayer. A righteous and devoted bearer of the Priesthood, a real missionary!

Before the baptism, many people were bearing their testimonies. When Al could not wait any longer, he stood and said, "I appreciate your wonderful testimonies, but simply cannot wait any longer—I want to be baptized. Could we please do it now?"

It was a very impressive occasion, for after the baptism three men of Jewish descent, who themselves were converts, stood in the confirmation circle.

It was also very interesting that before the confirmation, Brother Young said that the Jews, by virtue of their Jewish birthright and Jewish rituals, had been given a "new name." So as he confirmed Al, he was not only going to call him by his given name but also the new name which had been given him as a member of the House of Judah.

His wife, who had left Al here and had gone back home to be with the children, flew back bringing the rest of the little family for this spiritual and sacred occasion.

It has been a strong testimony to me that, first, the Lord does hear and answer our Prayers in time of need—and I was so desperately in need of help—and second, that one can only gain a testimony of the Gospel through the way prescribed by the Lord Himself, which is: faith, repentance, humility, and prayer.

Yes, it is then and only then, that we can know through the blessings and power of the Holy Ghost that Jesus is the Christ and that the true Church of Jesus Christ of Latter-day Saints has once again been restored upon the earth!

In August, Irene hosted His Eminence the Archbishop Iakovos, Primate of the Greek Orthodox Church of North and South America. He had come for the Greek Orthodox Youth of America 18th International Conference being held in Salt Lake City that year. It included eminent lecturers and representatives from the religious, academic, and political community. Irene hosted a "Consecration Banquet" in his honor, with many General Authorities present, including Elder Ezra Taft Benson who spoke in behalf of the ailing President McKay. The importance of these meetings with the Archbishop was reflected in a newspaper article concerning the events:

Article about the visit of Archbishop Iakovos
J.M. Heslop, *Church News*, 1969

President David O. McKay was honored last week "as a living example of the will of God" by His eminence Archbishop Iakovos, Primate of the Greek Orthodox Church of North and South America.

"You have been a great leader," Archbishop Iakovos, the spiritual leader of two million members, told President McKay. "God needs you in His service."

Archbishop Iakovos was honored with a special state dinner given by the First Presidency and attended by 45 General Authorities, their wives, and officials of the Greek Orthodox Church in Utah.

"I am glad to see you again. I remember with delight our visit of six years ago," Pres. McKay said.

The archbishop replied, "Thank you, I again express gratefulness for what you and the Church have done for my people in Greece and for our people here in Salt Lake City."

"Thank you for the honors Greece has given the Church," Pres. McKay said, referring to the Cross of the Commander of the Royal Order of Phoenix that has been signed by King Paul and presented to Pres. McKay. "I hope the friendship for which it stands will be eternal. There is nothing so precious as friendship, and through the years we prize the friendship of your nation and the Church," Pres. McKay continued.

While in Salt Lake City he toured Temple Square, attended a rehearsal of the Tabernacle Choir, and visited Welfare Square and the Granite Mountain record vaults.

During their visit, Irene hosted the entire Greek Church Council of North and South America, with a formal welcome on behalf of the Church and another tour. She helped organize a luncheon hosted by the First Presidency, under the direction of Elder Gordon B. Hinckley and Elder Thomas S. Monson. The Archbishop was given a special embossed copy of the Book of Mormon, signed by the First Presidency. While the Brethren were at this luncheon, Irene took the wives of these officials to lunch at the Lion House, and spent almost an hour, seated in a special room, telling them the history of the Church and answering questions about Mormon beliefs and doctrine.

Irene was then invited to attend a special Sunday morning Greek Orthodox Church service and luncheon. She learned that the Greek Orthodox Church was in grave financial trouble and church membership and attendance were declining. The council wanted to hold the conference in Miami, but the Archbishop insisted they go to Salt Lake. Irene commented:

> I had a gentleman come to me and say, "Mrs. Staples, I'm going to tell you something, and I want you to remember it: The time is coming—not now, but in the future—when a great force for good and the betterment of all mankind will come from your church and people here in Utah. It will have a great effect upon our nation and the world. I know that is true. There is a great and wonderful feeling here." He was so sincere and prophetic in his statement—that I almost expected him to end with "thus saith the Lord."

> Another question I was asked: "Are your Twelve apostles chosen because of their wealth, their prestige and their social standing?" How thrilled I was to answer that this had no bearing on it whatsoever. Following the ways of Christ, they were chosen as were the humble fishermen and others—from the lay membership of the church. Those who are pure in heart, humble, and with a great desire to serve the Lord and do His will.

> It also might be of interest to know that the wife of Father Elias of the local Greek Church told the group of ladies, "I have the best Mormon neighbors, and I go to Relief Society with them. It is a wonderful women's organization—you learn so much. And my children love Primary. They, too, go every week. They wouldn't miss it!"

As usual, Irene's good works did not go unnoticed. In a November 12, 1969, letter to Irene from Sterling W. Sill, Brother Sill expressed in a humorous way the great respect the Brethren had for the work Irene was doing: "I am sending you a letter from our good friend…whom you showed around the city a little while ago. They all seem to have so much fun I think I'll get me a disguise as a VIP and take the tour myself!"

On November 25, Irene was honored at Beehive Standards Night in her home ward. She had been chosen by all the young girls in her congregation as a woman "Worthy of Imitation."

They had a short program that presented some of Irene's accomplishments.

Highlights of 1969

February

8	Princess Irene of Greece
19	The Vienna Boys Choir

March

9	Sir Anthony and Lady Milward of England
25	Moshe and Edna Yegar, Israeli Consul General

April

7	Miss Universe, Gloria Diaz of the Phillipines
12	The Swedish Ambassador, Hubert W.A. deBesehe
15	A German Countess
28	A choir from the University of Seoul, South Korea

May

8	Vice President & Mrs. Spiro Agnew
9	Miss USA 1968, Dorothy "Didi" Anslett

June

13	The Osmond Brothers and guests
17	A United Church of Christ tour group
27	A German soccer team

July

22	Reverend Gerald Leo Tierney

August

23	His Eminence Archbishop Iakovos, Primate of the Greek Orthodox Church of North and South America, during the Greek Orthodox Youth of America 18th International Conference.
26	Lord and Lady Netherthorpe of London, friends of Elder Ezra Taft Benson

September

12	Reverend Faries McDaniel, Presbyterian Minister from Dallas, Texas
20	Lord and Lady Netherthorpe of London, friends of Elder Ezra Taft Benson, who returned for a second time
29	The First Lady, Mrs. Lyndon Johnson

October

2	A group of Hedrickites, or Church of the Temple Lot, Apostles and wives
6	Benjamin Abileah, new Israel Consul General

November

11	General George V. Underwood, Jr.
20	George Bush, Sr., Congressman

Statistics for 1969:

Total visitors hosted	17,162
Foreign visitors	683
Countries represented	53

The year 1970 was tumultuous for Irene. Sunday morning, January 18, the Prophet and President of the Church, David O. McKay, died. There were many friends and guests who attended the funeral held on January 22, like the Reverend Gerald Leo Tierney, who came to show his respects to President McKay.

In September of that year, Irene's home was robbed. But in spite of the ups and downs of life, her purpose held steady: she worked every day, seven days a week when necessary, to insure that visitors to Salt Lake, and specifically to Temple Square, had a wonderful, spiritual experience. They would then go home and spread the truth about the Mormons to the world.

Over the years, her status and importance to the progress of the Church did not go unnoticed by the Brethren. In one letter written March 23, 1970 to Irene from Sterling W. Sill,[2] he expressed (tongue in cheek) his gratitude for what Irene did for the Church:

> I think I would do pretty well in the world if you just always told me what I ought to do! Someday I'm going to vote for you to be the first female member of the Quorum of the Twelve!

Many others extended their appreciation for Irene's hard work. In a July 15, 1970 letter to Elder Mark E. Peterson, Kaye Burgon of Frontier Airlines wrote:

> I would like to comment on the excellent work that is being done for the Church by Mrs. Irene E. Staples, LDS Church Hostess. I have had occasion to work with Mrs. Staples on various occasions when Frontier Airlines has had influential people visiting Salt Lake City. Because of our desire to have these people better understand the Church and the rich history of our area, I have found the services of Mrs. Staples extremely helpful. I consider her position very important and valuable to the Church.

---

[2]See Appendix I, *Comments About Irene*

> She fulfills a service and need that, to my knowledge, could not be real-
> ized in any other way. From my experience, you could not have selected a
> more gracious, cooperative and understanding person than Irene. Her
> personality sparkles and certainly influences all with whom she comes in
> contact.
>
> If I might make an additional observation, I feel Mrs. Staples could use an
> assistant. She works very hard and puts in long hours."

This last comment was a serious concern for many within the Church: Irene was getting older, and the number of "special guests" was growing far beyond what she could handle by herself. Soon the problem would be remedied. Others, many others, would be called to assist in the important role of hosting the Church's guests from around the world.

Highlights of 1970

January

7	Ann Landers (famous columnist)
12	The American Baptist Board of Education
20	Reverend Gerald Leo Tierney

February

28	Agnes DeMille (wife of the famous movie producer)

April

14	The Israeli Consul General Michael Ravid; also the Director of Western States for the Government of Israel, the District Manager of El Al Airlines, and the local head of the Jewish Community Center

July

2	The President of Texas at El Paso University
12	Reverend Gerald Leo Tierney and guest

186

August

7   A German soccer team

September

11   The Boston Patriots football team (now the New
        England Patriots)
?   Margarete Hutter, Deputy Consul General,
        German Consulate, San Francisco

October

2   A group of World War I veterans
4   The Archbishop of Crete
6   His Eminence Bishop Charles B. Layoudakis of Crete
13   Ted Bryant, Congressman from New Mexico

November

22   The Ambassador from Argentina

Statistics for 1970:

Total visitors hosted   17,514
Foreign visitors   606
Countries represented   56

Irene Staples: Hostess to the World

Lehi's Cave

We have all heard people say, "If I don't do anything worse than that, I'll be all right." But isn't that a poor excuse for doing wrong—just the thought that one didn't do something worse!

I am reminded of the story of the boy whose father would have him drive a nail in a certain tree when he had done wrong. And when he had repented, he could pull the nail out.

After a while, the boy said, "What harm is there if I do wrong once in a while, as long as I repent and do good to make up for it?"

The father took the boy to the tree. It was still growing, but the trunk was full of holes where the nails had been driven and then pulled out. He said, "See, my son, no matter what you do in life, it makes an imprint on your soul for either good or evil, and the evil things leave an ugly scar that cannot be erased, just as the nail holes in this tree cannot be erased."

And so the leaders of our Church are continually pleading with us to live clean lives, both for our own good and so we may be an example to others.

Let us each and every day preach the gospel by living clean lives.

Irene

The relationship between the Mormon Church and Israel progressed rapidly in 1971. Irene continued writing letters to Moshe Yegar and other Israeli contacts, many of whom were asking the Church to help them find their ancestors through the genealogical program. As important as Irene's contacts were, she was not the only one making significant progress in establishing a relationship with Israel. Many of the Brethren were making their own contacts, and many people at BYU were developing contacts that would eventually lead to the establishment of the BYU Jerusalem Center in Israel.

One of the first signs of progress in this important relationship was the exchange program that began between Utah universities and Israel. The University of Utah and BYU started a program in which they would exchange professors for a semester or two. Much like exchange students in high school, professors in similar departments would trade places, each teaching in the other's university.

Irene's first challenge of 1971 was to convince the Brethren that she should not retire! Born in 1906, this year would mark Irene's 65th birthday—the usual retirement age for Church employees. But Irene was *not* ready to retire, and those within the hosting service could not imagine what they would do without her!

All kinds of personal and office politics ensued as the date of Irene's retirement neared. An example of this apprehension is conveyed in an April 30, 1971 letter from John Q. Cannon to Russell Williams:[1]

> Sister Irene E. Staples, a member of the Church Information Service staff, arrives at the 65 year retirement age on Sept. 29, 71. We request permission to continue her employment beyond that date. Elder Mark E. Petersen, who supervises the activities of this office, concurs in this request.

[1]See Appendix I, *Comments About Irene*

190

Functioning in the capacity of hostess, Sister Staples performs an exacting and extremely important service for the church, in a very effective way. She is thoroughly dedicated to her work and to the church, giving time and effort far in excess of regular or normal hours. As far as is known, her health is good and she is fully capable of carrying on. We have never succeeded in having her turn in adequate expense accounts, and the result is that substantial amounts of her own funds are expended on her job.

Reports are constantly received from persons who have visited here, attesting to the fine quality of her work, and it is known that she is primarily responsible for many converts to the church. Finding a replacement who could and would perform as she does would indeed be difficult.

Due to the efforts of her immediate supervisors, Irene was permitted to continue work for three more years. She was in good health, and her contacts in Israel were critical at this time in the Church's history. They *needed* her to stay and finish her work!

The Cave of Lehi

In February, Irene was contacted by Professor Joseph Ginat of Israel. Joseph was one of the first exchange professors to teach several semesters at the University of Utah. Consul General Moshe Yegar told Joseph to contact Irene, and she would "take care of him." And, of course, she did. Not only did she take him on the standard tour of Temple Square and give him a copy of the Book of Mormon, she helped him obtain housing and contacts within the city. Irene's gift of a Book of Mormon to Joseph Ginat would have a profound effect upon Joseph and lay the foundation for a spectacular revelation related to an archeological find in the land of Israel.

Irene immediately felt within herself the importance of Joseph Ginat to the relationship between the Church and Israel. This was expressed in a February 24, 1971 letter from Irene to Mark E. Peterson:

> Last week I entertained Professor and Mrs. Joseph Ginat from Jerusalem. He is a guest Professor at the University of Utah for this year...

> The Consul General of Israel, whom I hosted here and still
> correspond with, recommended that they should get in touch
> with me. We had a most interesting evening, discussing our
> Church with its beliefs and closeness with the Jews.
>
> I had invited several Jewish converts...and when Professor
> Ginat said, "I am very interested in your church, is it possible
> that I can learn more?" Little did he know he asked the
> "Golden Question", and I am arranging for Church discussion
> to be given to them by Sherman Young, Cleon Skousen, and
> others.
>
> I find that entertaining at home is the best way to get close to
> these people.

It was due to one of those "coincidences" that God seems to
put together, that a remarkable event came to light: the discovery
of the Cave of Lehi southwest of Jerusalem. The discovery of the
Cave of Lehi, and the revelation concerning its connection with
the Book of Mormon, was a significant step forward in the
relationship between the Church and Israel. Many Israeli visitors
had come to Salt Lake and felt the spirit that permeated Temple
Square, but most seemed to be waiting for something more —
some sort of proof that what they had discovered in the Mormon
Church was really true. That proof was about to be revealed, and
would send shock waves throughout the Jewish community,
especially since the connection between the Cave of Lehi and the
Book of Mormon was made by a Jew, Joseph Ginat. Irene
described how her relationship with Joseph developed:

> Joseph Ginat, the Israeli Deputy Advisor on Arab Affairs to
> the Prime Minister of Israel, Golda Meir, has taken a two year
> leave of absence to obtain his doctorate degree in Archaeology
> of the Middle East. He is also an authority on ancient scrip-
> ture and Middle East History.
>
> Although well supplied with references to attend New York
> University, from many top Government officials in Israel,
> including Golda Meir, Moshe Dayan, and others, he received

192

an unexpected invitation from the University of Utah to both work on his doctorate and to teach as well. This he accepted.

In 1970 the University of Utah had written to a university in Israel, and asked if there was a professor who would like to come and teach in the Middle East Department of the Anthropology and Archaeology Department.

Joseph Ginat was asked to fill this request, but he was not interested. He said that he had already made plans to go to New York University to not only teach, but also to work on his doctorate. The New York University had greater prestige and he had a cousin living in New York, which would add interest to his being there. He added, "Utah, where is that? I have never heard of the place. No, I am not interested. I have already made plans to go to New York."

He awoke in the middle of the night when a voice spoke to him. Whether it was an actual voice, or the definite words in a dream, he does not know, but he was awakened by hearing a voice say: "GO TO UTAH!"

He became wide awake, and was quite overcome and emotionally moved upon hearing this voice advising him to go to Utah. He knew he must go. He could hardly wait until morning, to go back to the university and tell them, that, regardless of where Utah was, he had changed his mind, HE WANTED TO GO TO UTAH!

He said, "Irene, I cannot say how this voice came to me, but, I HEARD IT! It woke me up, and I knew I had to go to Utah. This is truly what happened—someone told me that I must go to Utah. I hope there is a purpose in my coming here."

As Joseph Ginat began to read the Book of Mormon, he was touched by the Spirit and almost immediately felt it was true. He expressed many times how it would be impossible for anyone to write the first seven chapters of the Book of Mormon had they not actually lived in the land of Palestine. These chapters describe the travels of Lehi and his family as they attempted to flee Jerusalem. In the process, they traveled back and forth to Jerusalem several times. Joseph was convinced that the descriptions of their travels were specific enough, and fit the terrain and profile of Israel so well, that it would be impossible for anyone to write these chapters without having a firm knowledge of the land of Israel.

After Joseph began to believe in the Book of Mormon both spiritually and intellectually, he "happened" to read an article that was about to change his life. He had recently purchased a new book concerning recent archeological finds in Israel. One night the wind coming in the window fluttered the pages and stopped at an article written by Frank Moore Cross, Jr. (an expert from Harvard on Semitic cultures) concerning a recent discovery: while building a new road in the demilitarized zone between Israel and its southern neighbors, the Israeli military had discovered a cave with ancient writing on the walls. He [Cross] interpreted the inscriptions as being written by a prophet fleeing from Jerusalem during the Babylonian invasion—the same period of time that the Book of Mormon claims the Prophet Lehi and his family left Jerusalem!

This discovery started a chain of events established by Israeli law. From the establishment of the State of Israel laws had been written to protect *any* new discovery of archaeological significance. If someone were digging a foundation for a new building, or simply digging in a backyard garden, and happened across *any* ancient bones, pottery, graves, caves, etc., especially those that contained finds or information regarding ancient Israel, the site was immediately protected by law. This meant all work had to stop while archaeologists could be assigned to complete the digging, determine its importance, if any, and protect the discovery. Once the work of the archaeologists had been completed, the land or project would be returned to the owner. Due to these laws, as soon as the military discovered a cave with writing on the wall all work on the road was halted until research could be done on the cave.

The lead archaeologist assigned to this site had written a paper about what he found in the cave, and what was written on the walls.[2] As fate would have it, Joseph Ginat happened to read this archaeological paper shortly after reading the first chapters of the Book of Mormon. It did not take long for him to put the pieces of the puzzle together. The paper said it had been determined that the writing on the cave wall was dated back to 600 B.C....the very same time the Book of Mormon claims Lehi and his family left Jerusalem!

Irene describes Joseph's feelings of revelation and discovery:

> Joseph and Dalia's interest in the Church has been so outstanding that I took Joseph down to BYU where he had expressed a great interest to teach. After introducing him to Professor Wilkinson and explaining his background, Professor Wilkinson immediately gave his approval for him to teach summer school there for two semesters. He is also going to teach this winter at BYU Adult Extension classes in Salt Lake. Joseph often remarks that he is in a different world—he feels like he belongs with us!

> During this time a most unusual experience happened. Joseph obtained a new book from the University library on Archaeology for use in writing his thesis. After finding the chapter pertaining to his subject, he began to read when, all of a sudden, the pages turned over to a different chapter. This startled him and he wondered what had happened—but he began to read this new chapter.

> As he read, it became so fascinating he could not put it down. It told of a new archaeological discovery of a cave about 23 miles south of Jerusalem. Archaeologists could read and interpret the drawings and inscriptions on the walls, but, so far, they were at a loss to know who or what people put them there! However, there were five things they had definitely established:

---

[2]See Appendix 2, *Lectures on the Cave of Lehi,* and Appendix 3, *Drawings from Lehi's Cave.*

1. The drawings and inscriptions dated back to the time of Jeremiah—not later than 600 B.C..

2. They were not burial tombs, but were temporary shelters, or places of refuge.

3. The drawings are of people and ships.

4. The name given by archaeologists to the cave site is "Ancient Dwelling of Lehi."

5. There are three human figures with the inscriptions—one stands out from the other two.

The more Joseph read, the more excited he became. He stayed up all night reading and comparing the Bible, the archaeological book, and the Book of Mormon. He has come to the definite conclusion that this was the cave where Lehi's sons escaped to as described in I Nephi 3:27: "...and the servants of Laban did not overtake us, and we hid ourselves in the cavity of a rock."

Later, Joseph called me up at five o'clock in the morning and said, "Irene, I've got to talk to you. I've discovered something. I have to talk to you immediately!"

Joseph, an archaeologist himself, discovered a connection between the story of Lehi in the Book of Mormon and the Land of Lehi in Israel. While building a military road along a hill – they broke into a cave. In this cave, they found writings on the wall, dating back to 600 B.C. They found sketches of sailing ships, and wondered who in this mountain area would be drawing ships (about which they knew very little). The writings were asking Jehovah to forgive them, and to deliver them.

The sketches were of three men—one man with his arms raised in the attitude of prayer. This cave is in the Land of Lehi, about twenty miles southwest from Jerusalem.

Joseph said, "Irene, can you see the connection? You remember when Lehi sent his sons to Laban to get the records, and Laban refused to give the records to them? How Nephi suggested that they go back to the 'land of their inheritance,' and get the gold and silver and precious things which they had left there when they had started on their journey? Nephi

records that they took these precious things to Laban to buy
the records, and when Laban saw these things, he took them
and sent his servants to kill Nephi and his brothers, and
Nephi wrote:

> *And it came to pass that we did flee before the servants
> of Laban, and we were obliged to leave behind our prop-
> erty, and it fell into the hands of Laban. And it came to
> pass that we fled into the wilderness, and the servants of
> Laban did not overtake us, and we hid ourselves in the
> cavity of a rock. [I Nephi 3:26-27]*

They had to flee for their lives, and hid in the crevice of the
rocks. This cave is where they hid until the servants gave up
trying to find them! And while they were in the cave, they were
writing on the wall for Jehovah to deliver them and to forgive
them. They were drawing ships, for they knew that they would
be going on a ship to the new land. With the writings on the
wall, archaeologists can tell immediately the date—600 B.C.,
which is the exact date when Lehi left Jerusalem! This being
the Land of Lehi, it must be the cave where they stored their
precious things originally, and also where the sons went to
escape. The archaeologists definitely know that it wasn't a
burial cave, but have evidence to know that it was used as a
place of refuge or a hide-out."

Joseph knows this area of Israel very well. It is in a direct line
down to the Red Sea—to a place where the Bible indicates
they built ships. The "cave" is south of Jerusalem, and the
Book of Mormon tells of them "going down" to the wilderness by the Red Sea, or going back "up to Jerusalem." The
"up" and "down" denotes north and south according to the
customs of Israel speech. This, too, coincides with the area of
the caves from Jerusalem.

According to Joseph, no one in this area or at this time would
be drawing "ships," they were too far inland and knew nothing
or very little about ships, but would have drawn objects more
familiar to them such as houses, animals, trees, etc.

In that time people took their names from the places where
they lived, thus Lehi came from the Land of Lehi. His sons
knew this area, and when escaping to save their lives they naturally went to a hiding place with which they were familiar.

It is interesting...Joseph says that Mormonism is the religion for the Jews, for the beginning of Mormonism was in Jerusalem itself! Commencing with Father Lehi!

Joseph wants to do four things when he returns to Jerusalem next spring:

1. He wants to find new evidence of Lehi, his family, and the Book of Mormon in that area.

2. He wants to have this cave recognized in some way as belonging to Lehi and the Mormon people (of course, with permission of the LDS Church).

3. He wants to lecture throughout the Holy Land, telling his people about the Mormons and their connection with the Jews. They aren't just another Christian Church— the Christians have even persecuted the Mormons as they have the Jews—but are Israelite Christians. This is a big difference, he says.

4. At present, the people in Israel will not accept the missionaries—but after they hear the full story and have a true understanding of the Mormons then, he says, it will open the way for the missionaries to go into Israel and do a great work.

At the same time, discoveries were being made in South America that touched on a connection with Israel. One was the discovery of the "Tree of Life" stele, the other a carving showing a Mayan King with a "Star of David" as an earring. This engraving was found in Mexico, proving that the Jews came to America. Joseph commented to me on this last discovery as follows:

Joseph has a different interpretation of the enclosed clipping from the Deseret News showing a figure of a man with the Star of David as an earring. The article states the design on the head of the man is a ship, showing that they came to this country in ships.

However, Joseph says this is wrong. The design is a bird not a ship, and denotes that this person is from the tribe of Joseph. As evidence, Joseph cites Genesis 40:17, a scripture telling of the interpretation Joseph made of the dream of birds eating

> from the baskets on the head. Since then, the "bird" is the
> symbol of Joseph, and any Israeli would say the same without
> question.
>
> There is much more that I could tell, giving a background of
> Joseph Ginat and his lovely wife Dalia, who teaches Hebrew
> at the University of Utah, and could also tell many other inter-
> esting parallel stories which Joseph has discovered between
> the Bible, the archaeological discoveries, and the Book of
> Mormon. However, these can be more fully explained by
> Joseph himself.

In May, Joseph and Dalia Ginat came to see Irene and
brought her a beautiful necklace. Irene writes about Joseph's continued excitement of discovering the Book of Mormon and the
Cave of Lehi:

> Joseph is so enthusiastic, he wants to have the cave in the land
> of Lehi be made known to all tourists, to say: "This is where
> the Mormon Church started! Here is the evidence!"

In June of 1971, Joseph Ginat spoke at BYU, giving a lecture
concerning the connection between the Book of Mormon and the
discovery of the Cave of Lehi in Jerusalem.[3]

On July 15, Joseph Ginat and Irene met with President Harold B. Lee.[4] Joseph explained to President Lee his belief that the
cave near Jerusalem was the same cave where Nephi and his two
brothers hid when they fled from Laban's servants. He also described the wall drawings of men and ships. President Lee was
very impressed. Joseph suggested two things must be done: first,
that a monument should be placed on the Mount of Olives in
commemoration of Orson Hyde dedicating the land of Israel for
the return of the Jews; and second, that a monument should be
placed at the entrance to the cave, dedicating it to the Book of
Mormon and the sons of Lehi.

---

[3]See Appendix 2, *Lectures on the Cave of Lehi.*
[4]President Joseph Fielding Smith died within a few months after the death of the previous President, David O. McKay. Then President of the Church was Harold B. Lee.

Irene's hope was that she would have the privilege of being present at the dedication of these two great sites in the history of the Church. In time she would be instrumental in fulfilling the first suggestion, and although a monument was never placed at Lehi's Cave (due to the location of the cave in the de-militarized zone), she would get the opportunity to see the cave herself several times.

Joseph Ginat was privileged to meet with President Lee several times. On one of these occasions he was given a special blessing. Irene describes these visits, and the blessing Joseph received at the hands of the Prophet:

> When Joseph Ginat first came to Salt Lake, and made the connection between the Book of Mormon and the newly discovered cave in Israel, I told President Lee about him. He asked me to bring him to his office, which I did. After the first brief meeting, we were asked to come back when there was more time. At the second meeting President Lee asked, "Joseph, what do you think about Joseph Smith being a Prophet?" Without hesitating, Dr. Ginat replied, "Of course he was a Prophet. Look what he accomplished! He had to be a Prophet!" Then President Lee asked, "Then what do you think about the Book of Mormon being true?"
>
> Dr. Ginat turned to him and said, "President Lee, there are no words in the Hebrew or the English language to fully express how I KNOW THE BOOK OF MORMON IS TRUE!" Then President Lee asked, "Well then, what do you think about Jesus Christ being the Messiah?" Joseph hesitated and then replied, "That is a little more difficult, but I'm working on it!" I was there during the two meetings with President Lee. Many interesting scriptures were discussed relating to the Book of Mormon and the Jews.
>
> At the invitation to meet with President Lee for a third meeting, I told Dr. Ginat, that I felt he should go alone, just he and President Lee to meet together. He hesitated, and then asked me if I would meet him right after the meeting, which I did.

When Dr. Ginat walked out of that meeting over two hours later, I could tell from the look on his face that he had had a special experience. We sat down and he told me all the things he and President Lee had talked about, and then how President Lee had given him a special blessing. In the blessing he was told that the Lord had brought him here for a special purpose. He had been raised up as an instrument in the hands of the Lord to accomplish a great work for his own people and for the Lord. He was like Peter of old, called of God! This blessing is very sacred to Joseph, and he rarely speaks of it. When he came out of the meeting, the first thing he said to me was, "Irene, I will never be the same! This day is a memorable day which I shall never forget! I feel that today is the beginning of great things in my life!"

Yes, Joseph feels that he has a great mission to perform, and as he has told me many times, "Irene, there is something which just keeps pushing me on. I have a feeling within me which is impelling me to do what I can to bring our two people together. It is very important!"

Some Mormons, especially at BYU, say, "Why is Joseph doing this? Why is he trying to promote Mormon-Israeli tours, trying to get Mormon professors to teach in Israel, trying to get a student exchange program with the universities if it isn't for the money in it? He has to be connected with a travel agency and get a commission!"

It is a terrible accusation to make, and how far from the truth! It is important for us to make friends with the Jewish people so that they may come to know about the restored Gospel, and in the Lord's own due time we will be able to fulfill our great work with the Jewish people!

When Joseph Ginat did finally return to Israel, the revelations concerning the connection between the Cave of Lehi and the Mormon Church continued to expand. One of the most astounding stories told by Joseph about this connection occurred when he traveled to the Cave of Lehi to inspect it for himself. While visiting the site, Joseph spoke to a wandering Arab Bedouin, who was very familiar with the area around the cave, and relayed his

understanding of the ancestral home of a Prophet he called *Lehi*.
Irene writes:

> Last May, I [Irene] was invited by the State of Israel to be their
> guest for a two week visit to Israel. I had the privilege of being
> the first person from Utah to be taken to the Land of Lehi,
> and to see the remnants of this cave. I was also taken by Jo-
> seph Ginat to the top of the hill and shown the ruins of an
> ancient city. He pointed to an area and said, "Now look over
> there. Only last week I came up here. In fact, I can't stay away
> from this area. And while here I met a Bedouin shepherd
> who asked, "Why do you come here? No one comes out
> here! What is there that you are looking for?" I told him that I
> was interested in the people that lived in this area, and asked
> him if he knew anything about them. "Oh, yes, of course," the
> shepherd replied, and then his sheep started to go over to an
> area surrounded by a stone wall. Immediately he shouted to
> his son to get the sheep away from there; that the animals
> should not graze in that sacred place.
>
> Joseph asked the shepherd why the area circled around with a
> stone wall was so sacred, and the shepherd replied, "That area
> is where a great Prophet of Israel used to sit and admonish his
> people! It was here he judged and would bless his people.
> That is a very sacred place!"
>
> "Do you know his name?" Joseph asked. "Of course," the
> Bedouin replied, "his name was the Prophet Lehi!"

In October, Irene arranged a meeting between President Lee
and a group of Jewish government officials, which included Joseph Ginat. The relationship between the LDS Church and the
State of Israel was maturing quickly. Soon it would be formal-
ized, and the State of Israel would permit the Church to enter
Israel and establish an official branch of the Church! And that
would be just the beginning. Soon the Church would be permitted to lease land in Israel—something absolutely forbidden by
Israeli law for any *Christian* religion—and permit them not only
to build the *BYU Jerusalem Center* on the Mount of Olives, but

create a State park dedicated to a Mormon Apostle: *The Orson Hyde Memorial Gardens!*

Irene's Work Continues to Expand

Irene's work was not confined to Israel. She continued to host hundreds of people from around the world, and even some who felt the need to return to Salt Lake again and again. For example, the relationship between the Church and Greece had been growing for over a decade. In December, Irene again hosted His Eminence Archbishop Iakovos, Primate of the Greek Orthodox Church, and other church officials. The Archbishop had become a frequent guest of Irene's. Their visits always included a tour of Temple Square, the Tabernacle Choir, a visit with the President of the Church, Welfare Square, an organ recital, the genealogical vaults, and even an occasional dinner in their honor. Irene always gave them the time they needed to feel good about their visit.

Irene touched not only the rich and powerful. Sometimes her greatest success was in hosting "just regular folks" from all parts of the country. One conversion story was recorded in a *Church News* article dated April 16, 1977:

Salt Lake Visit was Overture to Baptism
Church News, April 16, 1977

Gene Morian knows firsthand how effective the Church's hosting program and guide service on Temple Square can be.

Coming to Salt Lake City as a nonmember six years ago...he spent several hours of his free time visiting Temple Square. He first came into contact with the Church in 1957 when he taught at BYU as a guest on the summer music faculty...

"When I was here six years ago, about a dozen of us went to see and hear the Tabernacle organ. That's where I met Irene Staples, then the Church Hostess, who has had a very significant influence in my wife and I joining the Church," Dr. Morian said.

"During the convention, I found myself going back to Temple Square during my breaks..."By the time Dr. Morian returned home to Virginia, Sister Staples had already contacted the bishop and stake president in that area. "Several members called on us and fellowshipped us," Dr. Morian said.

"We realized all of a sudden that we had been searching for something all of our lives and now had found the answer. We decided to invite the missionaries to come teach us and as we listened to the lessons, we were sure we had found something that we couldn't turn our backs on."

In April, Dr. Morian attended two conventions in the western part of the U.S...He decided to spend three days in Salt Lake City, where he again met Sister Staples, who introduced him to 14 General Authorities.

"At the end of each day, I'd call Betty and tell her about what was happening," Dr. Morian said. "As Sister Staples drove me to the airport, I asked her what the next step was. She said, 'Set a date for baptism.' She suggested the date be Betty's birthday, and said that she'd go to Virginia for our baptism—and she did."

Dr. and Sister Morian were sealed in the Salt Lake Temple a year later. During the year he continued to direct the Lutheran choir, one of the choir members also joined the LDS Church.

Highlights of 1971

January

7	John Glenn and wife Ann (astronaut)
20	Princess Irene of Greece, at luncheon
25	Joseph Ginat, exchange Professor of Anthropology at the University of Utah

February

3	Vincent Price (movie star)
17	Joseph and Dalia Ginat, referred by Moshe Yegar
20	Pat Boone family (famous singer)
25	The Assistant Secretary of Defense
28	Mrs. Moshe Dayan of Israel

March

10	Major General Robert R. Limiell and NASA VIPs
19	A group of 12 First Baptist Church ministers
29	Joseph Ginat and father-in-law

April

2	Wing Commander Charles Lynes
5	Mayor Charles Evers (first black Mayor in Mississippi)
21	Joseph Steinman, Israel
24	Joseph Steinman, Israel, returned
26	Joseph Ginat, taken to BYU, meets President Wilkinson and Dr. Hugh Nibley

May

18	The Ambassador and Consul General from Norway President of Dow Chemical
20	Dr. Wernher von Braun (rocket scientist) Joseph and Dalia Ginat and friends, dinner at Irene's home

June

3	General Charles G. Holle
17	Joseph Ginat, to BYU
24	Israel Consul, Ezekiel Carmel
30	The Aid Association for Lutheran Church

July

1	Hanna Catz, from Israel
9	Reverend David E. Evans of Holyoke, Massachusetts
11	Karl & Carla Malden (actor)
15	Joseph Ginat, meets President Lee and Elders Tanner, Benson, Peterson, and LeGrand Richards

16	Congressman Wilber D. Mills and wife
25	Baptist choir
30	Joseph Ginat & Dalia meet LeGrand Richards

August

8	Billy and Shirley Casper (professional golfer)
11	A Chinese table tennis group
12	A group of Arab exchange students

September

| 13 | Astronauts James Irwin, David Scott, Alfred Worden, all Colonels |

October

| 1 | Billy Casper, his mother and a Catholic Priest Bishop Noot from Holland |
| 12 | Lord and Lady Wells Prestel, England |

November

| 9 | Joseph Ginat and Yoseph Ben Charon, Israel |

December

2	His Eminence Archbishop Iakovos
7	Amnon Galen, Head of Public Relations, Tel Aviv Union
19	Yale University basketball team

Statistics for 1971:

Total visitors hosted	18,527
Foreign visitors	989
Countries represented	63

A Branch in Israel

> Teach your children, by your own example, the virtues of honesty and clean living.
>
> Teach them to heed to the admonitions of our Prophet and our General Authorities in all things.
>
> You can do this by your own example of obeying their admonitions. Why tell our children to obey if we do not obey ourselves?
>
> Let us show our appreciation of the Church and of our many blessings by serving the Lord—let us not complain but consider it a blessing and an opportunity.
>
> I remember when I was asked to speak at a PTA meeting. After writing my talk out I used my daughter, Mary Ann (who was 6 years old), as an audience. When I got through, I asked her how it sounded and she replied:
>
> "Oh, it sounds beautiful mother, if they will just know what you are talking about."
>
> Irene

In 1972, both the Mormon Church and the State of Utah doubled their efforts to embrace the Jewish community and the State of Israel. It was as though everything was coming together, at a perfect moment in time. That moment came at a state-wide celebration of the 24th anniversary of the creation of the State of

Israel. Irene was one small, but important, part of this united effort leading to the formal recognition of The Church of Jesus Christ of Latter-day Saints by the State of Israel.

In April, Irene was very busy with the Jewish community and Israeli government officials. She had been asked to help them prepare for their 24th *Independence Day*—a week-long celebration of the creation of the State of Israel. Irene took Joseph Ginat to the KSL TV and radio stations, where they were very generous in advertising the celebrations. The Tabernacle Choir was scheduled to sing several songs in honor of Israel.

Irene worked with Governor Calvin Rampton and his staff to prepare for the ceremonies ahead. She wrote the draft proclamation for the Governor, made arrangements for a special ceremony at which he was to preside in the rotunda of the capital, and coordinated many other details. Irene organized a similar ceremony with Mayor Jake Garn at the City Commission office. Following is the proclamation actually issued by the Governor of Utah concerning the forthcoming Israeli Independence Day celebration:

BY THE GOVERNOR OF THE STATE OF UTAH
<u>A PROCLAMATION</u>

WHEREAS, the Jewish Community of Utah, and the people from Israel residing in Utah, realize the value and need of international friendship and understanding, and,

WHEREAS, one of the most effective ways to promote such international goodwill is through an understanding of the people, their heritage, their culture, their faith, and their desire for a national home, and

WHEREAS, the people from Israel have made a great and notable contribution to the wealth, the welfare, and industry of the State of Utah, our 4th Governor, Simon Bamberger, being of Israel ancestry, as well as Louis Marcus Mayor of our Capitol City, State Legislators, and other local officials along with great and honored Religious Leaders, being of Israel ancestry, and

WHEREAS, this April 19, 1972, marks the 24th Anniversary of the proclamation declaring Israel a Free State,

NOW THEREFORE I, CALVIN L. RAMPTON, Governor of Utah, do hereby proclaim the week, April 17 to 22, 1972 to be,

STATE of ISRAEL INDEPENDENCE WEEK

in Utah, and do hereby urge the people of Utah to observe the week and participate in religious and civic ceremonies, and with traditional entertainments of Israel arts and cultures, thereby paying tribute to the State of Israel and those people who helped to develop the potentials of our great State, that we too join in their celebration and prayer, that there will be peace for their State and all people throughout the world.

IN TESTIMONY WHEREOF, I have hereunto set my hand and caused to be affixed the Great Seal of the State of Utah.

Done at the Capitol, Salt Lake City, Utah, this 12th day of April, 1972.

(Signed) By Governor Rampton
(Signed) By Secretary of State

Irene had the privilege of taking several Israeli government officials on her standard tour, and, after lunch at the University of Utah, to the granite mountain genealogical storage vaults. They were very excited and talked freely in Hebrew: "*They are unbelievable, overwhelming…and we have something in mind.*" It was not long after this visit that the Church was allowed to make copies of the names of all who had been killed in the Holocaust.[1]

The main reason the Consul General came to Utah was to extend a special invitation to the First Presidency to come to Israel, and officially open communications between the State of Israel and the Mormon Church! This privilege had never been given to any Christian church before, as there are laws in Israel forbidding *any* religion to proselyte or lease or own property in Israel.[2]

---

[1] See Appendix 4, *Salt Lake Institute Talk by Irene.*

[2] The Christian and Muslim religions which already had people and buildings in Israel were permitted to stay, however the law forbade the introduction of any new religion, or the lease or sale of property to any non-Jewish person, religion, or organization.

As hoped, on April 12, 1972, three Israeli government officials met with the First Presidency of the Church and extended a formal invitation for the Mormon Church to come to Israel. Irene was present when they met in the General Authority reception room with the President of the Church, Harold B. Lee, and Elders N. Eldon Tanner, Gordon B. Hinckley, and Mark E. Peterson. Irene wrote of the occasion:

> It was a thrilling occasion and one which will be recorded as the beginning of relations of the Church with Israel, and the very beginning of the time when the Church will be able to go into Israel to bring the gospel to this great people. It was thrilling beyond words for me to be a part of it, for it was with my writing the letter to Moshe Yegar several years before and hosting him, that all this association with the people of Israel has come about.

In May, Irene had a dinner party for the Ginats, as they were leaving for their home in Israel. Those who attended included President and Sister Harold B. Lee, Elder and Sister Gordon B. Hinckley, President Ernest Wilkinson, Dr. Truman and Ann Madson, Sherman and Harriett Young, Brother and Sister Green, and Brent and Helen Goates. They discussed the progress in the relationship between the Mormon Church and Israel, and showed the film *Ancient America Speaks*[3] just released by BYU.

In a letter written to Irene dated June 8, 1972, the current Consul of Israel, Benjamin Abileah, wrote to express his thanks for what both the Mormon Church and the State of Utah had done for the Jewish people, and to express his optimism for the future:

> Friends in the State of Utah have been sending us information, press clippings and programs indicating that Israel's 24th Anniversary was marked with outstanding events of high cultural value.

---

[2]A wonderful film documenting the many archaeological sites that had been discovered in South and Central America, proving the stories recorded in the Book of Mormon to be true.

> We are immensely proud and grateful for this demonstration of sympathy and understanding by the people of Utah and thus draw encouragement in these difficult years for Israel. The bettering of understanding between peoples through cultural and intellectual exchanges lays the ground for peace among nations.
>
> Kindly accept, Mrs. Staples, our heartfelt appreciation for your indispensable assistance and for all you have done for the success of this cultural presentation of Israel.

It seemed as though *all* of Irene's Jewish friends were leaving for Israel. The Ginats had already left, and now Moshe Yegar, Irene's first and perhaps most significant contact with Israel, was finally going home after living for six years in the United States. He wrote Irene on July 13, 1972 to express his gratitude for her friendship:

> In a few days' time we will be leaving the United States and return to Jerusalem on completion of six years of tour of duty in this country.
>
> One of the most interesting experiences we had in the United States and best friendships we developed was the opportunity given us to meet you. We hope that we will manage to maintain our relationship in future years and that we shall hear from you periodically.

All of this activity with Israel was to culminate in the State of Israel inviting President Harold B. Lee to come to Israel, and be permitted to organize the first branch of the Mormon Church in the Holy Land.

One humorous effect of Irene's close relationship with Israeli diplomats and contacts was their continued use of Irene as a contact, even *after* the Church had officially been recognized by Israel. Protocol would have dictated that the Church Office be contacted directly for appointments with the Brethren, especially after this significant event. However, *everyone* knew Irene, and knew that Irene would get things done! When people would want to notify the Church about Israeli diplomats coming to Utah, they often would call Irene instead of the proper Church office. Eventually, some began to complain that people in Israel

211

were contacting Irene directly, rather than going through proper channels. Irene herself may have been reluctant to give up the honor and prestige in which her calling as Official Church Hostess had placed her. In a letter to her supervisor,[4] Wendell Ashton, Irene explained the problem:

> The reason Elliot Bernstein, whom I personally know, called me to make his appointment for Abraham Sharir, is that Jews both local and in Israel have always contacted me. Even the local people have never called the Church Offices for an appointment with any of the General Authorities, they have always gone through me.
>
> Through the years I have built up a very good relation and friendship with them. They were kind enough to honor me on two special affairs the local and visiting Israeli people held here, one at the University of Utah and the other at the Jewish Center.
>
> When one feels close enough to call me at 12 o'clock at night to inform me of a visiting dignitary, you can feel assured they feel close to me. Which feeling I sincerely appreciate.
>
> This has paid off tremendously, as you know, resulting in the important contacts for President Lee and Elder Hinckley going to Israel, as well as President Oaks and others from BYU going to Israel during the holidays—for a most important contact.
>
> All this has been brought about through my close association with them. When you asked why Mr. Bernstein contacted me for the appointment with President Lee, I thought this might explain the reason. I sincerely hope that this close association will continue.

September 12, 1972, President Harold B. Lee, Gordon B. Hinckley and wives honored the invitation given them by the Consul General of Israel to visit their land, and left on a trip for London, Munich, Israel, and Greece. When they arrived in Israel,

---

[3]See Appendix I, *Comments about Irene*

they were met at the plane by Consul General Moshe Yegar and many other government officials Irene had hosted when the Consul had visited Salt Lake City.

On September 20, 1972, the first branch of the Mormon Church was established by President Lee and Elder Hinckley in Israel, with David Galbraith as branch president. Irene made this note in her journal about the event:

> President Lee assured the Minister of Religion that our Church would not come to Israel and proselyte underhandedly, and that we would not interfere with them and their religion. He later told the LDS group that proselyting in Israel would be different than ever before. But the time would come when we would be able to.

Also in September, a Church group was organized in Jerusalem to accommodate Brigham Young University faculty and students involved in a Near Eastern Studies program.

Future events stemming from this momentous beginning included the organization of the Israel District (1977), the dedication of the Orson Hyde Memorial Garden on the Mount of Olives (1979), and the dedication of the BYU Jerusalem Center for Near Eastern Studies on Mount Scopus (1989).

In October, BYU TV produced a program by Don Peterson that reviewed the many prophesies that were coming true concerning the Jews.

Highlights of 1972

January

16	The Mendoza Boys Choir, Argentina
	The Osmond Brothers
18	Admiral Tom Kelly

19   Joseph Ginat and Amnon Golan, go to BYU
        and meet President Oaks

February

6   Joseph Ginat, fireside
11   Israel Haskel, Jerusalem UN Fellowship,
        Land Management
25   Congressman Benjamin B. Blackburn, III
27   Mayor John R. Throckmorton, Pennsylvania

March

3   Major General Robert B. Smith
8   Stephen Kirsch and wife, Jews from Michigan
14   Joseph Ginat met with President Lee
21   Mayor Frank Rizzo, Philadelphia

April

4   Mayor Thomas Craig, California
5   John L. Harmon, Senator from California
10   John McManus, John Birch Society
        Mayor Frank Rizzo, Philadelphia, a second visit
12   Governor Rampton, Mayor Jake Garn and
        Commissioners, the First Presidency, Consul
        General of Israel Ezekiel Carmel, Joseph Ginat,
        Isaac Sower
16   Tabernacle Choir broadcast in honor of Israel
18   Israel Independence Day celebrations
22   300 members of the NAACP
25   Major William G. Weaver, Pennsylvania
27   Ambassador of Tunisia

May

15	Congressman Long
22	Congresswoman Shirley Chisholm

June

8	Joseph and Dalia Ginat, leaving for Israel
14	Ambassador Jacob Barmore, Israel

July

7	Lord Thompson of Fleet

August

2	A German soccer team
26	The Tabernacle Choir goes to Mexico
28	Consul General Roger Deon, Australia

September

13	J.C. (James Cash) Penny
12	President Lee and Gordon B. Hinckley leave for London, Munich, Israel, Greece
18	Mayor Louie Welch, Houston, Texas

October

15	Danny Bonaduce (Partridge Family TV star)
16	U.S. Naval Academy Glee Club
24	Vice President Spiro Agnew
31	Congressman Al Ullman

November

13	Governor Lars Eliasson, Sweden
29	2 Major Generals from Sweden

Irene Staples: Hostess to the World

December

19   Group of 12 ministers

Statistics for 1972:

Total visitors hosted	27,339
Foreign visitors	722
Countries represented	60

The End of an Era

My talk this morning is on doing a job well.

Whenever we are asked to do something, let's be happy to say: "I'll be happy to do it", and then let's do it the very best we can.

How happy our Heavenly Father is when he sees us doing what we are asked to do. If we are happy when we do a job, we can do it better. Let me tell you about a little postage stamp:

There was a little postage stamp,
No bigger than my thumb.
But still it stuck right to the job,
Until its work was done.
They licked it and they pounded it,
Until it made you sick,
The more it took a licking,
The harder it did stick.

So the stamp stuck to the letter,
'Till it saw it safely through,
There's none that could do better,
So...let's be stickers, me and you.

Irene

As usual, 1973 began as most years for Irene—working every day at a calling she loved and at which she was very, very good. However, as much as she wanted to continue serving as Church Hostess, her physical body was beginning to feel the strain, and those who worked around her noticed. Although Church policy required retirement at 65, Irene's time had been extended due to the many important contacts she had developed over the years, especially with Israel. However, now that Israel had officially recognized the Church, it seemed likely that Irene's time would soon come to an end.

In March, Irene was asked to represent the Church at the 25th anniversary of the founding of the State of Israel, a Jewish celebration attended by the Governor, Mayor, Justice of the Supreme Court, among others and, like the year before, the Tabernacle Choir sang a tribute of Jewish songs. Irene hosted the new Israel Consul General Yacov Aviad.

In April, Irene hosted Dr. Sami Said Ahmed, of Baghdad, who believes that Joseph Smith was a great modern day prophet, even as Christ and Mohammed were…he believes in Mormonism as the unifying world religion for which Islam has looked forward. Irene wrote:

> It was quite startling—the statements that Dr. Ahmed made concerning his belief and even testimony of the truthfulness of the Church. He left us with no doubt in our minds that he had a desire to join…He told Elder Delbert L. Stapley that it was a direct fulfillment of many prophecies.

In May, the new Church office building was being completed. In preparation for its opening additional hosts and hostesses were called to assist Irene, and a separate group called just for tours of the new building.

The highlight of the year came in May, when Irene was chosen *Woman of the Year* by the Utah Woman's Review. In their

Mother's Day issue, they had a lengthy article about Irene that described her experiences serving in the Mormon Pavilion and as Official Church Hostess, and included a beautiful picture of Irene standing in front of the Salt Lake Temple. It was one of Irene's most valued honors!

Irene continued to host all kinds of VIPs as an everyday part of her job as hostess. For example, in June she hosted several special guests of the State Department:

Iraj Alborz	Governor of Makuh, East Azerbaijan Province
Hossein Khaef	District Governor of Harsin
Iraj Maghsoud-Lou	Governor of Marivan, Kurdistan Province
Ebrahim Taghizadeh	Governor & District Governor of Masjed-e-Solieman, Kurdistan
Car Kempff	Consultant Geologist, La Paz, Bolivia

In August, the new General Church Office building officially opened and Irene went on tour with the Tabernacle Choir to Munich, Paris, and London. It was kind of a farewell tour for Irene, as her days as Official Church Hostess would soon come to an end.

Due to Irene's age, and the expanding needs of the Church, the hosting program was finally expanded to include many more hosts, and modified to include couples. An article in the Church's *Ensign* magazine described this significant change:

Church Hosting Service Expands to Meet Demand
Ensign, September 1973

A Church program initiated in 1965 to host visiting dignitaries has now grown so large that two couples, Brother and Sister W. Stanford Wagstaff and Brother and Sister A. Palmer Holt, have been called to assist the Church Hostess, Sister Irene E. Staples.

In addition, Sister Phyllis Sandberg has been named chairman in charge

of hostesses for the new General Church Office building.
Sister Staples has hosted many thousands of people since her call eight
years ago, and last year she assisted some 22,000 official visitors at
Church headquarters.

Many of the European guests to Salt Lake City have been invited to attend
the area general conference in Munich in August, as well as special recep-
tions and Tabernacle Choir concerts in Munich, Paris, and London. Sister
Staples will be traveling with the choir as she has done on their previous
concert tours.

"With the contacts I make here, I send thousands of referrals to the missionaries. I don't know what happens to all of them, but often I receive
reports of people joining the Church because of the work we have done
here."

In December, Irene helped with the decorations for the annual Sunday School General Board Christmas party.

Highlights of 1973

January

18	Mayor William Schaefer, Baltimore, Maryland
26	A group of 5 future Priests, referred by Father Gerald Leo Tierney

February

8	Mr. and Mrs. Al Thrasher, picture taken with First Presidency
19	Irene represents the Church at Jewish celebration
21	The Ambassador from Bolivia
22	Hadlai A. Hall, Assistant Secretary of the Army

March

2	Yacov Aviad and wife, new Consul General of Israel
3	Jewish celebration, 25th Anniversary of Israel
6	Admiral Thomas H. Moorer, Chairman, Joint Chiefs

of Staff
7   Reverend Lewis Green, Pentecostal Church
27 Brigadier General Hoyt S. Vandenberg, Jr.
    Major General James J. Gibbons and Lieutenant
    General William B. McBride

April

9   Major General Roy M. Terry, Chief of Chaplains
15 Walter Picard, German Parliament

May

2   Armando Toledano, Leader of the European
    Communities, Belgium
13 General George Doriot
17 Major General Bryce Poe, II
    Lord Mayor Rudolf Schlichtinger, Germany
    Mr. Tu Te-Chi of China, Chairman of the
    Kuomintang
18 Brigadier General Arman, Sweden

June

3   The cast of Disney on Parade
27 Major General James J. Gibbons, second visit

July

5   Congressman Luis Carlos Escobar, Columbia
10 A group of 40 members of a Methodist Church
    youth group
20 A group of Connecticut Eagle Scouts
22 A group of Belgium cadets

August

9   Dr. and Mrs. Lee Chang Kuei, China
12 A Japanese student group

| 21 | Congressman Lee H. Hamilton, Indiana |

September

5	Ngugen Chi and Ha Van Trung, Vietnam
14	Mayor Roman S. Gibbs, Detroit, Michigan
30	Danish choir boys

October

3	General Bryce Poe and wife
	Billy Casper (professional golfer)
10	A group of South African government officials
12	The Iowa State football team
30	A group of 20 Mexican journalists
	Reverend Malcolm McCullough, Chaplain General, Austrian Army

November

11	Mayor James A. Turnbach, Hazelton, Pennsylvania
13	Honorable Howard H. Calloway, Secretary of the Army
16	General Robert Scott (was baptized)

December

3	The Navy's show band
4	Dr. Julia de Olmos, Chief Legal Advisor of Foreign Relations, Bolivia
5	Colonel James G. Sandman
21	Brigadier General John C. Burney, Jr. and Colonel Frank S. Osiecki

Statistics for 1973:

| Total visitors hosted | 18,666 |
| Foreign visitors | 1,090 |

Countries represented   41

In 1974, it was made clear to Irene that this would be her last year as Official Church Hostess. Several events occurred to make it a banner year for her personally.

In March, Irene was interviewed on BYU TV about her work with the Church. The program discussed all of the progress and changes that had occurred while Irene was hostess for the Church, including the astounding relationship with Israel.

In May, Irene was invited to come to Israel, all expenses paid, as a *special guest of the State of Israel.* Irene would be able to see all of the friends she had made over the years, and experience for herself the Holy Land. It was while on this trip that the State of Israel made a *stunning* offer: to allow the Church to lease a parcel of land on the Mount of Olives. This land would eventually become the location for the Orson Hyde Memorial Park and the BYU Jerusalem Center. Irene wrote of her experience:

> After several years of hosting Israeli people and government officials, I received an invitation to go to Israel, as a special guest of the State of Israel, with all expenses paid, in recognition and as an expression of their appreciation for my devoted service to Israel and her people. This was a great surprise to me. Of course I was thrilled, not only for the trip but especially for the recognition of the friendship the Mormon Church had for the State of Israel and her people!
>
> I flew EL AL Airlines and will never forget the love and loyalty the Israeli people have for their country. As we approached Israel, a Rabbi in the plane announced, "We have arrived. We are flying over Israel. Let us give thanks to God for our safe arrival!" Then as he finished his sincere prayer, all the Jewish people on the plane began singing their National Anthem!
>
> What a beautiful, emotional thing to do! I immediately thought how thrilling it would be, and what a tribute to our great America if we did the same! Over the speaker a tribute

or the Pledge of Allegiance could be played, or a recording of the Mormon Tabernacle Choir singing our National Anthem with anyone on the plane who would like joining in the singing. Yes, we need more patriotism!

At the Israeli airport I was met by several Israeli friends and state officials who presented me with a beautiful bouquet of flowers as a special welcome! Also a limousine with a chauffer and a guide to take me to the "Hotel Continental" high on the top of the Mount of Olives, overlooking the City of Jerusalem and the whole valley!

As soon as I arrived the phone began ringing—friends and guests whom I had met in Salt Lake welcoming me to Israel. I was overwhelmed with invitations!

The State Department had the whole week's itinerary planned, leaving very little time to accept personal invitations. I was taken everywhere, even many places which the average tourist would not have the privilege to see.

I spent one afternoon with Consul Hesi Carmel, whom I had entertained in Salt Lake. As we were in Jerusalem, looking towards the Mt. of Olives, he said, "Irene, I have never forgotten the story you told me in Salt Lake, how the Prophet Joseph Smith called for Orson Hyde to go to Israel to dedicate the land for the return of the rightful heirs, the Jewish people! I feel that a Memorial should be established in honor of that great event! How he came here to the Mount of Olives, gathered stones and built an altar where he offered a special prayer that the land might be blessed, become fertile, nourished, and fruitful for the return of our people! In my Government position, I know of an acre piece of property. It is the largest and the most choice piece of property in this area (as he pointed it out to me). Do you think your Church would be interested in having that property free, with a 99 year lease, to create a beautiful garden. It should be called, 'The Orson Hyde Memorial Garden.' And Israel would be responsible to maintain it."

He then went into detail about the beautiful garden, with trees, shrubs, paths, water, lights, public facilities, and a large plaque giving the Orson Hyde prayer in three languages: Hebrew, English, and Arabic.

224

At that time the inflation in Israel was 150%, so it would cost about one million dollars to plant and create this beautiful garden! He also said it must be very secret, for many other Churches would want it—which happened, for no sooner was it given out that the Mormon Church was obtaining it than one of the world's churches announced their desire to purchase the land and offered a blank signed check saying, "Fill it out for whatever you want. Don't let the Mormon Church have it!"

I was very excited with the wonderful offer. I told Hesi that I did not have the authority, but I was sure the Church officials would be interested and for him to hold it until I presented it to the Church officials and he would hear from them. I most sincerely thanked him for the wonderful offer, and for giving us the first choice!

After I returned home, I immediately contacted the First Presidency of the Church. Yes, they were interested, and wanted more information. Arrangements were made, and Hesi Carmel and Dr. Joseph Ginat came to Salt Lake and brought all the blueprints and the design for the park.

The Church was very impressed with the offer and plans, and immediately began working on the details of the project!

They asked Elder Howard W. Hunter to take charge of the legal part of the project, and asked Elder LeGrand Richards to take charge of raising the million dollars through contributions from members of the Church and others who would be interested in contributing to such a wonderful project!

Immediately I presented Elder Hunter with my check, as I wanted to be the first one to contribute to this thrilling project!

Upon her return from Israel, Irene continued to host guests, knowing that her time was short. In June, Irene hosted Vice President Gerald Ford and family. She took them on her standard tour, to see the Tabernacle Choir, and organized a special lunch after meeting with the First Presidency. Two months later Gerald Ford would become president.

In August, Irene was asked to speak to the Huntington Beach, California Stake Youth Conference held at BYU. As over 300 attended, she ended up speaking twice. In addition, she hosted Elliot Richardson, former U.S. Attorney General.

As the year came to a close, many parties and special luncheons honoring Irene's service were held. In addition, many letters and cards arrived demonstrating the appreciation of the Church and many city and state officials for Irene's years of service. The following is an example of those cards and letters:[1]

December 17, 1974 letter from Elder Gordon B. Hinckley to Irene, about her retirement:

There are those all over the world who remember you with appreciation. I have met some of these, who, while visiting in Salt Lake City, met officials of the Church and State, but remembered only Irene Staples. You have opened many doors for the Church and have opened the minds of uncounted men and women in their attitude toward the Church. Baptisms have come of your efforts.

As you step down, there will be days of loneliness, but these will be sweetened by the memories of work well done.

It was obvious that regardless of Irene's *official* retirement, her work as a missionary and her relationships with contacts around the world would continue. In a letter dated December 13, 1974, from Irene to Elder Ezra Taft Benson, she expresses this desire for continued service:

Regardless of my retirement, it has been approved that I continue to be a representative of the Church with Israel. With several projects under consideration, and the contacts I have made there, they feel I should continue with my association with them.

I received a letter from Dr. Halbrech from Israel, whom you met with Dr. Joseph Ginat, expressing his great appreciation not only for the kindness extended to him, but also for the friendship of the Mormon people.

---

[1]See Appendix I, *Comments about Irene*

He has spoken to the leaders of Yad Vashem[5] and said they would be very glad to use our generous help in many ways, including the microfilming of the names of the 6 million Jews, and also obtaining documents of Jewish history. It sounds very promising.[6]

I also got a letter from Joseph Ginat, with congratulations concerning the Mount of Olives property. I will keep you informed of any further developments on either project which I may become aware of.

With Irene's retirement a reality, the entire hosting program for the Church would need to be reorganized and expanded yet again:

New Coordinator for Hosting Named by LDS Church Office
The Herald, Provo, Utah, Thursday, Dec. 28, 74

Salt Lake City—W. Stanford Wagstaff, Salt Lake City, a retired oil company executive, has been named coordinator of church hosting for the LDS church, the First Presidency announced recently...the new coordinator's wife, Oma W. Wagstaff, will assist her husband in his new calling in the Church's public communications department.

Mr. Wagstaff succeeds Irene E. Staples, who is retiring effective the end of this year after nearly 10 years as the Church Hostess. As many as 18,666 people have been hosted by the church in a single year.

Mrs. Staples was called to be the Church Hostess in 1965 after her release from a mission in the Eastern States. Since then she has met and entertained thousands of people from throughout the world, including royalty, ambassadors, religious leaders...

December 31, 1974 was Irene's last day as Official Church Hostess. The office had a luncheon for her, and Elders Mark E. Peterson and Gordon B. Hinckley spoke. Irene wrote about the event:

"They gave me a wonderful tribute. I have hosted over 100,000 people. The end of another era of my life.

---

[5]The Yad Vashem is the Holocaust Memorial in Israel that contains the archives of the 6 million Jews killed in World War II by Hitler's Germany.
[6]During Irene's visit to Israel as their special guest, she had the unusual privilege of being taken into the archives to see the records of the 6 million Jews, and immediately thought of the work for the dead!

227

> "Not knowing how long I would have this position, I decided to dedicate my full time to this calling...I have never taken a vacation or had a weekend free...some of my most memorable conversions were those when meeting guests on Saturday, Sunday, or on a holiday. I have never submitted an expense request for either the use of my car or for entertaining the hundreds of guests in my home... It was not a sacrifice to do this, but rather a blessing to me."

In a letter to Elder Gordon B. Hinckley after her release, dated January 13, 1975, Irene tried to say what was in her heart. After so many years of serving the Lord, and while reminiscing about the many spiritual experiences she had enjoyed, it was very difficult to put into words:

> Words fail to express my deep appreciation for the great kindness and friendship you have shown towards me through the years as the Church Hostess.
>
> You have been a tower of strength and guidance to me. Many times problems came up and had it not been for you standing behind me—I wonder if I would have been able to accomplish the work I was called to do.
>
> I have loved the work because I love the Church. I have been so very happy in seeing the lives of people change as they heard the Gospel truths and accepted them.
>
> Thank you so much for allowing me to stay on as long as you did. I sincerely appreciate this more than words can express.
>
> The beautiful tribute you paid me, Elder Hinckley, was so emotional to me that I simply "fell apart" and could not control my feelings. To have someone say such kind and generous words...thank you from the bottom of my heart.
>
> If at any time there is anything I can do for the Church or for you personally, please do not hesitate to call on me. God bless you! Irene

The amount of actual work Irene completed while serving as the Official Church Hostess, and the goodwill she generated for the Church, simply cannot be measured. In addition to the time spent actually hosting her guests on Temple Square, must be added the time taken to pre-arrange hotel rooms, transportation, interpreters, meetings with Church and State officials, luncheons and dinners, as well as the many times she took guests into her home. After every guest left Salt Lake City, calls would be made or letters sent to mission presidents, bishops, and stake presidents where the guests lived, to assure appropriate follow-up. Almost every guest was sent a letter of thanks, additional information, and an invitation to return. And, of course, not one person left Irene without being offered a copy of the Book of Mormon!

Highlights of 1974

January

15	Lieutenant General E.B. Roberts
16	U.S. Secretary of State Casper Weinberger
20	A group of doctors from China
26	Ambassador Masao Sawaki, Japan

February

12	Israel Consul General Ezekiel Carmel, photo with Elder Ezra Taft Benson and Gordon B. Hinckley
14	Rabbi Joel S. Goor, San Diego
21	Major General Francis Greenleaf and Lieutenant Colonel David Clark
26	Governor Rafael Hernandez Colon, Puerto Rico

March

6	Al and Paula Thrasher, met First Presidency and Bishopric
7	Roger Mudd (TV and radio journalist)
11	Hotel Utah groundbreaking
12	Today Show interview with President Kimball

22   Irene speaks on BYU TV
31   Major Tamio Yamashita, Japan

April

3   General Shiro Nishido and Colonel Tamura, Japan
18   The President of CBS, met with President
        Kimball and Choir
23   Anatole Davidov, Cultural Attaché, Russian
        Embassy in D.C., meeting with President Kimball
29   Mr. L.K.K'ung, Taiwan government
        representative, related to Chiang Kai-Shek

May

8   A group of Bolivian doctors
        Irene makes trip to Israel, as their special guest
14   Hagai Eshed, Chief Editor for Political Affairs,
        "Davar" Israeli newspaper
31   Archbishop Kanai, Japan

June

4   Consul General Maida, Japan
9   Vice President and Mrs. Gerald Ford, meeting
        President Kimball, luncheon
11   "Pale Moon," Indian Princess
        Alexander Schriener, Church Organist, honored
        for 50 years service, luncheon
24   Israeli group of diplomats: Samuel Mishori,
        Joseph Ginat, Hesi Carmel, Uri Plotnikov, photo
        with First Presidency
30   A group of 50 scouts from New York
        President Oaks and a group of 15 American
        Bar Assoc. members
        Honorable Anicets G. Barceal, Chief of Police,
        Philippines

July

5	A group of 50 young Jewish people
6	Dr. William A. Neville, Dean at Indiana University
13	Senator & Mrs. Robert Byrd
19	The Blue Angels, U.S. Navy pilots
21	Portugal cadets
22	A group of 8 rodeo queens
25	A Japanese group from 'Sister City' Matsomoto, Japan
31	Vice Admiral Emmett H. Tidd

August

10	An American Indian group
12	A German youth choir
17	Elliot Richardson, former U.S. Attorney General
22	Ernst Bruegger, Swiss Consul General

September

15	The International Assoc. of Fire Chiefs

October

11	David Zohar, Israeli Information Consul, Los Angeles
16	A group of FBI officials
18	A Finnish chorus
26	A group of Soviet Union guests
27	A group of 10 visitors from Yugoslavia
30	A group of 20 Japanese business executives
	Moshe Dayan, Israel, spoke at University of Utah

November

9	Telly Savalas (TV star)
12	A group of visitors from Egypt
22	Dave Lui, Vice Consul, Taiwan

December

5	Atomic Energy Commission officials
13	ABC executives
29	USO group and Joseph Jessel

Statistics for 1974:

Total visitors hosted	18,679
Foreign visitors	655
Countries represented	68

The Orson Hyde Memorial Garden

> With the thought that the home can best be fortified from within, the Church has made a special plea and has asked us to encourage you mothers to: "Put your house in order"
>
> Mothers, the big responsibility is yours! I say that because the mother is thrown in closer contact with the children than is the father. But the two together is the ideal plan.
>
> And how can we have better homes? This can be answered with one statement: by living the principles of the gospel.
>
> "If ye love me, keep my commandments."
>
> Love in the home fosters happiness, companionship, tolerance and respect for one another.
>
> Irene

Although officially retired during 1975, Irene continued to get calls from both Church and state officials asking her to host VIPs, or to organize dinners and luncheons, or even just to help decorate for special occasions. As usual, Irene was more than willing to do whatever she could to serve the Church and her community.

As her hosting schedule slowly diminished, Irene began to speak more often at ward and stake firesides, or anywhere there was an interest in her hosting work or what was happening in

Israel. For example, on February 14, 1975, Irene spoke at a Salt Lake Institute of Religion Devotional.[1]

On April 7, 1975, Irene left on her second trip to Israel. This time she brought with her some of her extended family.

In June, the Ginats returned to Utah for a welcome visit with Irene and the many friends they had formed while living in Utah for almost two years.

On August 14, Irene arranged a luncheon meeting between BYU President Dallin Oaks and Joseph Ginat at BYU.

On September 8, Irene invited a large group of friends to her home to hear Joseph Ginat speak. Joseph showed slides of archeological sites in Israel, talked about Lehi's Cave, and discussed ways to bring closer communications between Israel and the Mormon Church.

Although she was now 69 years old, in 1976 Irene continued to be active in both politics and social affairs. She was called upon to host an occasional guest on Temple Square, or to help organize special events around the state, such as luncheons and weddings. However, she was being used less and less in these capacities. As Irene found she had more and more time to herself, she began to spend much of her time working on her family genealogy.

Irene missed the activity and prestige of her calling as Official Church Hostess and occasionally began to feel lonely and depressed. For example, on May 30, Memorial Day, Irene went to Harold's grave to decorate it, and noted in her diary that she felt "all alone."

In April of 1976, Irene made her third trip to Israel, with some of her extended family.[2] This wonderful woman, even at 69 years old,

---

[1] See Appendix 4, *Salt Lake Institute Talk by Irene.*
[2] The author and his new wife traveled with Irene on this trip.

had enough energy to climb Mount Sinai with some of her children and grandchildren, and beat many of them to the top!

Irene continued to press forward with service on a number of fronts. On May 17, 1976 Irene was elected as a State Republican *delegate;* on May 26, she was elected *President* of the 'Classics Club;' and on July 16, Irene attended the Republican State Convention as a *delegate*. Irene also kept many speaking engagements. For example, on September 23, Irene spoke at the LDS Students Association of the University of Utah.

As another year passed, Irene continued to give as much service as age and opportunity offered. On January 4, 1977, Irene started to *volunteer* with the Genealogical Society. In May, she was again elected a *State Delegate* for the Republican Party. On July 6, she finally turned in to the Church Historical Library the *World's Fair Mormon Pavilion History* she had been working on, comprising three large volumes that included many letters, pictures, newspaper articles, and, of course, her own views of that event.

On October 26, the Brethren formally announced the *Orson Hyde Memorial Garden* project. The announcment took place in the new high-rise Church Office building, in front of a large mural of the Mount of Olives. Elder Wendell Ashton presided; Elder LeGrand Richards read the Church's statement to the media. Elder Howard W. Hunter, who was handling the legal and contractual work with Israel, answered questions. Irene had the privilege of attending this event and had her picture taken with the appointed officials.

The Orson Hyde Foundation had organized the million dollar project—all paid for through private donations. Elder LeGrand Richards was assigned to head the program. Both Dan Rona[3] and David Galbraith[4] helped coordinate the project from Jerusalem.

---

[3]The Branch President of the Jerusalem Branch of the Mormon Church in Israel at the time.
[4]The previous Branch President in Israel.

The Orson Hyde Memorial Garden would be one of 11 national parks in the Israeli park system. A newspaper article about the Orson Hyde Memorial Gardens describes the site:

Plans move forward / Hyde gardens to beautify area
By Carma Wadley, *Deseret News* staff writer, January 14, 1978

Jerusalem

Halfway up the northwestern slope of the Mount of Olives lays a five-acre tract of land surrounded by a rock wall. Today it is a pretty desolate area, covered only by rocks, weeds, a few scattered olive trees.

One day soon the plot will be covered by shaded walkways, a small amphitheater, and grove of trees, plants and shrubbery.
The Church has been asked to develop this tract of land into a park to be named in honor of Orson Hyde, the early Mormon apostle who traveled to Jerusalem in 1841 and who dedicated the land for the return of the Jews. The park will be part of the Jerusalem National Park System.

"The Orson Hyde Memorial Gardens will be the realization of a dream first envisioned by a prophet of God," said Daniel Rona, president of the Jerusalem Branch of the Church. "President Harold B. Lee and others have hoped that someday there could be a monument to Orson Hyde's dedication of the Holy Land. This garden, replacing the rubble around the old city, will be a fine memorial."

Members of the Jerusalem Foundation, a non-profit organization dedicated to improving life in Jerusalem, are equally enthusiastic about the Orson Hyde Memorial Gardens.

"The garden will bring enjoyment to hundreds of thousands of visitors," said Steven Rosenfeld, a member of the foundation who has been working with the Orson Hyde project.

Jerusalem is a city, he added, that has significance for the world's three largest monotheistic faiths: Judaism, Christianity and Islam.

"We are happy to have the Mormon Church working on this project," he continued. "Beauty is something that doesn't depend on culture or religion, but has universal appeal. They are developing this park for the benefit of all."

Mayor of Jerusalem Teddy Kollek, chairman of the Jerusalem Foundation, further explained the goals and work of the foundation.

"Jerusalem is, at one and the same time, an ancient city full of antiques and ancient monuments, and a modern city with the needs and problems of 20th century urban life.

"The purpose of the Jerusalem Foundation is to aid in solving these problems and to preserve the unique heritage of the city.

"With its limited means, the Jerusalem Foundation strives to bridge the social and physical differences within Jerusalem. It does so by adding the beauty of a park to a neglected neighborhood, by providing a community center or health clinic, by creating a playground or sports field for underprivileged youth, by promoting joint activities for Arab and Jewish youngsters, by establishing libraries, building synagogues, aiding churches of all denominations and by helping to restore historical and religious sites."

Within weeks after the conclusion of the Six-Day War, said Mayor Kollek, the late Prime Minister Levi Eshkol endorsed the idea of creating a national park around the walls of the Old City. Since then planning and actual development have progressed considerably.

The idea, in the words of C. R. Ashbee, one of Jerusalem's first planners, is to "isolate the Holy City, set it, so to speak, in the center of a park thus recognizing the appeal it makes to the world: the city of an idea."

The Orson Hyde Memorial Gardens will be one of 11 parks in the national park system. Others include the American bicentennial Liberty Bell Garden, the Zurich Garden, the Ophel Archaeological Garden, and the Garden along the Old City Walls and the B'nai B'rith Garden.

The Orson Hyde gardens is one of the largest projects in the park system and is in a very strategic location for attracting visitors.

Directly across the Kidron Valley is the Old City, with its ancient stone wall, famed Dome of the Rock mosque and other landmarks.

A few yards to the south is the peaceful Garden of Gethsemane, with ancient olive trees said to be the ones there at the time of Christ.

The one million dollar Orson Hyde Memorial Gardens project is being financed through private donations. This initial sum will pay for the development and building of the gardens. The government of Israel and the municipality of Jerusalem has agreed to provide care and maintenance for the property for 99 years.

The names of all who contribute funds will be inscribed on a scroll and placed in a time capsule in the stone wall of the grotto. A plaque will also be placed there with excerpts in three languages from Orson Hyde's dedicatory prayer.

Chairman of the board of trustees for the Orson Hyde Foundation is Orson Hyde White of Provo, with Elder LeGrand Richards of the Council of the Twelve as president and trustee.

As another year came and went, Irene's service, though slowed, continued at a brisk pace: on January 3, 1978, Irene again became a *volunteer* with the Genealogical Society.

Irene's service over the years did not go unnoticed. On March 2, Irene received the *Utah National Guard Minuteman Award* for the many years spent hosting top military officials; and later that same month was given the *Heritage Award* at a Lion House dinner.

At the April 2 General Conference, Irene took Joseph and Dalia Ginat to hear President Ezra Taft Benson speak. On June 7, she hosted the Jewish Cantor, David Serken, and took him to meet President Benson. On July 29 Irene spoke at the Brigham Stake, in Perry, Utah, with Dr. Russell M. Nelson;[5] and on July 30th took a large group from Israel on a tour of Temple Square.

On November14, Irene received the *Community Memorial Chapel Foundation Award.* The award "is limited to those individuals who have demonstrated distinguished achievement as founders, builders, leaders, and who, through unselfish service, have contributed significantly to the betterment of the communities of our country." The following newspaper article described the event:

Seven to Gain 'Living History' Honor
Salt Lake Tribune article, November 12, 1978

Seven persons will be honored by the board of the Honors Library of Living History Tuesday during a 6:30 p.m. banquet at the Lion House, 63 E. South Temple.

---

[5]Russell M. Nelson later became an Apostle.

Recipients will be Mr. and Mrs. Alf M. Engen, Mr. and Mrs. Sverre Engen, Mr. and Mrs. Sidney M. Horman and **Mrs. Irene E. Staples.**

The Honors Library of Living History, headed by Mrs. Frank O. Fonnesbeck, is a unit of the Community Memorial Chapel Foundation, 1324-18th East, "organized to preserve and perpetuate historic, cultural and patriotic values."

Mrs. Fonnesbeck said of the persons to be honored:

The Engen brothers and families have been very influential in skiing activities and developments for many years. Sidney Horman has served the community as a distinguished contractor and planner for civic development. Mrs. Staples is well known for generous volunteer work and artistic contributions for enhancement of dramatic productions throughout our area.

In December, as the year closed, Irene helped the General Authorities of the Church with their Christmas cards by hand lettering each one. Irene was well known for her wonderful calligraphy.

May 15, 1979, was a banner day for Irene. On this day, as recorded in her journal, she was "kissed by the Prophet!" Irene had been invited to a dinner at the Lion House; Jeffrey Holland[6] was speaking on his experiences representing the Church as a seminary teacher in Jerusalem. Before dinner, while everyone was still visiting with one another, President Spencer W. Kimball came up to Irene, put his arms around her and kissed her on the cheek! He remarked, "Sister Staples you are a wonderful, great woman." Irene expressed how very thankful she was to have been remembered.

On June 12, Irene submitted her *History of the Hosting Service* to the Church. Much like the history of the Mormon Pavilion, Irene had gathered material and pictures together to provide the Church with a concise history of her time as Official Church Hostess. The history was submitted to Margine Garff who was head of the volunteers, and is now part of the Church's historical records.

---

[6]Elder Jeffrey Holland was later called to be an Apostle.

On October 11, 1979, Irene left on her fourth trip to Israel, with a group of 50, to attend the dedication of the Orson Hyde Memorial Garden on the Mount of Olives. President Spencer W. Kimball, Elder Nathan Tanner, Elder Ezra Taft Benson, and Elder LeGrand Richards spoke. President Kimball gave the dedicatory prayer. Past Consul Generals Hesi Carmel and Moshe and Dvorah Yegar were there also. Irene sat with Joseph and Dalia Ginat. Irene wrote the following about the event:

> When starting this project, I was happy to know that the Church consulted and worked with the officials in Israel as to the design and all details, so they would feel that they were part of the project!
>
> The Church also used workmen from Israel in the construction of the project, and in many other ways, so that the Israelis could take pride in what they had accomplished. This would also bring a good friendly feeling between everyone.
>
> Finally the Orson Hyde Memorial Garden was finished, and special plans were made for the dedication!
>
> With a group of friends, I went to Israel for the dedication, which took place on the 24th of October, 1979.
>
> Hundreds of Mormons came from Utah and other places for the dedication. We all sat on the hillside; it was a beautiful warm day. A covered stand was erected for Jerusalem Mayor Teddy Kollek, and city officials, as well as for President Spencer W. Kimball and other Church Brethren.
>
> Mayor Kollek gave a very fine, friendly talk of welcome, and his appreciation for the privilege and pleasure of working with the Mormon people. He said that it was a very special experience, which he was very grateful for, and hoped that this friendship and association would continue through the years.
>
> President Kimball gave an inspirational Dedicatory Prayer, and the local Mormon Choir furnished the music.
>
> It was a beautiful spiritual occasion, and quite overwhelming, to realize that the Mormon Church was in Israel dedicating

240

the beautiful Orson Hyde Memorial Garden as a remembrance and in honor of when Orson Hyde was called by the Prophet Joseph Smith to go to Israel and there, on the Mount of Olives on Oct. 24, 1841, offer a special prayer that the land might become fertile, nourished, and fruitful, for the return of the rightful heirs ... the Jewish people! It was truly a day long to be remembered!

Coming for the Garden dedication was an opportunity for President Spencer W. Kimball and other Brethren to choose a piece of property for the BYU Study Abroad Building;[7] which they did, with President Kimball making the final decision and with Mayor Kollek's approval!

The Church erected a beautifully impressive and spectacular building, high on the hill overlooking Jerusalem. The Church has an organ or a musical concert once a week, in the evening, free to the public! They also conduct tours of the building, if so desired.

This program has been very well received by the people. The majority of Jewish people have a good feeling about the Mormon Church being there, and accept this beautiful building and garden as an asset to the City of Jerusalem!

We extend to Mayor Teddy Kollek our most sincere honor, and special appreciation, for the friendship and wonderful kindness he has shown to the Mormon Church! He is a great and an honorable man, and a great friend to give the Mormon Church the privilege of creating the "Orson Hyde Garden," and also to make it possible for the Church to obtain the property to build the BYU Study Abroad building! Each is a great credit to the Mormon Church, and to the beautiful City of Jerusalem!

God Bless him...for his great friendship, and for his kindness to our Church and to our people!

As I sat on the hillside during the dedication of the garden...I was filled with emotion, and my thoughts went back to January, 1967, 12 years ago, when as the Church Hostess I had the inspiration to write a letter to the Consul General of Israel,

---

[7]Later called the BYU Jerusalem Center.

> Moshe Yegar, inviting him to come to Salt Lake City to learn
> about the Mormon Church, and the love and friendship our
> people have for Israel and the Jewish people!
>
> Now I was witnessing the result of doing what I was inspired to
> do...write a letter, opening the way for the present friendly
> association of the Mormon Church with Israel!
>
> Since then, two important events have taken place, "The
> Orson Hyde Memorial Garden," and the BYU Study Abroad
> building!
>
> "I give the Dear Lord full credit. I am only thankful that this
> association has taken place, bringing peace and blessings to
> both people!"

On November 1, after returning from Israel, Irene took an
investigator on a tour. After the tour Irene stopped at the Church
Offices to give Brother Arthur Haycock[8] a donation check given
her by the investigator. Both President Spencer W. Kimball and
Elder Ezra Taft Benson came from their offices and visited with
her. They were kind and expressed happiness to see her. President Kimball said, "Whenever I think of you, Sister Staples, I
think of you with great admiration." What a wonderful compliment from the Prophet of the Lord!

---

[8]Personal secretary to President Kimball.

Epilogue

Irene's motto: Service above self.

Irene was getting old—even for her—and although her mind remained sharp, and she desired to do more, her physical body just would not permit her to do as much as she once had. The opportunities for Irene to serve as she once had were slowly disappearing.

On July 30, 1980, Irene took a group of investigators to see Elder Thomas Monson, who spent an hour with them. They also met with President Ezra Taft Benson.

On November 5, Irene had an evening out with President and Sister Benson, Rabbi Stanley Greenstein and his wife Judy and Cantor Maynor Gerber. They all went to hear the Jay Welch Chorale. This choir had been invited to go to Israel, but the trip was cancelled due to an airline strike.

In July and August of 1981, Irene was called as a missionary with Jerry Hayes,[1] to work at Lagoon's Pioneer Village for five weeks.

On May 2, 1983, Irene was asked by Arthur Haycock to hand write the place cards for the First Presidency dinner.

---

[1]Jerry Hayes was a car dealer in Salt Lake.

In March, 1984, Irene participated in making costumes for the play *Zion* put on by the Parleys Stake.

In August, 1986, due to failing health, Irene's family convinced her to move from her home on Virginia Street into a small Eagle Gate condominium just east of the Church Office building and Temple Square. Irene had become prone to falling, and the upkeep of her large home and yard had simply become too much for her. As an added incentive for the move, the condo was in the same building where many General Authorities of the Church lived. Irene would now be able to see the many friends she had made over the years a lot more often.

On January 19, 1988, Irene decorated tables for the *Thrasher Research Fund* dinner. During the dinner Irene was presented with a plaque: *"In recognition for service to the Thrasher Research Fund."* There was also a tribute read about Irene's service to the community. Irene had hosted the Thrashers several times, and was influential in convincing them to donate 14 million dollars to the Primary Children's Hospital!

To the end of her life Irene fought to be able to serve in some capacity. When her health began to fail, she still traveled to wards and stakes in the area to speak at firesides and special events. Her personal diaries document *over 500* speaking engagements!

Irene's life of service came to an end May 8, 1998,[2] due to complications after a serious fall. She was 92 years old.

Irene's life is an inspiration for anyone who wonders if *one person* can change the world. Irene was just *one woman*, yet through her passionate testimony of the Gospel of Jesus Christ, and her selfless service, she literally changed the world in which she lived! Tens of thousands heard her testify of gospel truths,

[2]See Appendix 5, *Irene's Funeral Eulogy.*

leading to hundreds, perhaps thousands of baptisms around the world. Through listening to that "still small voice" inside of her, Irene was able to follow the prompting of the spirit—writing letters and making contacts that helped open the land of Israel for the preaching of the gospel and the establishment of a branch of the Church in the Holy Land.

What can one person do? Irene's life is *proof* that one person can change the world they live in! If this small, red haired grand-mother, with nothing more than a passionate testimony of the Gospel of Jesus Christ, can rise from humble beginnings to liter-ally reshape the world, surely each of us has similar potential. For all who ponder the worth of one soul, for all who wonder what just one person can do to change the world around them, all they need do is look to Irene for inspiration and guidance. It doesn't take wealth, fame, or political power to influence the world in which we live. All it takes is a testimony of the Gospel of Jesus Christ and the desire to share it with others!

Irene Staples: Hostess to the World

Appendix 1: Comments about Irene

1962

June 20, Letter from *Stanley Russon,* YMMIA:[1]

My profound admiration and deepest gratitude comes to you for your costuming our "Evening in the Social Hall". Your tremendous talent coupled with your sweet spirit and willingness made our association the happiest of experiences.

All I can say about you is that you are "Perfection"!

1963

Oct. 21, Letter from the *General Presidency* of the Relief Society:

On behalf of the Relief Society General Board we wish to express our sincere appreciation for your assistance in the literature presentation "Album of America's Literature" presented in the Tabernacle...during the Relief Society General Conference.

This was a most effective and inspirational presentation...We appreciate you assistance in lending the lovely costumes worn...We thank you also for your assistance backstage with the changing of costumes during the presentation.

---

[1]Young Men's Mutual Improvement Association.

Irene Staples: Hostess to the World

1966

Nov. 29, Letter from Governor *Calvin Rampton:*

I want to express thanks on behalf of the state and myself for your cooperation and aid during the recent visit to Utah by nearly 100 European travel agents and travel writers.

You may be interested in knowing their response to our state and its attractions was most enthusiastic—and gratifying. One chief compliment heard from the foreign visitors was the warmth and friendliness shown them during their brief stay.

1967

May, Letter to *Mark E. Petersen* from *Weldon Matthews,* National Rep.:

The charm, enthusiasm, and personality of Mrs. Staples is superb and made a tremendous impact on our guest. Mr. Krakow is a world traveler, and he mentioned in his public talks, that he had never been entertained more hospitably.

Aug. 22, Letter from *Sterling W. Sill* to *Mark E. Peterson*:

I mentioned to you the other day what a great job I think Irene Staples is doing with the visitors that she visits with while they are in Salt Lake City. I am enclosing herewith a file on one of the latest of the ministers that she has discussed the Church with. I though you might like to see it.

I am familiar with other cases where she has done an equally good job. I think if we all did our work as well as Irene does the Church would be in pretty good shape.

Sept. 12, Letter from *Clarence Wonnacott,* Latter-day Saints Hospital:

What a wonderful missionary you are. I don't remember anyone so thorough in their hosting a foreign visitor.

Oct. 4, Letter from the *Central British Mission:*

I believe that if I were to write an article for the Reader's Digest on the most interesting person, you would have to be the subject for my article...We read the report on hosting Reverend and Mrs. D. Austin Bowen to the missionaries at the table. It was hard to keep back the tears as we realized what great missionaries there are throughout the Church.

1968

April 1, Letter from *Mrs. Joseph Yoder* of New York:

Reviewing our recent trip, my husband and I find that the afternoon spent with you was one of the most rewarding experiences of all. Thank you so much.

April 9, Letter from *Belle S. Spafford,* General President of the Relief Society:

Sister Staples, you are a wonderful missionary for the Church. You are gracious, informed, personally attractive, and you ideally represent Latter-day Saint womanhood in every way.

Nov 15, Irene journal entry

> While eating lunch at the Lion House with a friend, Elder *Spencer W. Kimball* came by and stopped to visit. He turned to my friend and, pointing to me, said," There is the Church's greatest missionary." Last month I sent referrals to 33 missions. I have received many letters and heard from people of many conversions from the referrals I have sent to the missions.

1969

Nov. 12, Letter from *Sterling W. Sill*:

I am sending you a letter from our good friend...whom you showed around the city a little while ago. They all seem to have so much fun I think I'll get me a disguise as a VIP and take the tour myself.

1970

March 23, Letter from *Sterling W. Sill*:

I think I would do pretty well in the world if you just always told me what I ought to do, and someday I'm going to vote for you for the first female member of the Quorum of the Twelve.

July 15, Letter to *Mark E. Peterson* from *Kaye Burgon*, Frontier Airlines:

I would like to comment on the excellent work that is being done for the Church by Mrs. Irene E. Staples, LDS Church Hostess. I have had occasion to work with Mrs. Staples on various occasions when Frontier Airlines has had influential people visiting Salt Lake City. Because of our desire to have these people better understand the Church and the rich history of our area, I have found the services of Mrs. Staples extremely helpful. I consider her position very important and valuable to the Church.

She fulfills a service and need that, to my knowledge, could not be realized in any other way. From my experience, you could not have selected a more gracious, cooperative and understanding person than Irene. Her personality sparkles and certainly influences all with whom she comes in contact.

If I might make an additional observation, I feel Mrs. Staples could use an assistant. She works very hard and puts in long hours.

1971

**April 30, Letter from *John Q. Cannon* to *Russell Williams*
about Irene's retirement:**

Sister Irene E. Staples, a member of the Church Information Service staff, arrives at the 65 year retirement age on Sept. 29, 71. We request permission to continue her employment beyond that date. Elder Mark E. Petersen, who supervises the activities of this office, concurs in this request.

Functioning in the capacity of hostess, Sister Staples performs an exacting and extremely important service for the Church, in a very effective way. She is thoroughly dedicated to her work and to the Church, giving time and effort far in excess of regular or normal hours. As far as is known, her health is good and she is fully capable of carrying on. We have never succeeded in having her turn in adequate expense accounts, and the result is that substantial amounts of her own funds are expended on her job.

Reports are constantly received from persons who have visited here, attesting to the fine quality of her work, and it is known that she is primarily responsible for many converts to the Church. Finding a replacement who could and would perform as she does would indeed be difficult.

1972

Feb 15, Letter from *John Cannon,* American Cancer Society:

I just had a call from Lane Adams in New York. Lane learned from Dr. Letton that the treatment Dr. and Mrs. Letton received in Salt Lake was far beyond their expectations and constituted a highlight of their lives.

April 6, Letter from *Ernest L. Wilkinson:*

The Church couldn't have picked a better person anywhere in the world for your present position than you.

April 24, Letter from *Preston Adams,* New England Life, to *Mark E. Petersen:*

May we extend to you the gratitude in our hearts for the super reception that your dear friend and mine, Irene Staples, accorded some dear friends of ours from North Carolina...The Robert McGhees were touched to the point that tears were rolling down their cheeks when they saw and heard, under Irene Staples' direction, the Mormon story in action. It wouldn't surprise me a bit that, through Sister Staples' extracurricular tour, these people could be converted to the Church.

Oct. 23, Letter from *Max J. Jones* of Thiokol to *Marvin J. Ashton:*

Last week the Aerospace Industries Assoc. of America held a convention in Salt Lake City...The purpose of this letter is to express sincere appreciation for an outstanding service rendered by Mrs. Irene Staples. Sister Staples arranged for 1) a special tour of the Temple grounds and Visitors Center, 2) audience at the Tabernacle Choir practice with the choir singing "Battle Hymn of the Republic", as a special request, 3) a special tour of Welfare Square and the Beehive House for wives of these men, and 4) a personal gift of a lovely book introducing each member to the "Mormon Church". Words fail me when I try to express the appreciation expressed by each of the visitors for these choice experiences...Please convey sincere appreciation to Sister Staples for an outstanding service. She is capable, dedicated and a very sweet person to represent the Church in this important capacity.

1973

May 26, Letter from *James Adams*, Principal:

You really thrilled a group of seminary officers on May 10, when you gave them the same treatment that Royalty might have received. Thanks so very much for your time and service. The attention they received...caused testimonies to grow so much.

February 6, Letter from Mayor *Jake Garn:*

I seem to constantly be in your debt. The gracious way you greet my guests and conduct the tour is unequaled. I am sure I will call on you many times in the next years. If at any time my office can be of assistance to you, please do not hesitate to ask.

1974

Letter from a young girl, *Debby Fell* from Maryland:

How is Charlie [*Irene's boots under her bed*]? He really gave me and Lisa a big, big scare. The dinner was delicious and I really enjoyed the parade, and the rodeo was great! And I love the building you work in is great! And everything you did for us was great. Love and a hug, Debby

August 19, Letter from *Junius Tribe:*

It is difficult to find words to adequately express our appreciation to you for the beautiful job you did for Mr. and Mrs. Russell C. Hughes and their relatives from the state of Illinois.

I only wish you could have heard their kind expressions of gratitude for your kindness and the way you gave of your valuable time to escort them and us through both the Visitors Center and the new Church Office Building. They informed us several times that it was the most memorable day of their lives and they would always remember it.

I have discovered that they are Lutherans and are deeply religious people, and I honestly feel that they will someday come into the Church.

October 28, Letter from *Debbie Austin:*

I wanted to thank you for the lovely talk you gave and for the answer to my prayer.

Earlier yesterday (Sunday) I had been reading the Book of Mormon. I had quite a few questions in my mind that needed answering. So I knelt in prayer asking for an understanding. Having no results I left for Sacrament meeting a little upset at having no answers.

Then, as you began to speak about the Book of Mormon, a warm peaceful feeling came over me and my questions were answered. I know that God lives and works in many mysterious ways. I also believe in prayer, and know that God hears and answers my prayers.

You are very special person and I have always admired you. You "radiate"!

Dec. 13, Letter from Irene to *Ezra Taft Benson:*

Regardless of my retirement, it has been approved that I be a representative of the Church with Israel. With several projects under consideration, and the contacts I have made there, they feel I should continue with my association with them.

I received a letter from Dr. Halbrecht, from Israel, whom you met with Dr. Josef Ginat, expressing his great appreciation not only for the kindness extended to him, but also for the friendship of the Mormon people.

He has spoken to the leaders of Yad Vashem (the Memorial and Archives of the 6 million Jews killed in the great holocaust by Hitler) and said they would be very glad to use our generous help in many ways, including not only microfilming the names of the 6 million, but also in obtaining documents of Jewish history. It sounds very promising. [Ed.: During Irene's visit to Israel as their special guest, she had the unusual privilege of being taken into the Archives to see the records of the 6 million, and immediately thought of the work for the dead.]

I also got a letter from Joseph Ginat, with congratulations concerning the Mount of Olives property. I will keep you informed of any further developments on either project which I may become aware of.

Irene Staples: Hostess to the World

Dec. 17, Letter from *Gordon B. Hinckley* to Irene, about her retirement:

There are those all over the world who remember you with appreciation. I have met some of these, who, while visiting in Salt Lake City, met officials of the Church and State, but remembered only Irene Staples. You have opened many doors for the Church and have opened the minds of uncounted men and women in their attitude toward the Church. Baptisms have come of your efforts.

As you step down, there will be days of loneliness, but these will be sweetened by the memories of work well done.

Dec. 31, Irene journal entry, *Irene's last day as Official Church* Hostess:

The office had a luncheon for her. Elder Mark E. Peterson and Gordon B. Hinckley spoke. They gave me a wonderful tribute. She has hosted over 100 ,000 people. "The end of another era of my life."

Not knowing how long I would have this position, I decided to dedicate my full time to this calling...I have never taken a vacation or had a weekend free...some of my most memorable conversions were those when meeting guests on Saturday, Sunday or on a holiday. I have never submitted an expense request for either the use of my car or for entertaining the hundreds of guests in my home... It was not a sacrifice to do this, but rather a blessing to me.

1975

Jan. 13, Letter from Irene to *Gordon B. Hinckley* after her release

Words fail to express my deep appreciation for the great kindness and friendship you have shown towards me through my years as the Church Hostess.

You have been a tower of strength and guidance to me. Many times problems came up and had it not been for you standing behind me—I wonder if I would have been able to accomplish the work I was called to do.

I have loved the work because I love the Church. I have been so very happy in seeing the lives of people change as they heard the Gospel truths and accepted them.

Thank you so much for allowing me to stay on as long as you did. I sincerely appreciate this more than words can express.

The beautiful tribute you paid me, Elder Hinckley, was so emotional to me, that I simply "fell apart" and could not control my feelings. To have someone say such kind and generous words...thank you from the bottom of my heart.

Irene Staples: Hostess to the World

Appendix 2: Lectures on the Cave of Lehi

Newsletter and Proceedings of the S.E.H.A.[1]

April 1972   Number 129

The Cave at Khirbet Beit Lei

By Joseph Ginat

Deputy Advisor on Arab affairs to the Prime Minister of Israel; 1970-72 visiting instructor and doctoral candidate in anthropology at the University of Utah; paper read at the 21st Annual Symposium on the Archaeology of the Scriptures, BYU, October 16, 1971.

An ancient cave was uncovered in 1961 in the course of road construction on the eastern slope of the hill Khirbet Beit Lei, according to Joseph Naveh, professor of archaeology at Hebrew University in Jerusalem, who was the first explorer after the discovery (Fig. 2). The cave is located five miles east of Lachish, about 10 miles west-northwest of Hebron, and 22 miles south-southwest of Jerusalem. (Naveh, 1963.)

Professor Naveh's Findings

On the walls inside the cave were found several ancient inscriptions in the Old Hebrew script and drawings of human figures and sailing vessels. As the vicinity of

---

[1]Society for Early Historic Archaeology at BYU.

the cave is far inland, the appearance of ships presents a problem to the investigator (Fig. 3). Naveh points out: "Whereas the human form is a common pictorial theme, the representations of ships found on the southern wall of the antechamber...provided an unexpected discovery: it is hardly likely that the inhabitants of this region had any connection with seafaring or fishing, and yet we have here two sailing vessels, schematically portrayed but realistic enough for all that" (p. 78).

Naveh dates the Hebrew script to the sixth century BC by comparison with other inscriptions found on monuments and ostraca of the period.

In the present paper I shall discuss the content of the inscriptions, utilizing Naveh's original study, together with a later analysis (Cross, 1970) by Frank Moore Cross, Jr., professor of Hebrew at Harvard University, an editor of *The Biblical Archaeologist*, and the leading American scholar at present working on the Dead Sea Scrolls firsthand.

Naveh concludes that this cave is a tomb but is more significant than an ordinary one: "We might hazard a guess that this burial cave belonged to a family of Levite singers. A hint in this direction may be found in the suggested contents of the drawings: a man with a lyre, a praying figure, and a man with headgear (priestly or Levitic?) (Fig. 4). Since it is unlikely that many ordinary fold were acquainted with the art of writing, the explanation that a number of Levites visited this cave is relatively plausible.

"What do these inscriptions purport to express, and why were they incised on the wall of the cave? Since no other examples are known so far, the explanation is not easy." (Naveh, p. 90.)

Naveh obviously feels this to be an important place, no doubt because of the cave's uniqueness and the fact that the Levites were spiritual leaders in Israel and important persons in its culture.

Dr. Cross' Findings

Cross agrees with Naveh's dating. He says: "...the Beit Lei inscriptions...are safely dated to the sixth century BC" (pg. 304). He disagrees with him, however, as to the supposed funerary significance of the three inscriptions. He arrives at this conclusion as a result of his differing translation of two of them (pp. 301–302).

258

Inscription A reads: "*I am Yahweh (Jehovah) thy God: I will accept the cities of Judah and will redeem Jerusalem.*" (Figure 5)

Inscription B reads: "*Absolve us O merciful God! Absolve us O Yahweh!*"

Inscription C reads: "*Deliver us O Lord.*"

Cross agrees with Naveh's decipherment only in the third inscription, but they both agree that the same scribe wrote all three and that all are closely related in character and context. Cross feels, however, that the writings and drawings "are not ordinary tomb inscriptions" (p. 304). He is sure they have nothing to do with those who were buried in the cave but suggests they may have been left by travelers or perhaps refugees who happened by and sought shelter.

One of the inscriptions, Cross points out, is a prayer for deliverance. Another is a plea to be freed from guilt. The third (Inscription A), which is worded like a prophecy from Isaiah or Jeremiah, quotes Jehovah as promising to accept and redeem Jerusalem and Judah. "It is very difficult," he adds, "to avoid the speculation that Inscription A is the citation of a lost prophecy . . . (p. 304)."

Cross conjectures that the three inscriptions may have been written there by someone fleeing before the Babylonian invaders who destroyed Judah and its capital city in 587 BC—perhaps even by a prophet or his secretary escaping from Jerusalem.

The Name Lei

What of the name of this place, *Khirbet Beit Lei*? "*Lei*" and "*Lehi*" are equivalent. The first biblical mention of Lehi is found in Judges *15:14–17*. In this passage two places bearing that name are mentioned. The first is the place where the men of Judah delivered Samson to the Philistines. The second is a nearby hill, Ramath Lehi (Ramah means hill), named by Samson after killing the 1000 Philistines. The *Khirbet Beit Lei* cave is in the same vicinity as the place named by Samson, situated on the ancient border between Judah and the Philistines.

Another example of two ancient sites located near each other and having the same name is that of the two cities of Arad, mentioned in Pharaoh Shishak's inscription describing his Palestinian campaign. This campaign, which took place in the fifth year of the reign of Rehoboam, king of Judah (c.925 BC), is known from two statements in the Bible: I Kings 14:25–26 and 2 Chronicles 12:2–9. It is also known from Egyptian sources. According to Yohanan Aharoni, chairman of the Department of Archaeology at Tel Aviv University, in his book, *The Land of the Bible,* "it is clear from the Egyptian text that the main objectives of the expedition were not the towns of Judah and Jerusalem but rather the kingdom of Israel on one hand and the Negev of Judah on the other" (p.285).

In the list of Negev settlements, the following is mentioned: h-q-r-m -r-d r-b-t -r-d n h-t y-r-h-m. Aharoni suggests that this may be rendered: "(the) forts (of) Great Arad (and of) Arad of the House of Yeruham." He further comments: "of these fortresses it is possible to identify only Great Arad, which is (Solomonic) Tell Arad, and the Arad of Beth-yeroham (the Jerahmeelite?) with Tell el Milh, the site of Canaanite Arad" (p. 289).

Both Samson at Ramath Lehi and Solomon at Great Arad perpetuated the name of a previous settlement by using it for a new site. In both cases the original place was connected with unpleasant memories. Lehi was where the Judaeans betrayed Samson into the hand of the Philistines" (Judges 15:12). Arad was where the Israelites were defeated upon their first encounter with the dwellers of Canaan: "And when King Arad the Canaanite, which dwelt in the south, heard tell that Israel came by way of the spies; then he fought against Israel, and took some of them prisoners" (Numbers 21:1).

Aharoni discusses the phenomenon of ancient place names continuing in use to the present day: "The names of places and regions were preserved in Palestine throughout thousands of years with surprisingly few changes. This is apparently due to two main causes:

"1. During various periods of its history the country's residents spoke Semitic languages more or less closely related to one another.

"2. In spite of the changes that took place in the population's composition, there was usually a continuity of settlement so that each new wave of residents inherited the older names from their predecessors." (Aharoni p. 96.)

The original biblical name is *Lehi,* pronounced "*lay-hee.*" The pronunciation "leehigh" has to be a later version. The word *lehi (lei)* means "cheek" in both Hebrew and Arabic but was also used as a proper name. In Arabic the word *khirba* (singular)

260

literally means "ruin." *Beit* in both Hebrew and Arabic means "house." Thus the name *Khirbet Beit Lei* means *"Ruin of the House of Lehi."*

A Prophet's Haven?

In my opinion, the cave was a place where refugees found shelter, as Cross suggests. Moreover, the inscriptions had nothing to do with the burials. It also seems logical, as Cross further suggests, that the writer was a prophet or his scribe. This would explain why, in Inscription A, he made bold to quote Deity in the first person.

Not only the ancient writer's use of the first person in speaking for God, but also the content of the inscription itself, bear examination. The text dates to the eve of the destruction of Jerusalem in 587 BC. The Northern Kingdom of Israel had fallen to Assyria in 721 BC. The Kingdom of Judah had also begun to crumble following the invasion of Sennacherib in 701 BC. Now, the armies of Babylon were moving toward Jerusalem, bent on total conquest. In such an atmosphere of despair only a prophet would dare make such a statement-prophecy accepting the cities of Judah and promising the redemption of Jerusalem.

Why would a prophet hide? A prophet is traditionally a messenger from God. We can find examples in the Bible where the Lord sends his prophets on dangerous missions, yet warns them that they must take care of themselves. Elijah is a striking example. In I Kings 17 he confronts King Ahab with a hard prophecy of impending drought. Then the Lord commands Elijah to hide beside a brook and later to change his shelter to the home of the widow of Zarephath.

In I Kings 18:4 is seen another significant example from Ahab's time in which Obadiah hides 100 prophets in two caves, fearing their assassination by Queen Jezebel. From this we also see that there existed numerous prophets whose names and activities are unknown to us from the biblical narrative.

Benjamin Mazar, professor of archaeology at Hebrew University, stresses the fact that in the period preceding the destruction of Jerusalem, spiritual leaders of the nation, including Jeremiah, prophesied the destruction and the Exile, but also the subsequent redemption of Zion (Mazar, p. 11). There were other important persons, then, contemporaneous with Jeremiah, who prophesied of the destruction and rebuilding of Jerusalem and the revival of the kingdom under the House of David.

Such outspoken statements may well have been cause for their having to flee the city.

The Human Figures

In the present cave, the persons who stopped at the *Khirbet Beit Lei* cave may have been engaged in a dangerous mission, in fulfillment of which they had to escape and find shelter. My hypothesis is supported by the human figures engraved on the cave wall, in which an emphasis on the leg muscles is clearly perceived. The distance of this cave down from Jerusalem is 22 miles, which is not an impossible distance for an athlete to run. But a man unaccustomed to such exertion would surely reflect in his drawings the strain felt in his own legs.

Similarly, the likeness of a praying man on the cave wall lends more meaning to Inscription B or C, or both. The former is a plea for forgiveness and the latter, a prayer for deliverance.

A prophet is a human being. Under dangerous circumstances he feels the need to bolster his self-confidence. Even though he is fully aware that he is carrying out the will of God, he needs additional encouragement. The cave was a stopping place, a shelter; it was not the final destination. His mission was not yet finished. We know from other examples in the biblical narrative that prophets who were involved in God's errands often asked for reassurance in two ways: (1) praying and (2) seeking a tangible sign.

Samuel prayed to God for the success of the Israelites in their encounters with the Philistines [I Samuel 7:5–6]. He prayed for guidance when the children of Israel demanded a king, having conflicting feelings about it himself [I Samuel 8:4–6]. The first example was during a critical time of war. The second was at a time of personal anxiety.

Elijah, in the famous encounter with the priests of Baal on Mount Carmel, prayed for success [I Kings 18:36–37].

Gideon, who was chosen by the Lord to deliver his nation from the Midianites, was convinced by the signs the angel gave that the latter came from God [Judges 6:11–24]. Yet, in the hour of organizing his forces he felt the need to strengthen his resolve and prayed, asking for additional signs.

262

When the Lord sent Isaiah for the second time to Hezekiah the King, telling him that his life would be spared for 15 years, the latter asked for signs. Though Hezekiah was not himself a prophet, yet he already had proof that Isaiah was one, for the latter had correctly foretold that Jerusalem would not be conquered by the Assyrians [2 Kings 19:15–37].

The temporary tenants of the cave at *Khirbet Beit Lei* prayed in order to strengthen their resolve in completing their mission. And what *was* their mission? From the inscriptions we cannot tell. Do the ships have any connection with their mission?

A biblical note may help us in this regard. From I Kings 22:48 we learn that King Jehoshaphat attempted to build up a merchant fleet at Ezion-Geber, or Eilat of today, but that his ships were broken. In 2 Chronicles 20:35-37 we learn that a prophet, Eliezer from Mareshah, prophesied, telling Jehoshaphat why his vessels were broken. Mareshah is a neighboring town to *Khirbet Beit Lei*. We may assume that the attempt to build the fleet, its failure, and the prophecy of Eliezer were known to the occupants of this cave, located so close to Mareshah.

In any case, if we add together the inscriptions, the praying figure, and the ships, the sum of them all indeed seems significant, especially in this particular cave, located down from Jerusalem and in the fields of the ancient House of *Lehi (Lei)*.

<u>Bibliography</u>

Aharoni, Yohanan
    1968   *The Land of the Bible.* Burns amid Oats: London.
Cross, Frank Moore, Jr.
    1970   *The Cave Inscriptions from Khirbet Beir Lei*
Maiar, Benjamin
    1968   *Jerusalem in the Biblical Period*
Naveh, Joseph
    1963   *Old Hebrew Inscriptions in a Burial Cave*

<u>EDITOR'S NOTES:</u> The "land of our father Lehi's inheritance" mentioned by the Prophet Nephi in the Book of Mormon, appears to have been a family estate somewhat removed from the city of Jerusalem itself. Students of the Book of Mormon should consider whether the Khirbet Beit Lei cave might have had some connection with this estate, which figured prominently in the family's departure from the Holy

City in 597 BC (the four sons having hidden for a time "in the cavity of a rock" (1 Nephi 3:16, 27).

In connection with the meaning and pronunciation of the name *Lehi* see, in addition to the above, Newsletter, 104.2, p.5, last paragraph.

In connection with the invasion of Judea by Sennacherib of Assyria about a century before Lehi's departure, as mentioned above, see also an extended discussion of this event in Newsletter, 119.0.

The Beit Lehi Cave
(Talk given by Irene, unknown date)

Twenty miles southeast of Jerusalem, in the Judean mountains, not far from the ancient fortress towns of Lakhish and Maresha, and in the vicinity of the modern Israeli village of AMATZIA, named after the King of Judea, lie the ruins of an ancient village named *BEIT LEI (LEHI)*, '*THE HOUSE OF LEHI*'.

In 1961, in the course of the construction of a military patrol road along what was at the time the Israeli-Jordanian border line, a bulldozer hit and partly destroyed the roof of a tiny cave; by mere good luck there was no damage to the walls of the cave on which ancient drawings and inscriptions in old Hebrew script were uncovered by the astonished workers.

Two archaeologists Dr. Joseph Naveh of the Hebrew University of Jerusalem and Dr. Frank Moore Cross, Jr. of Brandeis University, Mass., tried to decipher the large inscription on the wall. According to Dr. Cross this inscription reads:

"I am Yahweh thy God. I shall accept the cities of Judah and will redeem Jerusalem"

Who were the inhabitants of the *Beit Lehi* cave? Dr. Naveh believes that the inscription was engraved by a Levitic priest. Dr. Cross thinks that the inscription is the expression of a lost prophecy. As the name of God and his deeds are engraved in the first person, Cross concludes that the inhabitant of the cave was a prophet fleeing Jerusalem.

Joseph Ginat, an Israeli anthropologist who lectured at the University of Utah and BYU, believes the cave may have served as a hiding place for an important person who was seeking refuge.

The narrow size of the cave, its location on the slope of the hill at a safe distance from the village but quite close to the spring—the only source of water in the area—indicates that the cave was used as a hiding place rather than a normal living place.

Up on the *Beit Lehi* hill, there are many spacious and comfortable caves which served as regular living hamlets for the inhabitants of the village. In the early Christian period some of those caves served as hiding places for Christians fleeing roman persecution. One of those caves, on top of the *Beit Lehi* hill, has been rediscovered in 1900 by Stewart McAllister who described it as the rock cut chapel. This cave probably served as a chapel for the early Christians who were hiding in the area.

In 701 B.C., the village was destroyed by the Assyrian King Senaherib on the way to conquer Jerusalem.

The few survivors of the village had probably fled to Jerusalem. As the inscription found in the cave has been dated back to the Sixth Century B. C.—probably during the period of the prophet Jeremiah—the cave's inhabitants may have belonged to a family which once owned property in the village and returned to the place to seek refuge. In those days of distress it seemingly took a man of great vision to write words of redemption and hope like those engraved in the stone:

"And I will Redeem Jerusalem"

The drawings of sailing boats found in the cave are very unusual for a mountain area so far away from the sea. There is a possibility that the people who took shelter in the cave intended to reach the sea, thus drawing plans of vessels or merely expressing a hope to be delivered by God.

There was obviously a road connection between the *Beit Lehi* area and the Red Sea shores. Up to this day, several inhabitants of a village by the name of UTAH a few miles away from the cave are believed to be descendants of Israelites who lived along the shores of the Red Sea in the Arabian desert. Where does the origin of the name *Beit Lehi* come from? Bedouins, the nomad inhabitants of the area, whose traditions and legends are transmitted from generation to generation have an interesting version.

One of those settled Bedouins, Mahmoud Au Hassan Jaaoui, who lives in the neighboring village of IDNA and who dwells with his flock during the spring months in a cave on a nearby hill, said that the place is called after an Israelite prophet by the name of *LEHI* who in ancient days was sitting under an old oak tree judging his people. Around the old oak tree there is a stone fence which, according to the Bedouin, was erected in ancient times to protect the holy place. The Bedouins prevent their sheep and goats from approaching this sacred tree.

The area around the *Beit Lehi* cave is historically and archaeologically one of the most interesting areas of the holy land. Until now only relatively few surveys and excavations have been conducted in this area.

Further Confirmation of the Cave of Lehi (as related to Kevan Clawson by John Tvedtnes)

In 1972 a group of interested people from BYU, who were living and/or studying in Israel, traveled with Joseph Ginat to the site of Lehi's Cave in an effort to confirm whether or not the cave could in fact be the actual site of the "land of Lehi" as described in the Book of Mormon. Included in this group was the local villager that Ginat had met previously, and who had information about the sacred oak tree situated above the cave site.

While standing on top of the hill above the cave, and in front of the "sacred oak" that was surrounded by a short rectangular wall, the local Arab began to describe what he knew about the site. He said that this was a sacred spot, and that prior to the war of independence in 1948 the people of his village would come to this tree and sacrifice goats. He said the tree was sacred because a prophet named "Lahi" used to sit under the tree and teach the people. He added that they believed that it was bad luck to pluck branches off the tree and that anyone who did so would become blind.

Some of the group remained skeptical, since they knew that Ginat had spoken to the Arab previously. They decided to return to the site on their own. Several months later a small group including John Tvedtnes, Lamar Berrett, and David Galbraith returned to the area surrounding Lehi's cave. As they drove through the Arab villages located around the cave site, they looked for people they could speak to about the area and confirm the story they had heard.

At each small village they would look for someone they thought would be old enough to know the area and the ancient traditions associated with the area. When speaking to people, they were careful to ask "general" questions, making sure they did not lead them to say something they didn't actually know or believe to be true. "What do you know about the area?" "Is there a place in the area considered sacred?" "Is there a place locally associated with the name Lehi?"

Finally, at the village of Idna (the village closest to the cave site), they talked to a group of elderly men seated outside, drinking tea and playing backgammon. The one who seemed to be the eldest said he knew of a sacred site and could take them there. They brought the man into their vehicle and simply followed his directions—again being careful not to reveal that they had been there previously. For a while they did not know where the man was taking them, and assumed that he was leading them to a different location. But finally, they recognized the hill and the tree! He had brought them to the hill from the north. During their previous visit they had traveled to the hill from the south. It was clear that this man knew the area well. He took them to the cave and to the sacred tree above the cave. Once there, this ancient villager confirmed once again the story of "Lahi's Cave!"

There are some who remain convinced that this is *not* Lehi's cave, based upon their own interpretation of the ancient inscriptions and pictures on the walls of the cave. The specific facts concerning the cave and the sacred oak tree will always be circumstantial, and we may never know for sure whether or not this is in fact the land of Lehi as described in the Book of Mormon. But most who have viewed the evidence, circumstantial as it might be, are convinced that it is the real thing.

Appendix 3: Drawings from Lehi's Cave

Frank Moore Cross, Jr.'s interpretation:

Inscription A on west wall:

"Yahweh is the God of the whole earth; the mountains of Judah belong to him; to the God of Jerusalem."

"I am Yahweh thy God: I will accept the cities of Judah, and will redeem Jerusalem."

Inscription B on west wall:

"The mount of Moriah thou hast favored, the dwelling of Yah, Yahweh. Absolve us O merciful God! Absolve us O Yahweh!"

Inscription C on south wall:

"Deliver us O Lord."

Figure 1. Inscriptions A and B from a cave near Khirbet Beit Lei. The drawing is traced from a photograph and checked against the original now in the Israel Museum. Lines adjacent to the letters have been included in the drawing and a few more distant to suggest the character of limestone surface. However, most of the distant lines and scratches have been ignored.

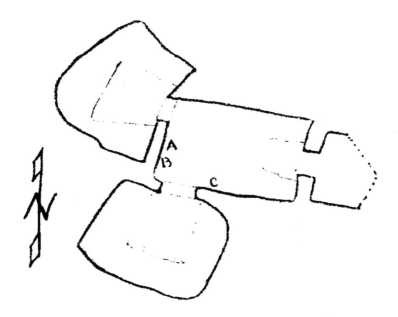

Fig. 2. Ground plan of the tomb at Khirbet Beit Lei. The letters A, B, and C show where the inscriptions were found. Redrawn by Vonda Louthan from Naveh, Fig. 1.

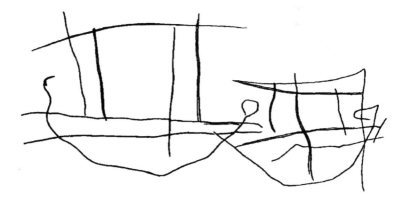

Fig. 3. Ships incised on cave wall. Redrawn by Vonda Louthan from Naveh, Fig. 7.

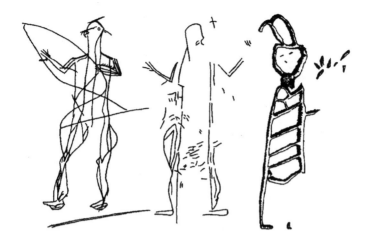

Fig. 4. Human figures incised on cave walls. Redrawn by Vonda Louthan from Naveh, Figs. 4, 5, and 6.

Fig. 5. A portion of Inscription A, redrawn from Cross, Fig. 1. This line reads—from right to left—"I will redeem Jerusalem."

272

Appendix 4: Salt Lake Institute Talk by Irene

Salt Lake Institute of Religion Devotional
February 14, 1975

Introduction by Hoyt W. Brewster, Jr.
(Friday Devotional Advisor)

"I was a stranger, and ye took me in." These words, recorded by the Gospel writer Matthew, have undoubtedly been directed at our guest speaker on numerous occasions. For the past ten years, Sister Irene Staples has served as the Official Church Hostess here in Salt Lake City. She has met and entertained thousands of visitors from throughout the world, including royalty, ambassadors, religious leaders, entertainers and other prominent persons.

Sister Staples, while you may be a "stranger" to most of us here in this audience, it is our privilege to "take you in." We are delighted to have you with us today.

Experiences of an Official Church Hostess

What a wonderful introduction! It makes me feel that if I were just about 100 years younger, I'd be a cute coed like once upon a time and as you are now.

What a sweet prayer of Carol's. How thoughtful it was of her to say, "And remember this little lady, that Thy Spirit will be with her." You know, young people, you can't do one thing right—unless you have the Spirit of the Lord with you. It's like the young boy who, after saying his prayer one evening, added, "And Heavenly Father, please take care of yourself, because if anything happens to you we're sunk!"

That is surely true, for I can tell you without the Spirit of the Lord I couldn't have done one thing, because many times, in hosting special guests, I have had to call on the Lord to help me. The big majority of the visitors are wonderful. But when you get a minister from Scotland who shakes his fist in your face and says, "Listen, you or no one else is going to keep me from going into that temple!", well, you have got to have the Spirit of the Lord with you to help calm him down. I really wanted to take him by the arm and say, "Okay, brother, you're wasting my time and yours too. Goodbye." But I kept thinking of the song, "School Thy Feelings Oh My Brother" that President Penrose wrote, and so I thought, "Be calm, Irene, be calm."

Well, incidentally—he didn't get in the Temple, and two days later I received one of the nicest thank you letters I have ever received, apologizing, and then saying, "You know, Mrs. Staples, you have taught me that true Christianity can rise far above the differences of religion," and then added, "If any of your people come to Scotland, tell them that my home is their home." Well, he'd be surprised if he knew I had made a public announcement and he'd get swamped with visitors over there. But that is the way my work has gone, and, of course, there have been many conversions.

How fortunate you are to have Elder Paul Dunn as your speaker next week. A while ago, he came up to me and said, "Oh Irene, I have to tell you! You know that couple you hosted from the Eastern States? I met them and they said to tell you that the whole family had joined." After hosting thousands of people, I wondered which ones they could be, and so I asked him what were their names. He didn't know. I asked him where they were from in the East—he didn't know. I asked him if he remembered where he had been—and he couldn't remember—he had been to so many places.

But he said, "I was told to tell you that the whole family had joined the Church, I delivered the message—and that is the main thing." So some family in the East joined the Church. Elder Dunn said so!

When I walked into this room, it took me back a few years when I had a Catholic Priest here. He was the spiritual advisor for one of the large Catholic colleges in upstate New York, and so I told him I would like him to see what we do up here on our campus. How surprised he was when he came in here and said, "Why you mean that you fill this chapel?" "Of course," I replied, "in fact, I had to speak at one of the wards up here not too long ago, and the Bishop got up and congratulated them and said that last Sunday they had 115% attendance!" I suppose they brought all their friends.

"Well," said the Priest, "we only have about 12% of our students attend Church." "Is that so," I replied, "I would suggest that you better join us."

I knew that he loved music and played the organ some. So as we walked over by the organ I asked him if he would like to play it. I told him that would be a memorable occasion for him to play the organ in a Mormon Church. As I went over to get a hymn book, he said, "No, never mind. I'll just play a couple of songs I often play in my Church, every chance I get." I was sure he would play the "Doxology" or "A Mighty Fortress," or some such hymn. But, do you know what—he sat down and played—"Come, Come Ye Saints" and "O My Father." Well, I'll tell you in the vernacular, I nearly flipped; as you young people would say. I was so moved to see this handsome young Priest, who was only about 35 years old (and that is real young when you get to my age), play those beloved songs.

At the Church Offices, he was asked if he ever ran into our missionaries, and when he answered, "No, he never did," I said, "Well, I can tell you why. Several years ago, the Catholic Church in that area called up the Chief of Police and said, 'Listen, the Mormon missionaries are here converting our people. You get rid of them. Get them out of here.' So the Chief of Police went out, picked them up, and told them if they didn't get out of there he was going to throw them in jail."

The young Priest answered, "But that is a Christian injustice!" And I replied, "Of course it is, but that is the Catholic Church for you, period!"

"Well" he said, "When I go back, I am going to see that this situation is changed." The General Authority present, or anyone else, knew that no Catholic Priest would go back and open the way for the missionaries to come in and convert his own parishioners. But two weeks later I had a phone call from this Priest and he asked me to go tell the Brethren that he had kept his promise—the way was now open for the missionaries to go into that area.

I could hardly believe it until the next morning I received a phone call from one of the councilors in the Mission Presidency, who said, "Irene, a miracle has happened! Yesterday this fine young Priest picked us up, took us to the city police, and stood there and demanded every right, every privilege and every protection for the Mormon missionaries who come into our area to proselyte. We were so overcome, that when we got back to where the missionaries lived, we fell to our knees and wept, and thanked the Lord for this miracle. Now the missionaries will be able to go back into this area."

Later, I received a phone call from this same Priest, and he said that he wanted to tell me that he was now a Mormon missionary. I got real excited and said, "Wonderful, Jerry." But later, someone told me that you never call a Catholic Priest "Jerry". Well, I did, and he seemed to like it. So I asked him to tell me what had happened, and he said, "No, I haven't joined the Church, but I was so disgusted with a new Catholic Priest who came into our Rectory. He didn't know a thing about the Mormon Church, and so I had to get my Book of Mormon and my Doctrine and Covenants and tell him the truth about the Mormon Church. In fact, I want every student in our college here, to know the truth about the Mormons."

I had to send him Church films, literature, and even talks of the General Authorities, and then he gave them examinations on these things, to be sure they understood what they had read and heard. You know the Lord can use these people better where they are, until the time comes when He wants them to come into the Church.

President McKay said, "Every member a missionary." Well, if we fall down, the Lord is going to use some of these other people and they will receive the blessings, won't they? Sure they will.

Let me tell you about a conversion of about a year ago. One of the Brethren called me and asked if I would host a Catholic nun, who was here for three days. I, of course, was happy to do so. She had been a nun for 25 years, and had been in the Convent since she was 13 years old. She was staying with his neighbor, and they didn't know quite what to do with a Catholic nun. But he told them not to worry; he would call Irene, which he did.

I met her and had her all afternoon. Every time I told her something, she would agree. There was no argument. She would say, "That's logical," or "How interesting," or "That's wonderful." And then she said, "Could I meet you again, I would surely like to know more. It is so interesting and so convincing." So I met her the following morning. I had a special film shown for her on Temple Square that really breaks the Catholic Church into pieces. Now I don't say anything against another Church — much, that is — but, anyway, this was a film, so it wasn't my fault what was in the film, right?

When we came out of the film, I wondered what her reaction would be. She stood there a minute and all of a sudden she threw her arms around me and sobbed and cried like a child and said, "Irene, it's true, it's true, I know it's true. I know where I am going. I want to be baptized!"

Well, don't think there weren't plenty of tears on my side too. To have the Holy Ghost testify to this lovely woman of the truthfulness of the Gospel. But I said, "No, Miriam, it would be wrong if you were baptized now. I could arrange for you to be baptized in the Tabernacle font, but when you would go back home among your Catholic friends, they would say, 'Now look what you have done. You have given up your sacred vows. That is the way the Mormons are, they put pressure on you and you have been moved emotionally, and now you are condemned for what you have done.'"

I told her it would be too difficult for her, and suggested that she go back to her home in the Southern States, and I would have the missionaries teach her. She should read the Book of Mormon and be baptized there. And then she said, "But will it take long?" "No," I answered, "it won't take long." (You who are missionaries here, you know that sometimes you have to work real fast, don't you, before old Satan steps in to confuse the investigator.)

But I said, "Look, its twelve o'clock. Let's go to the Lion House and I will buy your lunch." So as we went up South Temple and got in front of the Church Offices, I stopped and said, "You know, I feel very strongly impressed to take you in to meet one of the General Authorities." But the woman that she had been staying with, who was with us spoke up and said, "No, no we don't have time for that. I've been gone too long as it is. We've got to get home. We don't have time." But I said, "I feel so strongly that I would like her to meet Elder Bernard Brockbank. I was with him back at the New York World's Fair Mormon Pavilion for two years, when he was managing director there, and somehow I feel that you should meet him." But this woman insisted that she did not have the time, and wanted to get home. So I couldn't argue, and said, "All right, we will just go and have lunch."

As we got our trays, I suggested that we go way over in the corner of the dining room by ourselves, so we could visit and talk, which we did. Well, we were just ready to leave, when someone came up from the back and tapped me on the shoulder and said, "Hello, Irene, what can I do for you, what do you need me for?" Yes—you guessed it! I turned around and there stood Elder Brockbank! I said, "Elder Brockbank, how did you know that I needed you?" He just smiled and said, "Oh, just one of those things." Well, we went over to his office and spent at least an hour with him. He talked to her in such a wonderful way, and told her many things, explaining to this sweet sister the truthfulness of the Gospel. Just before leaving I said, "You know, Elder Brockbank, I am sure this sister will need a special blessing before she goes back home. Will you give her one?"

Elder Brockbank turned to her and said, "Would you like one?" And she replied. "Oh yes, but I am not a member of your Church." "But you are a child of God," he replied, "you deserve one.

And you young people, don't ever question about the Brethren talking directly to the Lord. They do! For in his most beautiful prayer, he was talking directly to the Lord, asking for special blessings for this lovely sister. How she would need His help and His blessings in the difficult days which would lie ahead for her. Such a beautiful spirit was there, in such abundance. He was pleading and talking to Heavenly Father, just as you would talk to your own father here, asking for help.

Well, the lady where the nun was staying, saw the miracle that had happened. Needless to say, this sweet nun returned home — the missionaries contacted her the next day, and three weeks later she was baptized.

Last June, I had the privilege of going through the Salt Lake Temple with her. She said, "Irene, I want to go back to Temple Square, where I received my first testimony of the truthfulness of the Gospel, and go to the Temple there."

She also told me that there are hundreds of Priests and Sisters who would leave the Church -- if they had someplace to go. But it is the only security they have, and what can they do, and where can they go? How thrilled she was to be so blessed. She looked like an angel as she walked through the Temple. It seemed almost as if a "halo" surrounded her, and tears of joy, often were on her cheeks.

Well, I could tell you many, many experiences like that, but as I was telling Brother Brewster, one of the thrilling experiences which will apply to you young people — is the fulfilling of prophecy concerning Israel.

Moshe Yegar

About seven years ago, I heard that the Consul of Israel for the Western States, with headquarters in Los Angeles, was coming here. I didn't know his name, or his address, but I felt inspired to find out and write to him, extending a special invitation to Salt Lake, and that I would be honored to have the privilege of taking him to many places of interest in our city, including of course all Church places, and also to meet some of the Church General Authorities.

And to you young people, let me suggest, that when you get an inspiration to do something-- do it. You are entitled to guidance and inspiration if you live righteous lives. And I say, "Don't argue with the Lord" when He is trying to give you guidance and inspiration as to what you should do. Let me tell you the result of the inspiration I had to write this letter.

I received a letter back from him immediately, expressing how happy he was to receive it and said that he would be delighted to see the places I had suggested. Well, I wish I had the time to tell you the whole story, but, needless to say, I spent a day and a half out of the three days he was here with him, and that's pretty good, especially when he came to spend the three days with the Jewish people in this community.

He was simply overcome with what he saw and heard, and the friendliness and the warmth of the people he met, for he had known nothing about the Mormon Church or its people before coming here. And as I said "Goodbye," he said, "Irene, you have no idea what this visit has meant to me." And then added, "Will you do something for me?" "I surely will," I replied, "What can I do for you?" And he said, "I know that your prayers are always answered." And I quickly replied. "Oh, I hope not..." For sometimes I am praying for the wrong things for my own good. But he said, "Please, will you pray to God and ask Him to open the way that I will be able to come back here and bring my wife, so she can see and hear the things I've experienced. Next to Jerusalem itself, Salt Lake is the greatest city in the whole world, and the Mormon people are the greatest friends. There is something different here. I can feel God's Spirit here. I want to come back!"

Well, about two months later he wrote a letter and said, "Your prayers have been answered. I have been promoted to the Consul General of the United States, with headquarters in Washington D.C. But before we go back there, the Jewish community here, in Los Angeles, want to send us on a week's vacation, with all expenses paid, to the Bahamas, to Mexico, the Hawaiian Islands, or anywhere we want to go. But we told them there was no decision to make, we wanted to go to Salt Lake City!"

Well, the people down there nearly died, and said, "Salt Lake, what is there in Salt Lake?" Well, he told them—as he had me, that next to Jerusalem itself, Salt lake City and its people was the greatest city in the world!

And so they came here. They were entertained royally wherever they went. They met the General Authorities and other Mormon people. The Orson Hyde Club of the BYU entertained them at a special luncheon and put on a program of Israeli songs and dances. It was a delightful occasion. They said they had never been treated so wonderfully anywhere in the United States.

With the Consul now in Washington, he would meet all the Israeli government officials who would come through, and he would say, "Oh no, you can't just fly out to San Francisco or Los Angeles. You have got to stop in Salt Lake!" And then he would proceed to tell them what a great city it was and what great people the Mormon people were. And then he would add, "You only have to know one person. Here is her name, and her phone number." So it has been my privilege to host and entertain all these top government people from Israel, all the way from General Moshe Dayan himself down.

I get so thrilled and so excited when I think of what is happening to bring forth the fulfillment of the great prophecies concerning the Gospel being taken to the people of Israel.

After presenting one of the gentlemen, who was here for some time, with a large, illustrated copy of the Book of Mormon, which he read immediately, I arranged for him to meet with President Lee, who asked this gentleman, "Well, Joseph, what do you think about Joseph Smith being a Prophet?" "Why, of course he was a prophet," he said. Then President Lee said, "Well, what do you think about the Book of Mormon being true?" and he answered, "There are no words in the Hebrew or English language to fully express how I know the Book of Mormon is true. The Book of Mormon didn't start in upstate New York, the Book of Mormon started in Jerusalem. It is our book as well as yours, and the prophets are our prophets as well as yours." Then President Lee said, "Well, then, what do you think about Jesus Christ being the Messiah?" Well, he hesitated, and finally said, "That's a little more difficult, but I'm working on it!" Yes, they themselves, the Jews, are going to convert themselves!

The Cave of Lehi

Later, this same gentleman called me up at five o'clock in the morning and said, "Irene, I've got to talk to you. I've discovered something. I've got to talk to you immediately!"

He is an archaeologist, and discovered a connection between the Book of Mormon and the story of Lehi with the Land of Lehi in Israel. When building a military road along a hill, they broke into a cave. In this cave, they found writings on the wall dating back to 600 B.C.. They found sketches of sailing ships, and wondered who in this mountainous area would be drawing ships which they knew very little about. The writings were asking Jehovah to forgive them, and to deliver them.

The sketches were of three men, with one man with his arms raised in an attitude of prayer. This cave is in the Land of Lehi, about twenty miles south-southwest from Jerusalem.

This archaeologist said, "Irene, can you see the connection? You remember when Lehi sent his sons to Laban to get the records and Laban wouldn't give them to them? How Nephi suggested that they go back to the land of their inheritance and there get the gold and silver and precious things which they had left there when they had started on their journey. Nephi records that they took these precious things to Laban to buy the records, and when Laban saw these things, he took them and sent his servants to kill Nephi and his brothers, and Nephi wrote, 'We had to flee for our lives, and we hid in the crevice of the rocks.' This is where they hid until the servants gave up trying to find them. And while they were in the cave, they were writing on the wall, for Jehovah to deliver them and to forgive them. They were drawing ships, for they knew that they would be going on a ship to the new land. With the writings on the wall, archaeologists can tell immediately the date—600 B.C., which is the exact date when Lehi left Jerusalem. This being the Land of Lehi, it must be the cave where they stored their precious things originally, and also where the sons went to escape. For the archaeologists definitely know that it wasn't a burial cave, but have every evidence to know that it was used as a place of refuge or a hide-out."

Last May, I was invited by the State of Israel to be their guest for a two week visit to Israel. I had the privilege of being the first person from Utah to be taken to the Land of Lehi, to see the remnants of this cave. I was also taken by the archaeologist to the top of the hill and shown the ruins of an ancient city. There he said, "Now look over there. Only last week, I came up here. In fact I can't stay away from this area. And while here I met a Bedouin shepherd, who asked, 'Why do you come here? No one comes out here! What is there that you are looking for?' Well I told him that I was interested in the people that lived in this area, and asked him if he knew anything about them. 'Oh, yes, of course,' the shepherd replied, and then his sheep started to go over to a certain area. Immediately he shouted to his son to get the sheep away from there, that they should not go there to that sacred place."

The archaeologist then asked the shepherd why that area circled around with a stone wall was so sacred, and the shepherd replied, "That area is where a great Prophet of Israel used to sit and admonish his people. He used to judge his people, and he used to bless his people. That is a very sacred place."

"Do you know his name?" the archaeologist asked. "Of course," said the shepherd, "his name was the Prophet Lehi!" See what is happening? The Jews are converting themselves with evidence of the Book of Mormon which they themselves are discovering in their own land.

The Holocaust Memorial

Two years ago, in April, I made an appointment with the First Presidency of the Church to meet three top government officials from Israel and there, in the Church Offices, these Israeli gentlemen invited the First Presidency of the Church to go to Israel, to open communication between the Mormon Church and the State of Israel!

Well, I can tell you, I just tingled all over, I was so thrilled. Yes, you can see prophecy being fulfilled, for it will be these top government officials who will open the way for the Church to go to Israel and bring the Gospel to these people. The following September, President Lee accepted this invitation and went to Israel. There he established the first branch of the LDS Church in Jerusalem, with Brother David Galbraith as president.

Let me tell you of an experience I had when I was there. I had fasted and prayed so hard that this trip to Israel wouldn't just be a regular sight-seeing trip. That somehow I would be able to open doors or do something special for the Church. One day as I was leaving the memorial to the six million Jews who were killed by Hitler, during the Second World War, a great feeling of compassion came over me, and I wondered what there was that could be done to compensate for their terrible suffering and for so many being killed. When we left the building, my guide stopped and said, "You know, Mrs. Staples, I don't know whether you would be interested or not, but I feel impressed to ask if you would like to go over and see the records of these six million who were killed in the holocaust. I am not sure whether they will let you go in or not, for no one is allowed in there. It is a very sacred place and no one, especially those who are not Jews, are allowed to go in there."

"Of course I would," I replied, "I would love to go there. I am very interested." And as we walked into the building, I waited in the front hall, while the guide went to the office of the Director of Yad VaShem. They were talking in Hebrew and the Director was shaking his head, "NO" — until the guide took out the letter showing that I was a special guest of the State of Israel.

The Director came up to me and said, "Mrs. Staples, we would be honored to take you through our archives."

Brothers and sisters, as I walked into that room, and the gentleman pulled out the drawers and showed me one of the genealogical sheets, it was one of the most thrilling experiences I have ever had, for — it was exactly that! There on the sheet was recorded all the information which is required on our genealogical sheets, and just exactly what we need for temple work. I was so impressed and excited when I saw them, I could hardly control myself with emotion. I told the Director that these records had to be protected, they could not be destroyed by some fanatic, or a fire or a bomb. I immediately told him about our Genealogical Library, and of our great Granite Mountain Vault. How we would be willing to come there, microfilm these records, give them a copy, and then put one in the vault for safe keeping. He and his associate became very interested, wanted to know more, and asked me to send them more information. Which I have done. I felt that I wanted to hold these records in my arms until this microfilming could be accomplished -- these records had to be preserved!

When I met with the General Authorities to report my visit there, and told them of this experience, I said, "In the Lord's own due time, when they build the Temple there, what will they do for names? Here will be the names of these six million Jews, pre-served for their descendants, who by that time—many of whom will have been converted—will be able to go into the Temple and do the Temple work for them." And then I added, "It might not be until during the millennium." And one of the Brethren spoke up and said, "That's not very long to wait, Irene."

Negotiations are being made to have this work done, and I am sure the Lord has had His hand in this great work.

And so, it has been a great privilege for me to be here with you young people. There is so much and so many things that I would like to tell you. But most of all---stay close to the Lord. Great trials are coming. I remember when President McKay, who was such a marvelous President, said how often he prayed to the Lord to stay His second coming, so that his people--you and I-- would be ready to receive Him.

No -- it isn't very long, and you young people will be part of the great millennium. Live righteously. I plead with you to live close to the Lord, and He will bless you with this great blessing, for He has reserved His special spirits for the last days, to bring forth and to help establish His Kingdom here upon the earth.

May this be your blessing, I humbly pray, in Jesus name. Amen.

Irene Staples: Hostess to the World

Appendix 5: Irene's Funeral Eulogy

Following is the eulogy given by her grandson, Kevan Clawson,[1] at Irene's funeral. There was a large crowd gathered to honor Irene, including President James E. Faust, who also spoke.

Hannah "Irene" Edwards Staples was born September 29, 1906 in Malad, Idaho. She was destined to become one of the great women in the Mormon Church, a woman who touched thousands of people and families, a woman who helped open Nations to the Gospel.

Irene's greatest pride was the knowledge that she was a descendant of Welsh ancestors who sacrificed everything to follow the Gospel of Jesus Christ. We will start there.

♦ Titus Davis was a shoemaker who lived in Wales.

♦ Titus married Mary Gwenllian Bowen and had several children

♦ Titus and his two oldest children, David and Gwennie, were converted by missionaries and became strong members. His wife however refused to be persuaded.

---

[1] The author of this book.

- The Davis' desire to join the Saints in Zion brought them to the difficult and profound decision to split up their family. Titus' wife, Mary, would not be converted, and with additional pressure from her minister and family she would not go to America.

- In the end, Titus and all of the children except one came to America, while Mary and one child stayed in Wales.

- The boat that took them to America was called the Amazon. And it just happened to be the same boat that Charles Dickens had visited in an effort to write about the Mormons. As he got to know the people on the ship, he was touched by their sincerity and honesty. He was especially moved by the hymns they sang along the way. As he listened to their music, he was drawn to one voice that seemed to stand out from the others: the voice of Gwennie Davis. He tried to convince her father to permit him to keep Gwennie in England, saying that he was sure she would become a Prima Donna. Her father left the decision up to her—staying in England to fame and fortune, or continue to Zion with the rest of the family. She chose to go to Zion.

- It would be on the wagon train going west that Gwennie would meet her future husband—John Edwards

- John Edwards was also from Wales, and, in fact, he and his family were baptized around the same time as the Davis family. The Edwards family was converted by Dan Jones.

- Dan Jones was a bodyguard of the Prophet Joseph Smith, and was also from Wales. He was with the Prophet in Carthage jail the night before his death, and was told by the Prophet that he would not die but would live to serve a mission to Wales. This prophesy was fulfilled as Dan was let out of jail to attempt to speak with Governor Ford to plead for the Prophet's life. His efforts were in vain, for the very next day the Prophet was killed. But Dan lived to serve a mission to Wales and changed the lives of our ancestors forever.

♦ The Edwards family also felt the burning desire to come to Zion, and though unable to sell most of their property prior to leaving, they had enough money to get to America. When leaving, they stopped to take one last look at the home they loved and saw their friends and neighbors looting their home of the things they had left behind.

♦ The trek west was not without great loss: they buried their mother somewhere on the plains of Kansas.

♦ One of John Edwards' many assignments was to return to the east to help guide the new emigrants to Utah. It was on one of these trips that he met his future wife, Gwennie Davis.

♦ After arriving in Utah, John and Gwennie were married and settled in Willard, where they successfully raised cattle in and around Promontory, Utah. They supplied the railroads with meat as the two railroads were completed and finally met on their land in Promontory, Utah. It was there that the Golden Spike was driven to symbolize the completion of the transcontinental railroad. In fact, John Edwards can be seen in the official picture taken of this event by those involved.

♦ Among the children of John and Gwennie was a son named David Titus Edwards. A burning desire to serve the Lord continued to burn in David's bosom, and he enthusiastically went on a mission to Pennsylvania. It was while on his mission that he met and converted the Fern family. Among the Fern children he was to find his future wife, Florence Edith Fern. They wrote to each other, and after his mission was completed they were married in the Salt Lake Temple.

♦ After their marriage they moved to Treasureton to work on one of his grandfather's cattle ranches. Their first three children were born there, David "Fern," Florence "Edith," and Mabel "Gladys." They were very happy.

♦ It was during this period, while serving in a bishopric, that David Edwards and his wife received their second endowments[2] in the Logan Temple.

♦ They moved to Preston, Idaho, where their forth child, Rex, was born.

♦ A change of events sent David to Salt Lake City to work as a mail clerk. However, he always got sick riding the mail trains (because they made him ride backwards), so he quit and went back to the ranch. Still dissatisfied, he decided to become a dentist.

♦ After passing the dental exam with a score of 100%, he moved to Malad, Idaho to start his practice. It was while living in Malad that their 5th child, Hannah Irene Edwards, was born.

♦ Soon afterward they moved back to Preston, Idaho, where he continued to practice dentistry. One of his patients was Harold B. Lee.

---

[2]The "second endowment" is an ordinance in the Temple whereby a person is sealed to Eternal Life by the Prophet. In other words, they had their calling and election made sure.

- After his mother died, David Edwards moved his family back to Willard to take care of his father and the family farm.

- This was a rough time for the family, as the farm had been neglected, and David worked hard to support his growing family. He also started a dairy farm to supplement the family income. It was during the 1st World War, which made their struggle that much harder.

- After moving back to Willard Irene finished high school, graduating from Box Elder High when only 15! She was intelligent, full of energy, and anxious to start out on her own.

- It was from her father that Irene received her intelligent and quick mind. It was from her grandmother, Gwennie, that Irene received her great talent as a milliner and dressmaker. It was from her mother that Irene received her love of flowers.

- She began by making dresses and hats for her dolls (out of chicken feathers!), then progressed to making hats for herself and her family.

- When Irene was 17, her father took her to the Paris Co. in Salt Lake City to look for work. While in the store, they admired the hat that Irene was wearing, and when they found out that Irene had made the hat herself they offered her a job at $5 a week. How could she refuse? She would be making the transition from chicken feathers to beautiful Ostrich plumes.

- Three years later, she became head of the Millinery Department designing and making hats for wealthy customers.

◆ During this exciting time, Irene often went to dances. In fact, she and a partner won a dance contest at Lagoon. It was at one of these dances that Irene met Harold Staples. As she put it, "He was nice looking, clean in his dress, and I remember how polished his shoes were."

◆ Irene moved to Idaho Falls, following an opportunity to manage and become part owner of a millinery company there. Though successful, she was very lonely. Several months later, Harold visited Irene and convinced her to marry him. In one of the few truly impulsive acts of Irene's life, she agreed to marry Harold immediately. Without informing her parents, she was married to Harold by a Judge in Pocatello, Idaho. In fact, Irene's parents learned of the marriage by reading about it in the newspaper! Sometime later Harold and Irene were sealed in the Salt Lake Temple.

◆ Irene gave up her position in Idaho, and she and Harold moved to Salt Lake City to start their life together. She once again took a job in a millinery department while Harold worked at the Piggly Wiggley store. After a while Harold started working for a car dealership, then started his own business selling used cars, and finally owned a car dealership in Bountiful.

◆ Desiring to become a "gentleman farmer," Harold persuaded Irene to move to the Cottonwood area. It was here that they developed lifelong relationships with families like the Fausts, and Irene began to blossom as a person dedicated to the Church and service.

◆ The parties and socials held at their home in Cottonwood were well known by all. Irene flourished:

Various Awards and Commendations

◆ Two national design awards while working for the Paris Co.

◆ Minute Man Award: National Guard, for service to the community

◆ Honorary Golden Gleaner Award

◆ Woman of the Year: Utah Woman's Review

Social Organizations

◆ Chairman, Ladies Literary Club

◆ Hostess, Western Governors Conference

◆ Receptionist, State House of Representatives

◆ Chairman, Welsh Ladies

◆ Director, volunteers at LDS Hospital (250 "Pink Ladies")

◆ Chairman, Salt Lake County Cancer drive

◆ Volunteer, Red Cross

◆ Officer, PTA

◆ Member, the Classics Club

◆ Member, the Top Hatters Dinner and Dance Club

◆ Member, the Bonneville Knife and Fork Club

Political Organizations

◆ Chairman, Salt Lake Women's Republican Club

◆ Board Member, Utah Federation of Republican Women

◆ Delegate, State & National Republican Conventions

Irene Staples: Hostess to the World

- Member, Republican State Central Committee

- Member, Utah Women's Legislative Council

- Board Member, State Fine Arts Council

Church Positions

- Tabernacle Choir Member

- Ward Choir Member (7 different Wards)

- Primary Activity Director

- Ward Newspaper Editor (twice)

- Junior Genealogical Class Leader

- Sunday School Teacher

- 2½ Minute Talk Supervisor

- Ward Relief Society Homemaking Leader

- Stake Relief Society Homemaking Leader

- Visiting Teacher Message Leader

- Participated in *Message of the Ages* with her family in the Tabernacle

- MIA First Counselor

- President, YWMIA (three times)

- President, Primary

- President, Relief Society

- Guide, Beehive House

- MIA Drama and Road Show Director

- Created over 200 costumes for the play "Promised Valley"

- Provided cleaning and rental service for Stakes performing the play

- Given Honorary Golden Gleaner Award

- Full-time Missionary at the Mormon Pavilion in New York

- Gathered and wrote 4 volumes of material on the History of the Mormon Pavilion

- Helped to organize the first Christmas Lights on Temple Square

- Official Church Hostess

- Gathered and wrote a History of the Church Hosting Service

- Volunteer at the Church Genealogy Department

- Created costumes for the play "Zion" for Parleys and Union Stakes

- Speaker at various Ward and Stake Firesides (over 500 times!)

Designs & Costumes

- Promised Valley musical. Irene spent a whole summer designing, making, mending, and shipping out costumes for this Church-wide play.

- University of Utah theater

- Summer Festivals

- Eventually, Irene persuaded Harold to move back to the city, to a home on Virginia Street. They had not been there long when Harold died of a brain tumor.

- With most of her children grown and married, and the last child (Richard) leaving on a mission, Irene's life was to change dramatically. She was called on a mission to serve as a hostess at the World's Fair in New York. She was soon to become known as "the flower lady" as she used her talents to create beautiful floral arrangements and corsages for her guests and the other exhibits at the fair.

♦ Her work at the fair, especially the ease with which she worked with the many dignitaries that she met, brought her to the attention of the Brethren in Salt Lake. Soon after arriving home from her successful mission, Irene was called to be the first official Church Hostess. She was responsible for caring for all of the dignitaries from around the world who came to Salt Lake. She served in this position for 10 years, and, conservatively, touched the lives of more than 150,000 people.

♦ Presidents, state officials, foreign politicians, business executives, royalty, and Church leaders were among the noted and the notorious she hosted.

♦ Her duties were not tied to the Church only: she was called upon by state and city officials, national congressman, military leaders, and private businesses and associations to host various dignitaries and socials.

♦ Perhaps the high point of her service as Church Hostess was her many trips to Israel and the relationships that developed as a result. The State of Israel invited her as their special guest, was invited to return again by the Consul General, and made four additional trips to this sacred land. She became a close friend of Moshe Dayan. In fact, at the age of 71 she climbed Mount Sinai with some of her children and grandchildren.

- With her help, the door to Israel was opened and a relationship between the LDS Church and the State of Israel became permanent.

- The key to her success as a hostess was that she approached all of her guests on a first name basis, with kindness and courtesy. Irene said of her work: "*I have entertained royalty on rocking chairs on the front porch.*"

- Her genuine love of other people could easily be felt by all who came in contact with her. And her love of sharing the Gospel with others made her the perfect missionary. She said of her work:

- "*My job is to extend tolerance and understanding to all nations and people.*"

- After being released from her calling as Church Hostess, Irene continued as a "hostess" whenever called upon. Her contacts around the world and in Utah kept her very busy.

- She also turned to genealogy, and soon accomplished a great deal in tracing her ancestors. Her research goes back prior to the 11th century.

- Unfortunately, the last days of her life were spent in a nursing home. But anyone who knew her will quickly forget this small dark portion of her life and remember Irene as she really was and is: a vibrant woman of passion who loved the Gospel of Jesus Christ, and dedicated her life to sharing it with others.

Irene's One and Only Practical Joke

Charlie, the man who sleeps under her bed. Irene had a pair of her grandfather's brown boots arranged to poke out from beneath her bed as if they belonged to some unknown guest.

Irene's Sayings

♦ "Talents are meant to be used in the service of our fellow-men."

♦ "The best way to thank me is to ask me to do something else."

♦ "My greatest joy is in service to others."

♦ "I have always felt that a person must have a balanced life in all fields of endeavor to achieve his highest potential. This involves a willingness to help others."

Family Memories

♦ Chuck-a-Rama and a purse full of rolls and a piece of chicken (Irene's favorite place to eat, especially with her grandchildren, was an all-you-can-eat restaurant—where she would always carry out something for a "snack" later).

♦ Secret candy in church (Irene always kept some kind of candy in her purse, to help her grandchildren get through boring sacrament meetings).

♦ Red velvet and dingle dangles (Irene's home was always filled with pink colors, red velvet, and crystals hanging from lamps and chandeliers).

- A large painting of a mother and her children (in Irene's living room, hung prominently on one wall, was a picture of a mother and flying cherubs [children with wings], as her way of saying she was a mother *first*).

- Crab dinners (one of Irene's most popular dinners for her family).

- Dresses and drapes (Irene was well known for making costumes, dresses, and drapes for family and friends).

Personal

- The most profound experience of my life, a dream of the Savior of the World, was a direct result of Irene's influence. That very night Irene had taken me to Temple Square and arranged for a special showing of the film "The Three Witnesses." This film, and the spirit that I carried home with me, prompted the marvelous dream.

- I went to Grandma Irene's for Family Home Evening every Monday night for months after coming back into full activity in the Church, and prior to my mission, and then again after my mission.

- Our birthdays were very close together, hers on the 29th and mine on the 25th, so we often celebrated together.

- I got my red hair from Grandma Irene.

- I was called to the Pennsylvania Mission and found my future wife there, just as Irene's father had.

No one is perfect. We all have our faults, and Irene was no different. But when she comes to Judgment Day, and her life is placed in the balance, there is no question that the good Irene did in her life will far outweigh any bad she may have done. We can only hope that when we die the same can be said of us.

There is an ancient Jewish tradition that, after death, the spirit stays behind to see where the body is buried. If this is true, then Irene is here with us today. I want her to know that we love her, and that we will only remember the things about her that make us smile.

Index

If you enjoyed this book, you will enjoy these other books from

Walking the Line Publications

Books by Kevan Kingsley Clawson

Becoming A Great Missionary:

A Training Manual for Missionaries, Members and Priesthood Leaders
Forward by Anne Pinnock

The Atonement of Jesus Christ

An in-depth study of the doctrine of the saving atonement of Jesus Christ.

The Second Coming of Jesus Christ

An in-depth study of the doctrine of the second coming of Jesus Christ.

Raising A Worthy Missionary:

A Spiritual Guide for Parents of Young Children
How to teach your children to become great missionaries.

By Kevan Kingsley Clawson
and Terri Hopkins Clawson

By John and Nancy Hopkins

The Enhanced Old Testament

Interesting facts and stories from ancient writers and historians about the people, places and events relating to the Old Testament.

Obtaining Your Calling and Election

An in-depth study of the doctrines of faith, hope and charity; and how a person receives their calling and eletion to the Celestial Kingdom.

Mongolia: The Circle in the Clouds

Stories from the Hopkins humanitarian service mission to Mongolia.

Books can be obtained at any LDS bookstore around the world! (If they are our of stock, they can order them for you.) Or, simply go on-line to: www.amazon.com and search for the book title or author.

For retail stores and bulk purchases (#10 or more books), contact:

Granite Distribution
868 North 1430 West
Orem, UT 84057
(Toll Free 1-800-574-5779
Fax (801) 229-1924

www.walkingthelinebooks.com

WALKING THE LINE PUBLICATIONS